WRITING.COM

CREATIVE INTERNET STRATEGIES

TO ADVANCE YOUR WRITING CAREER
REVISED EDITION

MOIRA ANDERSON ALLEN

D1016322

ALLWORTH PRESS
NEW YORK

07   06   05   04   03   5   4   3   2   1

Published by Allworth Press
An imprint of Allworth Communications, Inc.
10 East 23rd Street, New York, NY 10010

Cover and interior design by Jennifer Moore

Page composition/typography by Integra Software Services Pvt. Ltd. Pondicherry, India

ISBN: 1–58115–270–1

Library of Congress Cataloging-in-Publication Data:

Anderson Allen, Moira.
Writing.com : creative internet strategies to advance your writing
career / by Moira Anderson Allen.—Rev. ed.
p. cm.
ISBN 1-58115-029-6
1. Authorship—Computer network resources. 2. Authorship—Marketing.
3. Electronic publishing. I. Title.

PN142.5.A53 2003
025.06'80802—dc21
2003004456

Printed in Canada

TABLE OF CONTENTS

INTRODUCTION TO THE SECOND EDITION

INTRODUCTION TO THE SECOND EDITION:

ANOTHER BOOK ABOUT THE INTERNET? WHY? ... AND WHY A SECOND EDITION?

WHEN I FIRST WROTE THIS book in 1998, the obvious question was: With so many guides to the Internet, do writers really need another one? At the time, however, most books claiming to be "writers' guides" to the Internet focused on topics such as "what is a URL" or "how to use e-mail." Others were simply directories of useful sites—information that, unfortunately, tends to go out of date before a book even sees print. None addressed the specific issues of how writers could use the Web to enhance their business or skills.

My goal for the first edition, therefore, was to show the connection between the Internet and the business of writing. How had the Internet *changed* the business of writing? What was its effect on the marketplace, on publishers, on how one dealt with editors, on research, on building skills? Rather than explain what a search engine was, the book was designed to show writers how to use search engines effectively to research articles. Rather than providing generic tips on how to set up a Web site, the book was designed to explain how to create an effective *author* site to promote your books, your writing, your career. In short, its purpose was to demonstrate how the Internet was making the business of writing more effective, productive, and successful.

So why a second edition? Simple: A lot has changed since 1998. When I first wrote this book, writers were just beginning to explore the Web. Only a few publications in *The Writer's Market* listed Web sites or e-mail addresses. There were only a handful of really good "writing megasites" (such as the lost and lamented Inkspot.[1] When I spoke at writing conferences, I often found myself talking to writers who hadn't even "logged on" yet (and to some who didn't even have computers). Today, a much larger percentage of writers are online, the Web abounds with sites for writers, and the majority of writing markets accept queries and submissions by e-mail.

The Internet has helped writers in some areas, but harmed them in others. The dot.com boom crested in 1999, when investors were willing to throw money at anything with a .com in the title. "Content" was considered

---

[1]For several years, Inkspot (founded by Debbie Ridpath Ohi) was the premiere Web site for writers. I became its managing editor in 2000. In 2001, Ohi sold the site to Xlibris, which shut it down (much to writers' dismay) in 2001 for lack of funds. In an attempt to salvage some of the content (and its general purpose), I was able to transfer many of its articles to Writing-World.com, which now attracts more than 80,000 visitors per month.

one way to mine the gold everyone believed to be lurking in the Internet hills, and for a brief time, amateur writers had the opportunity to post anything they wished online and (sometimes) get paid for it. A classic example was Themestream, which offered writers ten cents a "hit" for whatever they chose to post. Ultimately, however, such sites found that advertisers weren't ready to shell out hundreds of thousands of dollars for ads—and when those sites crashed and burned, as Themestream did in 2001, thousands of writers were left unpaid.

Electronic book publishing also saw a flurry of optimistic predictions in 1999 and 2000, attracting hundreds of authors with the lure of bypassing the hidebound editorial channels of print publishing. Stephen King made headlines with his first e-book, a novella called *Riding the Bullet*—and made them again when, a year later, he shut down his second e-book project, the serialized novel *The Plant.* But most of those optimistic predictions failed to materialize—and major publishers launched expensive electronic publishing arms only to scale them back or shut them down a year or two later.

The purpose of the second edition of this book, therefore, is to take a fresh look at the Internet and answer the question, "What does it mean to writers *today*?" This edition looks at what has changed, what is new, what is still working and what isn't. It looks at new opportunities for writers, and also at some of the new perils and pitfalls that await unwary travelers in cyberspace. It still offers plenty of information for the writer venturing online for the first time, but it also offers a wealth of material for Net-savvy writers who have been surfing for years.

WHAT'S NEW IN THIS EDITION

In addition to the previous edition's chapters on research, networking, and markets, this volume offers new chapters on:

- Fighting online piracy
- Web resources for screenwriters
- Scams and pitfalls for writers
- The "mechanics" of the Internet, including information on viruses and virus hoaxes
- Tips on creating your own e-book

Old chapters have also been extensively revised and updated. The chapter "Paperless Publishing" in the first edition, for example, has now been split into three chapters, one on creating an e-zine or e-mail newsletter (including information on how to promote a publication and find advertisers), one on electronic publishing, and one on subsidy and print-on-demand publishing. The chapter on electronic rights has been updated to cover recent e-rights lawsuits, while the chapter on markets looks at changes in the online marketplace, and some new types of "nontraditional" markets (such as electronic greeting cards). I've also incorporated chapters and chapter sections by other expert authors, such as MaryJanice Davidson (author chats), Debbie Ridpath Ohi (author showcase and syndication sites), lawyer Charles Petit (electronic piracy), Loralei Walker (freelance job sites), and Lenore Wright (screenwriting).

The other key change is the way this book handles links to online resources. Each chapter includes a list of online resources at the end. Sites that are referenced in these end-of-chapter lists are indicated in SMALL CAPS and are included in the alphabetical list of sites in Appendix A. (Sites that have been referenced in a previous chapter will not be re-referenced in subsequent chapters; in this case, the small caps indicate that you will be able to find the complete URL in the alphabetical appendix.)

In this edition, I have chosen to include the larger appendix of "best online resources for writers" as a separate electronic file, rather than waste paper and ink on a printed list of resources that may be largely obsolete by the time this book goes to press. This electronic directory (which will contain approximately two thousand sites) will be available as an Adobe PDF file that can be downloaded directly from the Allworth Press Web site, and it will be updated at regular intervals. To download the file, go to *www.allworth.com/Catalog/WP280A.htm* and follow the instructions there.

And finally, for more information on writing, I invite you to visit my Web site for writers, Writing-World.com (*www.writing-world.com*), which offers more than 350 articles for writers, along with a host of other resources, such as contest listings, market information, and a free biweekly newsletter. See you there!

—Moira Anderson Allen
www.writing-world.com
moirakallen@writing-world.com

<< CHAPTER 1 >>

WRITERS AND THE INTERNET: WHERE ARE WE TODAY?

WHEN I WROTE THE FIRST EDITION of this book, I argued that for writers, getting online was a *really good idea*. I saw it as a way to improve one's writing business by enhancing one's ability to conduct research, contact editors, save money, network with other writers, and take advantage of skill-building resources, such as online classes and critique groups.

Today, if you're serious about writing and getting published, being online isn't just a good idea. It has become a necessity, for one simple reason: This is where your market is. Today's editors expect writers to be able to communicate and submit manuscripts by e-mail, review guidelines on a publisher's Web site, and more. A writer who can't be contacted "instantly" via e-mail is a writer who is likely to miss out on assignments; a writer who sends a SASE for a publication's guidelines before researching those guidelines online will be viewed as a writer who "hasn't done her homework."

If you're a book author, there's a second reason to be online: The Internet is where your readers are. Book publishers are providing less and less promotion for their authors, but the Internet provides a far-reaching and inexpensive way for authors to market their work directly to the reader. Authors use their Web sites to share sample chapters, connect with fans, announce forthcoming titles, and even sell books directly. (Chapter 11 describes a variety of ways to promote one's book on the Web.)

In short, the Internet no longer simply offers a range of "cool" resources for writers (though it offers an abundance of those). Instead, it has become the arena in which writing business is conducted. Being online is no longer simply "helpful" to a writer's career; it has become essential.

THE ADVANTAGES OF THE INTERNET

FOR THOSE WHO ARE JUST "logging on," here is a brief overview of some of the primary advantages to writers of being online. (If you're a more experienced Net-user, surf on down to the next section to find out what has changed for writers online over the past four years.)

THE INTERNET WILL SAVE YOU MONEY

One of the first things I always did with a new copy of *The Writer's Market* was comb the pages for new magazines and send for sample copies. At $3 to $5 each, however, the cost of samples could add up quickly (especially if many turned out to be inappropriate markets). The Internet offers an alternative: the ability to review publications online. Many magazines post samples of current articles, and some archive back issues. While you don't get the entire "feel" of the magazine (ads, illustrations, layout, and so forth), you do get a chance to see what is being published—and what has already been covered. In addition, many publications post their guidelines online, saving you the cost of a SASE (and the endless wait for those guidelines to arrive).

More and more editors are willing to accept queries and assigned manuscripts by e-mail, which translates into significant savings on envelopes, paper, postage, computer disks and mailers, and trips to the post office. When you start tapping international markets, those savings increase dramatically—and you'll never have to wait in line at a post office to buy International Reply Coupons (which no one likes anyway). You can even buy your postage online from the UNITED STATES POSTAL SERVICE Web site (*www.stampsonline.com*).

The ability to interview experts by e-mail will also save you phone (and in some cases travel) costs. Many experts prefer e-mail interviews, as this gives them the opportunity to review your questions and answer them on their own time, rather than under the time pressure of a direct interview. "Long distance" doesn't matter; you can interview an expert on the other side of the globe just as easily as someone in your hometown.

THE INTERNET WILL SAVE YOU TIME

To a writer, time is money—and the Internet enables us to use our time more efficiently. Seeking an answer to a question at a library could take hours, days, or weeks; finding that same answer online could take minutes. What's the currency in Ghana? How do you say "glass" in French? How many angels can dance on the head of a pin?[1] A simple search can bring the answers to your desktop in seconds.

Thanks to e-mail, questions can now be asked and answered in something very near the speed of light. To get clarification from an editor or a source, you no longer have to play telephone tag, and most editors would rather communicate by

---

[1] The currency of Ghana is the "cedi" (which is divided into 100 pesewas). The word for glass is "verre," not to be confused with "vair," a heraldic term for a type of fur—and possibly the original source of Cinderella's slippers. As to the angels, it is rumored that OSHA regulations now restrict the number to four, and require the angels to wear safety helmets and glasses. (See "FAQs About Christmas," *www.alharris.com/holidays/faqxmas.htm*.)

e-mail than in person. Queries are often answered more quickly (although, as more writers take advantage of this option, I've noticed that the response time on e-mail queries for some publications is just as long as for surface mail.) The ability to e-mail a manuscript automatically extends any deadline by at least a week; you can literally send it the morning it is due. E-mail also makes it possible to quickly negotiate an assignment or contract; you can discuss specific clauses or issues by e-mail until an agreement is reached.

THE INTERNET WILL KEEP YOU CONNECTED

Writing has traditionally been described as a lonely profession; now, however, it is only as lonely as you want it to be. A thriving writing community flourishes online, with forums, chats, and discussion lists that welcome both the "newbie" and the established professional with open arms (or at least open mailboxes). On the Internet, you're not limited to the pool of writing talent available in your local community; you can share ideas and tips with writers at all levels of expertise from around the world. In a single week, I might discuss pet loss with a correspondent in Australia, fax an article to a writer in Singapore, or learn how to properly wield a two-handed sword from a writer in Scotland. These groups can provide the basis for genuine, long-term friendships with writers you may never meet in person, as well as "partnerships" with people who can give you honest feedback on your work. Plus, there's something magical about the discovery that one of your favorite writers is a member of your discussion group!

THE INTERNET CAN BRING YOU WORLDWIDE EXPOSURE

When you publish online, your readers respond—and writing often becomes a dialogue instead of a one-way transaction. Those readers include editors, and while writing for online publications rarely brings in the big bucks, it *does* provide opportunities for international exposure. I've had articles reprinted in South Africa, and brochures requested from Russia, Pakistan, and a monastery in Switzerland.

THE INTERNET ENABLES YOU TO BE SUCCESSFUL NO MATTER WHERE YOU LIVE

The Internet transcends geographical boundaries. No longer are you limited to the research resources of your local library; you now have access to libraries around the world, including a host of primary and specialized resources that you could never access "just down the street." Want to find a list of the British crews that sailed against the Spanish Armada? It's online. Need the text of a recent state or federal bill, plus the arguments and testimonies for and against it? They're online. Care to learn how to speak Klingon? That's online too.

The Internet also provides access to experts around the world. A simple search not only gives you vital background information for your article, but also provides you with names and e-mail addresses of potential interviewees. You can also be in instant contact with an editor anywhere in the world; it's just as easy to contact an editor in Hong Kong as in New York. You can even conduct your banking online, and accept payments from overseas markets electronically.

WHAT'S CHANGED—AND WHAT HASN'T

MAKING PREDICTIONS ABOUT HOW THE Internet would affect the business of writing was a popular pastime for several years. Some of the predictions were positive (depending on your point of view)—a year or so ago, pundits confidently declared that electronic books would be outselling print books within five years. Other predictions foretold doom and gloom—concerns over database-protection proposals in the late 1990s, for example, caused many to believe that information would no longer be "free" but would be available only at a heavy cost to researchers.

Some predictions have come true. Others have fallen by the wayside. In addition, factors that no one counted upon—the changing economy, growing problems with online security, and simple human nature—have affected the course of Internet development. Here's a look at where things stand in several areas that directly affect writers.

WRITING FOR THE WEB: A NEW WORLD, OR NOT?

A common perception in the 1990s was that writing for the Web would be completely different from writing for print publications. Writers were warned that they would need to develop an entirely new style and approach. Readers, we were told, didn't want to read "long articles" on the Web; they wanted to scan, to skim through bullet points, to read material that was short and concise.

We were also told that the traditional approach of "beginning, middle, and end" would no longer apply. Instead, the Web would use hyperlinked texts—a sort of "choose your own adventure" approach to information. Instead of giving readers linear documents that they would read from start to finish, we were to offer stand-alone chunks of a paragraph or two. The reader would then navigate his or her own path through the material, choosing which "chunk" to read next.

There may, indeed, be readers out there who enjoy hopping from one random chunk of text to another, and there are certainly those who won't read long articles. However, it does not appear that the Web has actually *changed* people's reading habits. People who like in-depth, linear, coherent articles will read those articles online; those who don't probably didn't read such articles offline in the first place.

While you'll still find plenty of articles claiming that "writing for the Web is different," the majority of online content follows the same traditional linear pattern as print writing. Indeed, much of it *began* as print writing, and was then posted online by magazines, newspapers, publishers, universities, and individuals. Fiction e-zines offer short stories that still follow the classic "beginning, middle, and end" format, and the Web abounds with lengthy treatises running to hundreds of pages.

Moreover, many publications have found that readers can be frustrated by "interactive" approaches. A site that offers a paragraph or two of information and then requires you to click to a new page is immensely annoying. (This style, by the way, has nothing to do with presenting information more easily; it's simply to boost a site's "hit" count.) While early Web articles tended to be loaded with internal hyperlinks, editors quickly discovered that this had the effect of leading the reader *out of* the original article (and often away from the Web site altogether); now, many editors prefer to list links at the end of an article.

Multimedia was also predicted to be the "big thing" that would distinguish online writing from dull print pages, and one can certainly find multimedia presentations online. However, most writers lack the ability or interest to build (or program) complex audio, video, or graphic elements into their writing. Further, multimedia effects create lengthy download times, which are a nuisance for folks using slower modems (and, quite often, for folks using faster connections as well).

If you're just getting started writing for the Web, therefore, fear not: You won't have to change your writing style to accommodate the "electronic" reader. Most Internet publishers look for exactly the same thing print publishers do: high-quality writing, accurate information, and professional presentation.

THE ELECTRONIC MARKETPLACE

In the first edition of this book, I predicted a growth in electronic markets for writers. In 1998, the dot.com boom was just beginning, and new e-zines, content sites, and other writing venues were blossoming on the Web. Granted, most didn't pay much—but the general feeling was that as revenues increased, pay rates would follow.

Sadly, that prediction has not come to pass. Instead, the electronic marketplace is steadily shrinking. I keep a file of electronic markets for my e-mail newsletter, *Writing World*,[2] and each time I check the list, markets have disappeared. The collapse of the dot.com boom brought about a corresponding collapse of several major "content" purchasers (such as Pets.com). Other sites have reduced their rates, closed their doors to new freelancers, or imposed more demanding contracts. While new e-zines pop up all the time, most are nonpaying, and many that do pay offer only minimal payments (e.g., $5 per article).

The problem, of course, is revenue. In 1998 and 1999, everyone assumed that dot.coms would make money; however, no one was quite sure how. One approach was to sell advertising space at sky-high prices (Themestream offered banner ads at $50,000 on up), on the basis of "eyeballs"—if 50,000 people visit a page, that's 50,000 "eyeballs" checking out your ad. Unfortunately, "eyeballs" didn't translate into sales—and advertisers began to realize that they weren't getting much bang for their buck.

When ad revenues failed to materialize, many publications turned to the "paid subscription" model. However, readers who had been accustomed to receiving a publication for free often balked at being asked to pay a fee. Inside.com, for example, began charging $14.95 per month for its formerly free publication (considerably more than one would pay for a year-long subscription to many print magazines). It later dropped the rate to $4.95 per month, but folded shortly thereafter.

For writers, the bottom line is simple: If a publication isn't receiving revenue from ads or subscriptions, it can't afford to pay for content. (Of course, some sites

[2]Available free from *www.writing-world.com*.

seem chock-full of ads and *still* don't pay ...) Consequently, writers aren't seeing any growth in the number of paying online markets—or in the rates that those markets pay. (Ever-optimistic e-writers can find a list of paying electronic markets in the online resource directory for this book.)

PRINT MARKETS IN CYBERSPACE

It isn't all bad news, however! While the electronic marketplace isn't growing as anticipated, the print marketplace has established a huge presence in cyberspace.

The vast majority of U.S. periodicals now have Web sites, which makes it far easier for writers to research potential markets. Many publications post their guidelines online or make them available by e-mail. (Sometimes those guidelines can be a bit hard to find; I'll discuss this further in chapter 5.) A magazine's Web site will usually have up-to-date staff contact information, making it a more reliable source than printed market guides.

More importantly, most editors are now willing to accept queries and *solicited* manuscripts via e-mail. This has become even more true since the anthrax postal scare of 2001, when many editors literally refused to handle their slush pile. The key word here is "solicited"—editors rarely want to see unsolicited manuscripts by e-mail. Editors also have very precise requirements as to how queries and manuscripts must be submitted; for more information, see chapter 6.

Book publishers have also gone online, and, like magazine publishers, are posting their guidelines, catalogs, and even sample chapters and author interviews. Some, like DEL REY (*www.delrey.com*), offer extensive resources for readers. Some even offer free electronic editions of their books. As with magazines, book publishers' Web sites enable the writer to get the most up-to-date information on submission guidelines and contacts.

ELECTRONIC PUBLISHING

The area of online writing that produced the greatest number of predictions—and the most exuberant predictions—is electronic publishing, or "e-publishing." Pundits confidently stated that e-books would become the reading vehicle of choice within five years. Some believed that all previously printed books would soon become available in electronic format. Many predicted that "resistance" to e-books would melt away as readers discovered how convenient they were. New technologies would create the "perfect" handheld e-reader. Meanwhile, bookstores would add "print-on-demand" kiosks that would enable them to download an electronic text and print a book for a customer on the spot.

Stephen King helped fuel these predictions by launching an electronic novella, *Riding the Bullet*, that sold half a million copies in the first week. At about the same time, several major print publishers launched electronic divisions, intending to bring out electronic editions of their backlist, new electronic titles, and simultaneous electronic and print titles.

Most of those electronic divisions have now either shut down (e.g., Time Warner's iPublish) or been dramatically cut back (Random House's @Random). Stephen King himself discontinued his serialized e-novel, *The Plant*, due to lack of sales. Time Warner Trade Publishing chairman Larry Kirshbaum noted, when shutting down iPublish, that "the market for e-books has simply not developed the way we hoped," and that "hitting a thousand-copy sale with an e-book is like selling a million copies of a print book."

One of the big problems has been the price; many print publishers sold their electronic editions at the same price as their hardcovers. Readers rightly rebelled, asking why, if production costs were so much lower for e-books, those savings were not being passed on to the consumer. A second problem was the lack of interest in handheld readers, perhaps because many consumers felt that they would prefer to spend $300 to $600 on *books* rather than on a device to *read* those books. Finally, many readers continue to resist the *idea* of reading electronic books; as Kirshbaum noted, "No reading device comes close to reproducing the experience of reading a book."

This is not to imply that e-books are dead, or even dying. In fact, they are thriving, as many e-published authors will tell you—but they are thriving in the context of the small press rather than the mega-publisher. While only about one percent of all books sold at the time of this writing are electronic, that's still a lot of books.

ELECTRONIC RIGHTS

Electronic rights have become a battlefield between writers and publishers. Ironically, the biggest demands for electronic rights come from print publications. Magazines wish to secure the right to post material on their Web sites—even if (a) they don't *have* a Web site, or (b) they don't post articles on it if they do. While some magazines do offer an extra fee if material is posted online, many do not. Worse, due to lawsuits like the *Tasini* case (see chapter 8), many publications have found it "easier" to simply demand all rights to an author's work, bypassing the issue of whether writers should receive extra compensation for electronic use.

Electronic rights have also become a hot issue in book publishing. While some publishers have already attempted to launch electronic divisions, others simply want to secure future electronic rights—or ensure, at the least, that those rights aren't used by anyone else. A significant case in this area is that of *Random House v. RosettaBooks*—in which Random House sued an electronic publisher for producing electronic editions of former Random House print titles (more on this in chapter 8 as well).

A SELF-PUBLISHER'S PARADISE?

Anyone who can put up a Web site can become a publisher—or so it has been said! Thousands of authors have flocked to the siren call of "post it and they will come" Web publishing, loading their poems, stories, and full-length novels onto the Web in hopes of finding an audience. As a result, the Web is flooded with some truly abominable writing. Worse, "publishing it yourself" (specifically, posting your unpublished works on a Web site) is generally considered the sign of an amateur—and an indication that the work is, in fact, unpublishable.

However, posting unpublished works on your Web site can have even more serious consequences. There is a growing tendency on the part of publishers to view such work as "previously published"—i.e., even though they don't take the work itself seriously, they are taking the claim of *publication* seriously. This means that many publications will treat such previously posted work as a reprint, if they are willing to accept it at all. Web publication, even on a personal site, is considered by many to be a use of "first rights" or "first electronic rights."[3] If you post your novel on your Web site, you run a serious risk of ruining your chances of ever getting it commercially published.

Many writers post their works under the mistaken impression that editors and publishers will "find" them and decide to publish them. This simply doesn't happen. Editors and publishers get more than enough slush in their mail; they don't need to cruise the Web looking for more. Nor is it wise to post material on your site in hopes that other writers or readers will "critique" it for you. If you want feedback, the best approach is to join a well-managed critique group (see chapter 4).

Conversely, posting previously *published* work online can be a very effective self-promotion tool. The fact that the work has already been published declares that you are a professional writer—and editors often *are* willing to visit your site to review online clips (especially if you are querying by e-mail). Sample chapters of a published book, or samples of your published short fiction, can be an excellent way to attract readers to your published novel. Posting this type of material also does not "consume" any rights that you can't afford to lose; it's simply another type of reprint. (Just make sure that you actually own the electronic rights to the material before you post it.)

ELECTRONIC PIRACY

A big concern for many writers is whether, by posting their works on the Web (or by submitting them to an online critique group), they will make themselves vulnerable to electronic piracy. How easy it will be, writers think, for someone to simply pull something off one's Web site and put it up somewhere else, or sell it, under another name.

Electronic piracy *does* occur—but situations in which one would-be author plagiarizes another are rare. One factor that works in the writer's favor is the vigilance of the online writing community: When a woman plagiarized an article that appeared in the now-defunct e-mail newsletter *Inklings* and sold it to another newsletter, writers who subscribed to both newsletters noticed the similarity between the two pieces and exposed the theft within hours. In the long run the original author actually benefited, as the second newsletter sent her a payment for the stolen material!

Far more common is the unauthorized electronic use of material that originally appeared in print. Occasionally, this sort of piracy is practiced by a lone individual (such as the fan of Harlan Ellison who posted scanned copies of Ellison's books to an AOL newsgroup); more often, it's practiced by mega-corporations. A case in

---

[3]Many writers are confused by the issue of "use" versus "licensing" of rights. Many believe that rights are used only if a piece is sold to a publisher. However, an author can "use up" rights by self-publishing a work, even if it is never sold. Thus, online self-publication can indeed be a use of "first" rights—and once those rights are used, they are gone forever. For more information on rights in general, see "Rights and Why They're Important" by Marg Gilks, at *www.writing-world.com/rights/rights.html.*

point is the now-defunct Contentville, which offered articles, dissertations, books, and other materials for sale. Hundreds of authors found that their articles were being sold on the site, even though they had never sold the electronic rights to those pieces. Contentville had somehow managed to acquire the archives of hundreds of magazines from a database firm that, supposedly, only had the rights to provide those archives to libraries and educational institutions.

Staying *off* the Web, therefore, is no protection against piracy! Instead, being online can actually be a benefit, as one can take steps to search periodically for stolen material. (Chapter 9 provides tips on how to search for stolen works, and what actions to take if you discover that your work is being used without your permission.)

PAY-PER-CLICK, PROFIT-SHARING, AND WEB GUIDES

In the traditional print market, the circulation of a publication is generally known. When you sell an article or a story, you're paid a flat rate for that material—and it goes into a publication that is sent out to a certain number of subscribers. Online, however, circulation is a constantly shifting entity. While ten thousand people might visit a particular online publication in a month, perhaps only a hundred may click on *your* article or story.

Consequently, Web publishers have struggled to develop methods by which writers could be paid "by the reader" rather than by the piece. A writer's revenue would be determined by that writer's popularity, or ability to attract readers. The result has been a variety of "profit-sharing" models that base a writer's payment on the number of visitors that writer attracts. One approach was the "pay-per-click" method most commonly associated with Themestream. Themestream (which began as "OscarTech") planned to sell advertising space (and other products) based on "eyeballs," and it planned to attract those eyeballs by loading its site with content. To get the content, it offered writers ten cents per visitor—and the writer could put up absolutely anything he or she wanted on the site.

Writers flocked to Themestream, thinking that this was a great deal. For a time, it was. Before long, however, Themestream cut payment to two cents a visitor. Then, when ad revenues still didn't materialize, it began to change the rules on what qualified as a "visitor"—and finally, not too surprisingly, it went bankrupt in early 2001, leaving thousands of writers unpaid. Several other similar "pay-per-click" sites, such as TheVines and TerraShare, followed.

Other sites offering a form of revenue sharing include Suite101.com and About.com (formerly TheMiningco.com). Suite101.com offered writers a flat rate that, ironically, decreased the more one contributed. If one wrote one article per month, one was paid $15; if one wrote two, one was paid $20 ($10 per article); if one wrote three, one was paid $25 ($6.25 per article). About.com offered revenue shares based on the number of visitors, ad click-throughs, and so on; the actual amounts paid to writers are a closely guarded secret, and About.com "guides" are asked not to divulge what they are paid.

By early 2002, hard times hit these sites as well. Suite101.com announced in January 2002 that it would no longer pay its contributors—but urged those contributors to go on hosting sites more or less "for the love of it." About.com began to prune its site, cutting out hundreds of topics; its market value dropped by several million dollars. About.com is currently being sued by a number of editors who claim that they have not received the payment they've been promised. Another revenue-sharing venture, WebSeed Publishing (which provided hosts with their own domain name and site templates), shut down completely in late 2002.

The moral of this story is simple: Don't fall for the lure of a site that promises to let you post anything you want—and to pay you a share of advertising revenues based on the number of visitors you're able to attract to your pages. The old-fashioned approach of getting paid for your writing up *front* is still the best model for writers!

THE MORE THINGS CHANGE ...

WHILE IT MIGHT APPEAR ON the surface that the Internet has made huge changes to the business of writing, in many cases those changes are superficial. The Internet provides a wealth of tools and resources—but it's important to remember that these *are* simply tools and resources. They are not necessarily fundamental changes to how we write, or what we write, or even whom we write *for*.

While more and more editors may want submissions by e-mail, for example, this is simply a change in the *mechanism* by which we contact those markets. It is an improvement, perhaps, over older mechanisms—just as air mail is an improvement over Pony Express. The way we transmit our material doesn't necessarily change how we *produce* that material, however; we must still know how to write an effective query, a solid article, an interesting story. Similarly, while the ability to network with other writers may be enhanced by our ability to make connections online, what we share with those writers—tips, success stories, commiserations on rejection, and mutual support—is no different from what we've shared in "real-world" writing groups.

Most importantly, the Internet has not changed the need for *good writing*. When Internet access became inexpensive and easy, thousands of would-be writers and writer wannabes flocked to the Web, hoping to find an audience for their material. That audience, however, never materialized—because *readers* still want high-quality writing, regardless of the medium in which it is published. In short, while the Internet may change *how* you communicate, it is far less likely to change *what* you communicate. It is simply a tool, just like your typewriter or a goose-quill pen. The purpose of this book is to help you use that tool to your best advantage.

RESORUCES

GENERAL WRITING RESOURCE SITES

Eclectic Writer, The
www.eclectics.com/writing/writing.html
Lots of articles on various topics;
scroll down for the menu, as the
top of the page advertises books
for sale.

FictionAddiction.NET
http://FictionAddiction.net
A huge site, with loads of articles,
resources, links, and a free
newsletter.

Fiction Factor
www.fictionfactor.com
As the name implies, this site focuses on
resources for fiction writers, including an
extensive market section and a free
newsletter.

Forwriters.com
www.forwriters.com
Though this site tends to emphasize
resources for writers of speculative
fiction, it has something for everyone,
including an excellent research section.

Misc. Writing
www.scalar.com/mw/index.html
Offers a number of excellent resources,
including a comprehensive "FAQ"
that answers most of a new writer's
"getting started" questions. Also has
links to newsgroups and other writing
resources.

Preditors and Editors
http://anotherealm.com/prededitors
Categorized links to a wide range of
resources, including agents, publishers,
articles, associations, and more.

RedInkWorks
www.redinkworks.com/writing_tips.htm
Loads of links on a wide range of writing
topics.

WordWeaving Archive
*www.wordweaving.com/
archives_index.html*
You'll find a ton of useful articles in this
archived collection.

WriteLink
www.writelink.dabsol.co.uk
This U.K. writing site offers a great list of
markets and contests, plus an e-mail
newsletter and several writing contests of
its own.

WriteLinks
*www.writelinks.com/Creative/Links/
crea06.htm*
This site offers extensive links to
literary agents, book publishers,
contests, and magazines. Unfortunately,
they don't appear to have been
updated recently; the contest links
seem to be from 2001 and earlier,
and the magazine section is still
"under construction." Nevertheless,
 some useful stuff can be
found here.

Writer's Resource Center
www.poewar.com
Loads of articles on the business and
craft of writing.

Writers Write
www.writerswrite.com
Links, critique groups, a writing
"university," contests, job listings, book
promotion services, classifieds, a guidelines directory, and The Internet Writing
Journal.

Writing-World.com
www.writing-world.com
Hosted by the author, this site offers more than 350 articles and a number of other resources, including contest listings, markets, and a free biweekly newsletter.

ONLINE PUBLICATIONS FOR WRITERS

Children's Book Insider
www.write4kids.com/aboutcbi.html
Web site and monthly print newsletter for children's writers, offering writing tips and new markets (paid subscription).

Worldwide Freelance Writer
www.worldwidefreelance.com
Articles and information on international markets.

Writers Weekly
www.writersweekly.com
A weekly e-mail newsletter listing markets and jobs for writers, plus links to online articles and columns.

Writing for DOLLARS!
www.writingfordollars.com
A monthly newsletter offering tips and markets.

Writing World
www.writing-world.com/newsletter/index.shtml
A free biweekly e-mail newsletter edited by the author, offering feature articles, an "advice" column, markets, publishing news, and contest information.

<< CHAPTER 2 >>

THE MECHANICS OF THE INTERNET

I N 1998, GETTING ONLINE WAS a fairly straightforward process: You bought a modem, signed up with an ISP (or a service like AOL), and that was it. Today, writers face a multitude of choices regarding hardware and software—and a host of other perplexing technology issues. While it's not within the scope of this book to address all the possible technologies that one can apply to the use of the Internet, this chapter will look at some of the basic decisions that a writer needs to address, including setting up an ISP account, choosing a Web site host, and protecting against computer viruses.

ACCESSING THE INTERNET

UNLESS YOU'RE STEPHEN KING, chances are that your budget for writing expenses is tight. Your time is also valuable, particularly if you're managing a day job or a family along with your writing activities. These are factors to keep in mind when choosing how to connect to the Internet—whether you're going online for the first time or making decisions about your existing service.

There are four basic connection options:

- A dial-up account through a general service such as AOL, Earthlink, or Juno
- A dial-up account through an independent ISP (Internet Service Provider)
- DSL
- Cable

A dial-up account requires a modem. In the United States, most dial-up services support a transmission rate of up to 56 k; outside the United States, the rate tends to be slower. For unlimited Internet access, an independent ISP will generally provide the least expensive service. Fees are typically $9.95 per month, for which one can usually obtain e-mail hosting (often with more than one address) and anywhere from 5 MB to 10 MB of Web hosting space. The downside is that most ISPs are local, which means that you'll have to pay long-distance fees if you wish to access the Internet or your e-mail while out of town—and you'll generally have to switch ISPs and change your e-mail address if you move.

Services such as AOL and Earthlink charge more than most local ISPs, but have the advantage of being national; you can access your e-mail or the Internet from anywhere, and you never need to change your e-mail address when you move. AOL offers a range of plans, including "light use" at a cost of $9.95 for five hours of Internet usage (including e-mail) per month; additional hours cost $2.95. Unlimited access can be purchased for $23.90 per month, or $19.95 if one signs up for a year in advance. Earthlink offers a similar service for $21.95 per month. AOL and Earthlink also offer access to their own "communities" (including chats and newsgroups) and other resources that aren't available to nonsubscribers. Juno offers free Internet access if you're willing to put up with constant advertising on your screen—including pop-up ads. Its paid service, for $9.95 per month, offers "less advertising and fewer pop-up ads"; it's worth noting that one can get access through an independent ISP for the same price with *no* ads.

DSL and cable offer much faster connection speeds. DSL, for example, provides a download speed of up to 1.5 MBps (megabytes per second), and an upload speed (e.g., when you're sending e-mail or uploading files to your Web site) of up to 128 kps (kilobytes per second). The speed of cable is similar.

It's important to note that while the *capability* for high speeds may exist, the actual speed may vary, depending on traffic rates at different times of the day. Even at their slowest, however, DSL and cable generally provide a huge improvement in the speed at which you can download your e-mail or view Web pages—and if you spend a lot of time surfing, conducting research online, or networking, this is an option well worth considering.

Another "plus" to cable or DSL is that you can connect—and use—more than one computer at a time (though you'll have to pay extra to set up the connection). With a dial-up account, while you can connect multiple computers and their modems to the same line, you can't *use* them at the same time.

The downside to DSL and cable, of course, is the price. The monthly cost of DSL or cable is generally around $49.95. In some areas, this includes modem rental (which you may or may not end up owning after a period of time); in other areas, you either have to rent a modem for an extra charge or buy your own. In addition, cable installation costs apply only to a single computer; you'll have to pay for a router, wiring, and installation if you wish to connect more than one. Another downside is that these services aren't available in all areas. While cable is becoming increasingly widespread (as it generally uses the same lines as cable TV), DSL service is still very limited, because one must be within a certain radius of a DSL "hub." Finally, a cable or DSL connection is of no use when you're traveling; you'll still need some type of dial-up connection to access the Internet or e-mail on the road.

You may also wish to consider a combination of services. For example, I maintain both a cable connection and an ISP dial-up—the latter primarily for when I'm traveling or as insurance against the occasional times when the cable goes down. That doesn't happen often, but when it does, it's bound to be a day when something important is due!

CHOOSING AN E-MAIL SERVICE

IN MANY CASES, YOUR E-MAIL service will be included with your Internet connection service (whether dial-up or cable). However, this is not your only option, and may not even be your best option. For example, if you have your own domain, you can't use your domain name in an AOL or cable-based e-mail account (although you may be able to redirect your mail through an alias). However, you can have an e-mail account anywhere, or multiple accounts, and access them all through a single connection. For example, your dial-up or cable connection might be local, but you might choose to host your Web site (especially if using your own domain name) on another ISP in another state because of lower rates or better services. You can set up another e-mail account with that ISP and access it through your local dial-up or cable connection. All you need to do is specify the locations of those accounts in your e-mail "client" program (e.g., Microsoft Outlook or Eudora). Your e-mail host will provide you with the access information needed to send and receive mail.

An alternative to "regular" e-mail is Web-based e-mail. Web-based e-mail services, such as YAHOO! and HOTMAIL, are generally free. The primary advantage of such a service is that you can access it from any computer at any time; you don't have to have the access codes programmed into your e-mail client. Another advantage is that you can keep the same e-mail address forever, no matter where you live; you won't have to worry about changing it if you move.

Web-based e-mail systems have a number of disadvantages, however. Accessing one's e-mail online tends to be much slower than downloading it through Outlook or Eudora; your e-mail loads at the same speed as a Web page (since it *is* a Web page). The size of your "mailbox" is also limited (often you can store no more than 2 MB of mail at a time). If your limit is exceeded, incoming messages will bounce until you've cleaned out your inbox. However, since Web-based e-mail is not automatically downloaded to your hard drive, you must transfer it manually if you wish to save messages offline. Some accounts also limit the *length* of messages you can receive, place a cap on the size of message attachments, or prohibit attachments altogether. (For an extra fee, many providers offer options such as longer message lengths or increased storage space.)

Another annoyance many users have experienced with Web-based accounts is the actions taken by providers to screen spam. While the desire to block spam is certainly admirable, many providers (such as Yahoo! and Hotmail) make arbitrary decisions as to what messages will be treated as spam based on their length or the originating address. Among the types of messages often blocked (without the user's permission) are e-mail newsletters sent from majordomo or listserv addresses. If you don't include the return address of such newsletters in your "address book," such messages will often be routed to your "junk" or "trash" box.

WEB HOSTING AND DOMAIN NAMES

IF YOU WANT TO SET up your own Web site, you now have a number of options. Perhaps the first issue to address is whether you wish to register your own domain name. Until recently, this could only be done through NETWORK SOLUTIONS; however, it's now possible to register and manage your domain through a variety of different sites. (See Resources, below, for sites that list domain name registries.) Domain name registration generally costs from $15 to $35 per year, depending on the number of years you sign up for. It is now possible to register a name with any of the following suffixes: .com, .net, .org, .biz, .info, .us, .ws, .cc, .bz, and .tv. (If you are not in the United States, you may need to use a country-specific suffix, such as .ca for Canada or .co.uk for the United Kingdom, though .com and other suffixes are also available to international domains.)[1]

Next, you'll need to select a host for your Web site. While most ISPs offer Web space, not all offer domain hosting. For example, if you wish to place your site on Yahoo!, you'll need to use a "geocities" address; on AOL, you'll have an AOL address. (It is, however, possible, through Network Solutions, to register a "virtual" domain name that points to another address.) Generally, you'll need to use an independent ISP to host your site.

Before choosing a host, consider which of the following options you might wish to incorporate into your site:

- **Extra space.** Most ISPs offer 10 MB of space, which is ample for a typical author's site. (With more than seven hundred pages, my Writing-World.com site still requires less than 30 MB.) If you feel that you'll need more than 10 MB, you can generally purchase additional space for a small fee.
- **E-mail addresses and forwarding.** Find out how many e-mail addresses you'll be provided with your Web site. Some providers offer only one, and charge for extra addresses; some provide up to ten. Multiple e-mail addresses are useful if you want to automatically filter your e-mail (e.g., have "information requests" go to one folder, "orders" to another).
- **Technical support.** What type of support does the provider offer? While most providers may claim to offer "24/7 support," the reality may be somewhat different. Some support lines, for example, require you to leave a message, and you may not receive a response for a day or more. Some providers will accept requests for help by e-mail; others require you to visit their Web site and complete an online "help" form (which, again, may not be responded to

[1]You do not have to live in, or host your domain in, a specific country to obtain a domain name with that country's suffix. For example, you can obtain and host a .co.uk domain in the United States—or a .com domain in the United Kingdom.

for 24 hours or more). Find out, as well, whether your provider will give you any assistance in actually setting up your site.

- **Hit counters.** Some providers will give you a "hit counter" for every page on your site; others offer a counter that registers the hits to one page or the site as a whole, but not to individual pages. Some don't offer counters at all, but require you to obtain this from another party. If hit counters are important to you (they do provide very useful information, as I'll discuss in chapter 12), find out what your options are before signing up.

- **Web tracking.** Many providers offer Web tracking as part of their "business" package. Such tracking gives you far more information than a hit counter. For example, it usually distinguishes between "hits" (the number of times any element on a page, including a graphic, is viewed), "page views" (the number of times a specific URL on your site is visited), and "distinct visitors" (the number of people who visit your site). You'll be able to find out where your visitors come from, what sites are referring them to you, what keywords are being used to locate your site, and more. However, Web tracking won't tell you the hit rate for every single page in your site; it will only track the most popular pages.

- **CGI scripts.** If you wish to include forms or sign-up boxes on your site, you'll need the ability to incorporate CGI scripts and have the results sent by e-mail. Some providers only offer this option for "business" hosting, and you may have to contact your ISP to have "form mail" enabled.

- **Password protection.** Some providers will enable you to include a directory that visitors can only access if they have the password. This can be useful if you wish extra security for some of your information—or if you are charging a fee for some of the information on your site.

- **Unix, NT, Front Page, etc**. Most providers offer both Unix and Microsoft NT servers. Find out which is the best option for you, based on the type of program you are using to create your site. There is often an additional charge for "Front Page" hosting.

- **Shopping cart or e-commerce services.** If you want to sell a product (such as an e-book) through your Web site, you may want to set up a shopping cart (although, as I'll discuss in chapter 17, there are other ways to handle such sales). These services are generally available only through "business" hosting and can be expensive.

- **Billing.** Many providers automatically bill your credit card each month, which is convenient. However, keep in mind that site hosting is a deductible expense; it's a good idea to ask the provider to send you an invoice for your records every month, even if the fee is still being deducted automatically.

Setting up a Web site does not have to be a complex process. Many software programs are available to help you with the task—and if you prefer to do it yourself, HTML is not at all difficult to learn. Chapters 12 and 13 offer more tips on developing an effective author site.

UNDERSTANDING DOWNLOADS

SOONER OR LATER, YOU'RE almost certain to need to download a file from the Internet. Sometimes this is an easy process; sometimes it can be more complicated, depending on the file format.

Adobe Acrobat PDF (Portable Document Format) files are among the most common types of downloads. A PDF file is like an electronic photocopy of a text or illustration; it captures the image of an electronic document just as a photocopy captures an image of a hard-copy document. This has become one of the most common formats for e-books, and is also a popular way to save and transmit scanned documents.

To read a PDF file, all you need is a recent version of the Adobe Acrobat Reader, which is available free for any platform and for many different languages. Often, this will come with your browser software; if you don't already have the Reader, see Resources, below, for a link from which you can download a copy.

Some people experience problems with PDF downloads, however, particularly when downloading through Internet Explorer. While Netscape offers the option of saving the file rather than opening it, Explorer will attempt to open the document while it is downloading. If the file is large, or loaded with links, this can cause your system to freeze or crash. Windows users can generally bypass this problem by *right-clicking* on the document, which indicates that the file is to be saved rather than opened.

Larger files are often compressed into .bin, .sit, .hqx, .zip, or similar formats. In some cases, your browser may not be equipped with the proper "expansion" program to open this type of file. Most of these files can also be opened with StuffIt Expander (see Resources), which is available free from ALADDIN SYSTEMS.

You may also encounter Microsoft Word or Excel file downloads. Before downloading such a file, be sure that you know that it is coming from a reputable source, as this type of file *can* be infected with a computer virus. Generally, these downloads will work with either a Mac or PC. Another type of program that works only with Windows is an .exe file; again, be cautious with these, as they can contain viruses.

If you wish to *create* a download, that's easy to do as well. Simply post a file on your Web site with a link from which people can access it. Include the title and file format in the URL; for example, if it's a PDF file, the link should be something like "http://www.mydomain.com/directory/title.pdf." A Word file should be listed as "title.doc," an Excel file as "title.xls," and an executable file as "title.exe."

If you'd like to create PDF files but don't wish to purchase the Adobe Acrobat program for $249, you have two options. One is to "try out" Adobe's Web-based PDF service, which allows you to convert up to five documents at no charge. You can convert additional documents by subscribing to Adobe's online service for $9.99 a month (or $99.99 for one year)—again, an inexpensive option if you have only a few files to convert. For more information, go to the Adobe Tryouts page (*www.adobe.com/products/tryadobe/main.jhtml*).

If you expect to create a large number of PDF files, or if you wish to be able to modify those files after they have been created, I recommend that you purchase the Acrobat program. This will enable you to edit your files (by adding or deleting pages), hotlink URLs, hotlink your table of contents to the pages within the document, change the pagination, and more. If you anticipate creating your own e-books, the program is well worth the money (more on this in chapter 17).

COMPUTER VIRUSES AND VIRUS HOAXES[2]

EVERY DAY, I RECEIVE four or five e-mail messages with subject headers like "A funny game" or "Some questions" or "Your password." I don't have to open them (or their attachments) to know what they contain: the Klez virus.

As I write this, the Klez worm is the latest of a seemingly endless stream of viruses. At present, some 250 viruses are known to be "in the wild" (i.e., "out there"). Some are relatively harmless, though annoying, such as worms whose primary purpose is to reach other computers via an infected host's address book. Others are far more dangerous, designed to corrupt, overwrite, or destroy your data and eventually bring your system to a halt.

While a virus can damage your computer, the fear of viruses can damage your ability to use the Internet effectively. Since most viruses are transmitted via attachments, many people are afraid to open *any* attachment. Some are even afraid to open their e-mail itself, having heard (incorrectly) that simply opening an e-mail message can activate a virus (it can't). Many editors refuse to accept attachments due to virus concerns. To make matters worse, the constant barrage of virus hoaxes keeps many users in a constant state of jitters (more on that below).

The best protection against computer viruses isn't simply a good antivirus program. The best protection is knowledge. Once you know what to look out for, you don't have to worry needlessly—and you'll be better able to spot dangers when they *do* arise.

ATTACHMENTS: TO OPEN OR NOT TO OPEN?

Antivirus advice ranges from "don't open any attachments" (too broad!) to "don't open attachments from anyone you don't know" (not broad enough). While there's no point in assuming that every attachment is infected, knowing the sender is not enough; many of the viruses I receive are from people I know, whose systems happen to be infected. Once you know what to look for in the e-mail carrying an infected attachment, however, you'll find viruses fairly easy to spot.

The first clue is generally in the subject header. Is your friend really sending you "a funny excite game" or "a WinXP patch" or "free XXX pictures"? Be wary of generic subject headers like "some questions" or "can you help me?" or "seeking advice." If you see this type of subject header, with an attachment—and especially if you see it more than once, from different senders—you can be pretty sure it signals a virus.

---

[2]This section was originally published in my "Net//Working" column in *The Writer* in October 2002 (*www.writermag.com*).

The next clue will be in the text of the e-mail itself. The Klez virus, for example, does not include a message; all you receive is a subject header and an attachment. If you get a blank message with an attachment, therefore, it's wise to delete that attachment even if the subject header *doesn't* look suspicious.

Other viruses pull a random chunk of text from the infected host's file and slap it into the e-mail. This text will make no sense, as it's simply a portion of a paragraph with no context. Thus, if you receive an e-mail message that makes you go "huh?" and it has an attachment, delete that attachment.

Another clue is likely to lie in the file name of the attachment itself. While many viruses are carried in .exe files, worms like Klez often send attachments with suffixes like .bat, .pif, .scr, and .vbs. In other cases, the names won't make sense; I received one titled simply "a." The good news is that viruses are rarely (if ever) found in *legitimate* files such as .jpg, .gif, and .pdf.

If you receive an e-mail with even one of these clues (let alone all three), simply delete the attachment without opening it. Again, a virus cannot infect your system *unless* you actually open the attachment; you cannot be harmed simply by opening the e-mail. (The exception to this is if you are using Outlook and it is set to "preview" attachments—which is really the same thing as opening them. In that case, clicking on your e-mail will pop the attachment into the preview window, thereby opening or executing it. Viruses with .vbs extensions can be activated in this way.)

DETERMINING IF YOU'RE INFECTED

E-mail attachments aren't the only means by which viruses are transmitted. Downloads can be another source—especially if you frequently download files from unprotected sources, such as bulletin boards. Disks can also be infected—and an infected disk can spread a virus to your system simply by being "read" from your disk drive. (If you share disks or obtain disks from other individuals, be sure that your virus-checking program is set to scan any disk that is inserted in your disk drive.) A file downloaded directly from the Web generally cannot infect your system unless you actually open (or execute) that file—so again, it's wise to set your virus program to check files as they download to ensure that they are safe. If you *do* "contract" a virus, you may not become aware of it immediately, as most viruses spend time *infecting* your files before actually *destroying* any files. This is so that you will be more likely to pass those infected files on before having any indication that your system is, in fact, compromised.

The best way to determine whether your system is infected is to run a high-quality antivirus program—and update that program regularly. Most antivirus software can be set to operate in the background, checking for viruses every time you open a program, download a file, or insert a disk. If you don't download files or use disks from others (such as shareware software), you may prefer to simply scan your computer periodically for viruses. However, once your system is infected, keep in mind that you may not be able to repair or retrieve all the files that have been corrupted. If too much damage has been done, antivirus/repair programs may not help; if, for example, your system has shut down entirely, you will probably have to take the computer to a repair shop.

If you have an e-mail "worm," you may not find out until people tell you that they've received it from you. However, the fact that someone has received an infected e-mail from you may not always indicate that your computer is infected! Versions of the Klez virus, for example, use "address spoofing" to prevent a recipient from knowing exactly where a virus came from. In "spoofing," the virus selects one e-mail address from the infected computer's address book as the target, and another as the "from" address.

Many Macintosh users have been confused by address spoofing. The Klez virus doesn't affect Macs—but if your e-mail address is in someone else's infected computer's address book, it may appear that you are sending out viruses, even though your system is clean. (The majority of viruses do *not* affect Macs—the Mac operating system doesn't even recognize a .exe file—but Macs *can* be affected by viruses that are carried by, and target, specific programs such as Microsoft Word or Excel.)

HOAXES AND ALARMS

Just as prolific as actual viruses are virus *hoaxes*—e-mails that warn of some dangerous new virus that will do horrible things to one's computer if one opens a particular e-mail or attachment. Unfortunately, far too many people accept (and spread) these "warnings" without question.

Fortunately, most virus hoax messages are easy to spot. If you have to scroll down through dozens of addresses before you even reach the message, you can be sure that you're looking at a hoax. The second "sure sign" of a hoax is the line, "please forward this to everyone in your address book." Hoaxes may also contain phrases like "reported on CNN" or "reported by Microsoft." (If a warning is genuine, it will include links to official virus/antivirus Web sites, such as SYMANTEC or McAFEE.) Some hoaxes instruct you to delete a particular file from your computer; never do so until you've verified that the warning is accurate! (For example, as I write this, an e-mail is circulating advising people to delete the JDBGMGR.EXE file from their computers—though this file is actually a legitimate Windows operating file.) If you're not sure, check a site like VMYTHS for the latest information on hoaxes.

Besides refraining from passing on unsubstantiated "warnings," you can do other things to help reduce fears about viruses. It's good network etiquette, for example, to refrain from passing on unsolicited attachments. If you find an image or file that's just too cute to keep to yourself, *ask permission* before forwarding it to your friends. Most discussion lists have an unspoken rule against posting attachments; violating that rule can result in some serious flaming. Finally, if you *do* send someone an attachment, make sure that you include a relevant subject line *and* a personal message that explains what the attachment is. Don't just say, "Here's something cute"—that could too easily be mistaken for a virus message.

There's no question that viruses cause hundreds of thousands of dollars in damage every year. However, fear of viruses should not prevent you from networking and gathering information online—or simply enjoying yourself. Being informed is the best defense!

RESERVES

WEB-BASED E-MAIL

Hotmail
www.hotmail.com

Yahoo!
www.yahoo.com

FINDING ISPS AND HIGH-SPEED INTERNET PROVIDERS

AT&T
www.linksys.com/attbroadband
Provides cable Internet services.

Computer User ISP/Web Hosting Directory
www.computeruser.com/resources/isp

Cox Communication Services
www.cox.net
Provides cable Internet services.

DSL Service Providers and Availability Search
www.dsl-service-providers.net
Find out whether DSL is available in your area, and locate service providers.

Find an ISP
www.findanisp.com
Lists eight thousand ISPs in United States and Canada. Search by criteria such as price, platform supported, and specific services.

List, The
http://thelist.internet.com
A list of ISPs, searchable by various criteria.

Looksmart ISP Finder
www.looksmart.com/ispfinder

SITES LISTING/COMPARING DOMAIN REGISTRIES

Domain Registries
www.domain.registries.net

Network Solutions
www.networksolutions.com
The original domain name registry, but by no means your only option. The site offers several useful tools, including "Whois" (to find out who owns a domain) and a domain availability search function that suggests "similar" names if the one you want is taken.

RegSelect
www.regselect.com
Includes price comparisons for single- and multiple-year registrations.

Webmonkey Reference: Domain Registry
http://hotwired.lycos.com/webmonkey/ reference/domain_registries
Domain registry information.

DOWNLOAD TOOLS

Acrobat Reader
www.adobe.com/products/acrobat/ readstep2.html

Aladdin Systems
www.aladdinsys.com
Produces DropStuff, DropZip, StuffIt, and StuffItExpander.

WinZip
www.winzip.com

VIRUS AND VIRUS HOAX INFORMATION

Antivirus Software
http://antivirus.about.com
Includes information on current viruses, links to antivirus software sites, and loads of other information.

Hoaxbusters
http://hoaxbusters.ciac.org
Information on various Internet hoaxes

and scams, including how to recognize a hoax.

McAfee
www.mcafee.com
Provides antivirus software. For virus information, including news, a glossary, and information on hoaxes, go to *www.mcafee.com/anti-virus/default.asp.*

Symantec
www.symantec.com
Provides antivirus software and information.

Urban Legends Reference Pages
www.snopes.com
Check out e-mail hoaxes and urban legends before passing them on.

Viruses online and offline
www.lctn.com/util/virusfaq.html
FAQ and glossary about computer viruses.

Vmyths: Truths about Computer Security Hysteria
www.vmyths.com
If you're not sure whether a warning might be a hoax, look it up here.

<< CHAPTER 3 >>

CONDUCTING RESEARCH ONLINE

RESEARCH HAS ALWAYS BEEN ONE of a writer's most time-consuming tasks. One could spend hours, days, even weeks tracking down an elusive bit of information or locating an expert to interview on an obscure topic. Today's shrinking library budgets, dwindling collections, and (in many areas) diminishing hours compound the problem.

Enter the Internet—and a solution to many writers' research needs. While the Internet is no substitute for a library in some cases (just as there is often no substitute for a good book), in others, it offers unparalleled access to material that has never before been easily available to writers. Plus, location is no longer an issue: You can conduct the same research whether you live in New York or New Guinea.

On the Internet, no topic is too obscure. You don't have to know much (if anything) about a subject to go online and find enough information to build a coherent query, gather the basic facts and figures to fill in the background of your article, and locate an expert to interview for the substance of the piece. This means you can cover a broader range of topics, pitch to a wider range of markets, and sell more articles.

VIRTUAL LIBRARIES VERSUS REAL LIBRARIES

WHAT CAN YOU FIND ON the Internet that you can't find in that venerable library building down the street? The differences begin with the way information is organized online and the ease with which you can find material that might not be available at your local library. For example:

- The Internet offers up-to-the-minute information and research results. Scholarly papers may appear online as soon as they are published or approved. It could take months for that material to appear in book form in a regular library.
- The Internet offers older material that traditional libraries can't afford to archive. Since electrons are inexpensive, it is easy for universities, publications, and other sources to archive huge amounts of older (and positively ancient) material online.
- The Internet makes it possible to find information without knowing exactly what you're looking for. While you can search a card catalog by subject, you have to have an author name or catalog number to actually locate the materials themselves. Online, you don't have to know what has been written on a topic, or by whom. Simply type in a keyword, and you'll be taken directly to the information you're looking for. And it won't be checked out by someone else when you find it!
- The Internet enables you to search on details as well as subjects. Searching for details in a traditional library involves a "top-down" approach: First you must define the general subject, then the books on that subject that are most likely to contain the details you want. Then, you must search the indices of those books and hope that your details were considered worthy of indexing by the author. Online, you can start your search at the detail level (e.g., was Cinderella's slipper made of glass or fur?) and have the answer in minutes.
- On the Internet, information leads to more information. Once you've found a site that addresses your topic, it will usually lead you to other sites (and other experts).
- The Internet puts you in instant contact with authors, experts, and other interview sources. Most material on the Internet includes a contact address, which gives you a chance to communicate directly with the person who provided the information or conducted the study. This makes finding an expert far easier than combing through directories or telephone books.

By far the most significant advantage of the Internet, however, is its ability to connect you with information that you couldn't possibly find anywhere else—even through interlibrary loan—including:

- **Government documents.** Bills, proposals, legal documents, legislation—and the official arguments and testimonies for and against such legislation—can now be found online, not only for the federal government, but also for most states and a number of towns and counties. Many of these are "mirrored" on other sites. Several universities, for example, maintain extensive collections of legal materials, while institutions like the ASSOCIATION OF RESEARCH LIBRARIES (ARL) post just about every imaginable legal document related to changes in copyright law.
- **Government studies.** Besides posting contemporary legal documents, many government sites also post the results of studies, projects, and other types of research. The LIBRARY OF CONGRESS, for example, offers a huge selection of

digital documents, recordings, oral histories, and other materials (go to the "American Memories" section of the site for details). NASA offers a wealth of information on space exploration and related topics.

- **Primary source documents.** Due to the efforts of universities and private individuals, thousands of primary materials are now online—historical journals, diaries, records, letters, texts, and other documents that were formerly nearly impossible to find—because many have never been published or collected in book form. Try the HISTORY/SOCIAL STUDIES WEB SITE FOR K–12 TEACHERS for links to such materials.
- **Original texts.** Medieval manuscripts, ancient texts, sagas, classics, historical records, and other hard-to-find documents—translated and untranslated—are posted on various sites. Check the ONLINE BOOKS PAGE for a list of more than 18,000 e-texts on the Web.
- **Current research studies.** Find the latest discoveries and developments in science, medicine, history, astronomy, and any other topic through journal articles, research reports, and conference proceedings. Most of these are posted through university Web sites and professional databases.
- **Clearinghouses and directories.** Several sites have attempted to collect links to all sites on the Web relating to a particular topic—such as Georgetown University's LABYRINTH, a directory to everything medieval. Such clearinghouses are far often more effective than search engines in tracking down information on a specific subject. For more information, see Directories, on page 29.
- **Databases.** Much of the information on the Internet is stored in databases, which cannot be searched by search engines. For more information, see Databases, below.
- **Journals.** Once, professional, technical, and scholarly journals were available only to subscribers. Now, many post their contents online. (Many, however, still require a paid subscription.)
- **Newspapers.** The latest news is available online from a variety of sources, including newsfeeds such as Reuters. Older stories are usually archived in fee-based databases. Smaller papers, however, often provide free access to back issues. You can also access newspapers around the world for an international perspective—including English-language and non-English papers. For a local slant, try one of the hundreds of regional papers online. Start your search for newspapers through an online newsstand such as NewsDirectory.com (you'll find a list of electronic newsstands in the Resources section of chapter 5).
- **Magazines.** Looking up an older article from a consumer magazine has become much easier, as hundreds of publications now provide complete archives of back issues online. You can also find archives of semi-scholarly publications like *Military History Quarterly (http://militaryhistory.about.com)* and *British Archaeology (www.britarch.ac.uk/ba/ba.html).*
- **Books.** Thousands of free, classic, and public-domain books are now available as e-texts. PROJECT GUTENBERG focuses primarily, but not exclusively, on literature and fiction. This is the place to go for the books you remember from

childhood, plus hundreds of novels, short stories, and other materials. The ONLINE BOOKS PAGE offers links not only to literary e-texts, but to hundreds of scholarly, technical, professional, and historical documents (such as studies, conference proceedings, and public-domain government documents).

- **Private organizations.** Thousands of groups, agencies, organizations, associations, medical institutions, research centers, and benevolent associations that formerly offered free literature by mail now post that information online. This provides the researcher with a wealth of tips, background basics, statistics, and current research news on an incredible range of topics.
- **International governments.** To find out basic facts about any country in the world, just look for that country's Web site. Some focus primarily on tourism. Others offer statistics, historical data, information on currency, weather, and language, and more. International information can also be found through a host of travel and tourism sites.
- **Educational materials.** Instructors, teaching organizations, and many other agencies have provided huge quantities of teaching materials, often consisting of links to informational sites that might be of benefit to instructors or students. These often provide a good starting point for researchers as well.
- **Commercial organizations and businesses.** While some commercial sites are little more than electronic catalogs or storefronts, you can also find useful information from commercial sources. Just be sure to filter fact from hype.
- **Individual experts.** Personal and personal/professional sites are often excellent sources of information. For example, members of the Society for Creative Anachronisms have posted vast quantities of obscure, hard-to-find historical information (such as lists of "historical period" names and genealogies) online. Personal experts also include hobbyists, fans, activists, and authors. Some provide useful information onsite; others develop link sites that will take you to the best sources of information on a particular topic.

CHOOSING EFFECTIVE KEYWORDS

PERHAPS THE GREATEST CHALLENGE in using search engines is choosing keywords that will bring the best results. The difficulty lies in the fact that search engines use indexes rather than topical guides. Thus, while you could look up "cats" in a library card catalog and find a selection of subject-specific entries, searching on the word "cats" online will give you thousands of irrelevant results. Your goal should be to find a keyword (or set of keywords) inclusive enough to produce a range of useful results, yet exclusive enough to filter out the chaff. The following techniques can help:

- **Choose the term most likely to be used by your preferred source.** If you want veterinary tips on cat care, for example, keep in mind that most animal care professionals will use the word "feline" rather than the word "cat," which means that a search on "feline care" will produce better results. If you're looking for tips from (or for) average cat owners, however, a search on "cat care" may work better.

- **Use specific or unusual terms.** If you want to find information on "cancer in cats," searching for "feline oncology" will pull up veterinary pages and exclude most personal "cat memorial" pages. A search on "feline lymphosarcoma" will narrow the results even further.
- **Consider how your topic might be indexed in a book.** If you bought a book on cat care, topics such as "how to feed a cat" would be listed under such keywords as "nutrition," and "diet." Combine those keywords with your primary subject (e.g., "feline nutrition," "feline diet") to refine your search.
- **Think like the author of the site you're seeking.** If you were writing an article on feline nutrition, what words or phrases would you use? How would you title your site? If you'd call your site "Ten Tips on Feline Nutrition" or "How to Feed Your Cat," try running searches on those phrases.
- **Brainstorm variations on keywords and phrases.** Rather than just searching for "feline nutrition," try searching under "diet," "care," "feeding," "food," or any other variation you can imagine.
- **Use phrases instead of single words.** Searching on words that are likely to be paired, and on complete phrases, can get you to a specific site more quickly. Most search engines consider any word combination placed in quotes to be a phrase.
- **Use multiple keywords.** A search for Cinderella's slipper, for example, will work better if you search for "Cinderella" and "slipper" and "glass." Most search engines now use "and" as a default when multiple keywords are entered, returning only those sites that include all the selected words or phrases. (In the past, you had to specify "and" with the appropriate symbol or Boolean operator; thankfully, search engine logic has now caught up with the rest of us!)
- **Use NOT to exclude unwanted results.** A search on "limericks," for example, will bring better results if you specify "NOT Ireland." (On some engines, the minus sign [-] is used instead of the word "NOT.")
- **Use the most obvious keywords first.** It's possible to overspecify a search word or phrase and exclude useful results. Often, what you want can be found under the most obvious terms. When I wanted an Anglo-Saxon name for a character, for example, a simple search for "Anglo-Saxon names" brought immediate results.
- **Check the meta tags of your results for other keyword options.** If you've located one or two useful sites, check the source code of those sites for meta tags (located at the top of the document). Those tags can give you hints on other keywords that can be used to find related materials.

SEARCHING WITHOUT ENGINES

SEARCH ENGINES ARE WONDERFUL, BUT there are many things they cannot do. They cannot, for example, retrieve information from directories or databases that require a secondary, onsite search function. Thus, a search engine won't retrieve book titles from an online bookstore database, or terms and phrases from a reference guide or dictionary. They often can't locate information embedded within download-only files, such as .zip files and .pdf files. Nor do they always provide access to the most recent documents on the Web: Search engines may be as much as two to three months behind in indexing sites, so they may not provide access to materials posted within the past few weeks.

Fortunately, other tools can help you dig further into the Web for information that search engines miss. These include:

META-SEARCH ENGINES

How do you know if your search engine is giving you the best results? One way to find an answer is to run your search query through a meta-search engine, which submits your request to several different search engines at once and then compiles the results. To test the results of different search engines, you could run a query through a meta-search engine such as DOGPILE and specify that it provide the results by engine. That way, you can determine which regular search engine provided the best answers to your query.

Some researchers swear by meta-search engines; others find them less satisfactory. In general, meta-search engines allow you to determine the sources you want searched (i.e., which regular engines), the maximum number of desired results, how the results should be sorted (i.e., by keyword or by search engine), and an upper limit on search time. Some also allow complex searches or the use of Boolean operators, but not all. Most don't provide the option of tailoring a more advanced search. For a more detailed discussion of how such engines work, see INTERNET TOOLS FOR THE ADVANCED SEARCHER.

DIRECTORIES

On the surface, directories like YAHOO! look much like search engines: You enter a keyword and get a list of results. Underneath, however, there is a difference: While search engines build indexes automatically, directories are compiled through human selection.

This can be both an advantage and a disadvantage. The advantage is that human selection filters out irrelevant and inappropriate entries that might pop up under a normal search query. When you search Yahoo! for "writing," for example, you won't be flooded with dozens of "read my writing" sites, or lists of writing classes from twenty different universities.

On the other hand, you have no guarantee that this selection process uses the same criteria you would have chosen. You can't be sure that a directory will include every worthwhile site on a topic, or even those sites that you consider worthwhile. It may also include many sites that you'd choose to omit. In addition, many directories rely on sites being submitted to them, so if they aren't informed of a worthwhile site, it won't be included in the directory.

Nevertheless, directories can be an excellent place to start a search. Besides search directories, you can find a number of excellent online directories and subject-specific directories such as MY VIRTUAL REFERENCE DESK.

DATABASES

Huge quantities of information—including statistics, records, research results, figures, lists, compilations, and data of every description—can be found through online databases. Databases fall roughly into three categories (with respect to how they are accessed):

- Databases that can be accessed only by members of a particular profession or association, such as certain medical or technical databases
- Databases that can be accessed by the public for a fee, such as archives of magazine and newspaper articles
- Databases that are free to the public

This final category includes dictionaries, encyclopedias, directories (such as telephone and address directories), compilations of articles or texts, reference utilities (such as stock quotes, currency converters, and weather guides), and many other resources. Such databases can often be a quick and easy way to answer a complex question—and they contain a wealth of information for researchers.

One way to find databases is to simply search on the term you want to find (or the general topic area) and the word "database." For example, if you want information on medieval history, try searching on "medieval history" AND "database" (or even just "medieval" AND "database"). Or, check a database list such as DIRECT SEARCH or MY VIRTUAL REFERENCE DESK.

PORTAL SITES

While many sites call themselves "portals," I use this term for subject-specific sites that offer extensive resource links. WRITING-WORLD.COM, or example, could be described as a *clearinghouse* of writing information, while Georgetown University's LABYRINTH is a *portal* for medieval history sites.

Portals range from major directories sponsored by university departments to sites handled by private individuals with a passion for a particular topic. They usually offer better sources of links than more generic directories or search engine "recommended sites," because they are compiled by people with a knowledge of and interest in the site's subject. Such sites offer a number of advantages, including:

- **Comprehensive coverage.** A good portal will usually offer the best and most complete set of links on a subject. You'll find links that search engines miss, and you're also likely to find that further searching keeps bringing you back to the same links listed on the portal.
- **Screening.** Good portal hosts check linked sites for content and accuracy. You can be confident, in most cases, that irrelevant, inaccurate, or inappropriate sites have been excluded.
- **Timeliness.** Portals may offer links to resources too recent to be indexed by search engines. Good portals also check old links regularly, removing dead links and updating those that have moved.

Not all portals are perfect, of course. Many offer only limited collections of links, don't seek out new resources, and never clean outdated URLs from their files. Once you find a good site, however, you'll find that it takes you places that even the best search engine might have missed. Therefore, when you hit a portal, it's usually wise to explore that site's resources before going back to your regular search.

WEBRINGS

Webrings are a means of linking together useful or interesting sites on a particular subject. You're very likely to come across a Webring in the course of your research, and when you do, you can use its directory to locate related sites. Just click on the "list all" or "directory" button on the Webring menu, and you'll be taken to a list of all the sites that are members of the ring.

EVALUATING INFORMATION

ONCE YOU FIND A SITE, how do you know if it's any good? After all, anyone with a modem can post absolutely anything online, with no regard for accuracy—so do you dare trust the material you find on the Web?

Unfortunately, the Internet offers just as much *misinformation* as *information*. One classic example is an article that appeared in *The Boston Globe* in July 2000, touching on the grim fates of the fifty-six men who signed the Declaration of Independence. This article was based on an e-mail that has been making the rounds since about 1995—an e-mail that was also passed along as "fact" by Ann Landers. As *American Journalism Review* columnist Carl Cannon pointed out, this e-mail (and the resulting *Globe* article) was, in fact, almost entirely false.[1]

According to the oft-quoted account, five signers of the Declaration were captured by the British and tortured to death as traitors, while nine fought and died in the Revolutionary War. In reality, no signers of the Declaration were tortured by the British, while two were merely injured in the war (none died). One signer who supposedly "died in poverty" actually became governor of Pennsylvania.

The Internet is also a hotbed of urban legends, hoaxes, and scares. You've probably gotten an inbox-full of "virus threats"—characterized by the tell-tale phrase, "Please pass this on to everyone you know." You've probably heard that the government is about to start charging everyone for using e-mail to help subsidize the Post Office (it isn't). Even accurate information (such as the news that certain cold medicines were to be withdrawn from the market) gets circulated long after its "time," until it becomes misinformation simply because it is out of date.

How can you determine whether the information you find is accurate? It's impossible to be 100 percent sure—but by asking the following questions about everything you read, you'll improve your chances of getting "the right stuff."

[1] "The Real Computer Virus," by Carl Cannon, *American Journalism Review*, April 2001, www.ajr.org/article.asp?id=225.

- **Does the author, site, or information appear to exist primarily to support a particular point of view?** Why is this information online in the first place? Does the material contain an obvious bias toward a particular point of view, agenda, or belief? If so, chances are that the material will at least be slanted toward that bias—even if it is, itself, factual—and there's also a very good chance that information that does *not* support the author's views will be omitted.
- **Does the site seem "overly emotional"?** It's often easy to spot "emotional" sites—they're full of **bold-face phrases** and LOTS OF CAPS. They often look as if the author is "shouting" at you. If a site uses phrases like "Don't believe what those Commie bastards in government are trying to pull off!!!" I'm inclined to believe that the author has an axe to grind—and that accuracy may not be his highest priority.
- **Is the author trying to sell something?** I'm always wary of sites that purport to offer "valuable medical information" that "doctors won't tell you"—but that just happens to be available in the author's book, or that supports a line of products such as supplements or exercise equipment. That doesn't mean that an author who is trying to sell a book is necessarily providing misinformation—but if the information seems primarily offered as a sales pitch, beware!
- **Who is the author?** Does the author have any credentials? The Internet is a place where absolutely anyone can post anything. Keep in mind, however, that a *lack* of credentials does not necessarily mean that the information will be inaccurate; the Internet is also a place where thousands of ordinary folks post highly accurate information, based on their personal research. If the author doesn't have credentials, look for references (e.g., a bibliography) that can help confirm the information provided.
- **Who is the host?** Is the site sponsored by a reputable organization? Or is it sponsored by an organization with a vested interest in promoting a particular viewpoint? Note that a suffix like ".edu" does not mean that the information is sponsored by a university (and therefore accurate); it simply means that the site is hosted on a server based at an educational institution. Nor does the suffix ".com" necessarily indicate that the site is "commercial," as this suffix is used by thousands of private individuals who offer excellent and accurate information.
- **Is the site up to date?** In Netscape, you can check on how recently a site has been updated by going to the "View Page Info" command. This will bring up a window that gives some basic information on the site—including the date of the last update. Another way to determine if a site is current is to test a few of its links. If you find that most of the links are "dead," you can assume that the author has not updated the information recently.
- **Does the information agree with other sites on the same topic?** When I see ten sites that list Shackleton's death on January 5, and only one that lists it on January 4, I'm inclined to believe the voice of the majority. By reviewing several sites on a topic, you'll get an idea of what the "accepted facts" are—and be able to spot a site that seems to be "out of step" with those facts.
- **Does the site offer links to other resources?** A biased informant may not offer links to other sites that would enable you to check out counter-arguments.

If links are provided, are they balanced or do they lead to only one side of the story? How current are the links? If the majority of a site's links are outdated, this is an indication that the author isn't maintaining the site or isn't keeping up to date with new developments.

Here are some other ways to protect yourself—and your writing—from inaccuracies:

- Never assume that information in an *unsolicited* e-mail (e.g., something that is passed on to you by a friend, or through a discussion list) is factual unless you have checked it thoroughly or are familiar with the original source. E-mail has been the most prolific source of legends, myths (like the "signers of the Declaration" story), virus hoaxes, urban legends, and outdated information. E-mail gets forwarded forever—and it seems to appeal to the gullible, who pass on stories like "I passed out in a hotel room and woke up without a kidney." Hoaxes also include warm-fuzzy stories, such as tales of sick children needing prayers or greeting cards.
- Check the URBAN LEGENDS REFERENECE PAGES for stories that are too good (or too bad) to be true. (For example, Osama bin Laden does *not* own Snapple!) Similarly, check VMYTHS.COM for information on possible virus hoaxes.

Above all, use your common sense. Information that appears in the most reputable of domains may not be free from bias or inaccuracies; conversely, information located on an intensely personal Web site may prove highly valuable. Where lists of criteria fail, good judgment can prevail.

E-MAIL INTERVIEWS AND SURVEYS

WHILE WEB RESEARCH IS a great way to flesh out an article, you may also need to conduct interviews with experts on the subject—and here, too, the Internet can help. First, you can often locate experts using the search techniques described above. When conducting your research, you're also likely to find sites hosted by experts who are willing to give you interviews, or by organizations that have a staff of experts. If you wish to talk to a few experts, you may be able to handle this with individual e-mail interviews; if you wish to get information or opinions from a larger group, you may be able to do so through an e-mail survey.

E-MAIL INTERVIEWS
Besides being a wonderful alternative to the long-distance phone call, e-mail interviews are often appreciated by busy experts who don't have time for a face-to-face or telephone interview. It enables you to compose questions carefully rather than "on the fly" and gives your interviewee time to respond carefully as well. E-mail also offers a good way to follow up on a traditional interview, when seeking clarification or additional information.

E-mail interviews are especially useful when the interviewee's information will constitute a small part of your article or, alternatively, when the article will be based almost verbatim on the interviewee's words, as in a "Q and A" interview or similar piece. They are also appropriate when:

- You know exactly what questions you want to ask. (This often requires some background knowledge of the subject.)
- The subject is relatively impersonal. (An e-mail interview wouldn't be appropriate for discussing a tragic or deeply personal issue.)
- The interview can be conducted with a limited number of questions.

E-mail interviews are less effective when you're trying to develop a profile or catch a personal glimpse of the interviewee—a profile that would include not only the individual's words but also your observations of the person's appearance, actions, skills, emotions, tone of voice, etc. They are less effective if you don't know enough about a subject to develop useful questions, or when you're more likely to get information from the natural flow of questions and answers than from a predefined script. In an e-mail interview, you can't change direction if a more promising tangent emerges from the conversation; you can't nudge the interviewee back on track if the conversation strays or ask immediate follow-up questions if your first questions don't elicit enough information.

The following strategies can help you develop and refine an e-mail interview:

- Determine your goals before writing your questions. Decide exactly what you need to know, then develop questions that will best elicit that information.
- Ask open-ended questions rather than questions that can be answered "yes" or "no." For example, instead of asking, "Do you enjoy writing children's books?" ask, "What do you enjoy most about writing children's books?" or "What are some of the things you enjoy about writing children's books?"
- If necessary, explain why you are asking a particular question, so the interviewee has a better idea of the response you're looking for.
- Let the interviewee know what audience or market you're writing for, so she will know how detailed or technical the information should be.
- Keep your questions as clear, uncomplicated, and short as possible.
- Keep your list of questions as short as possible. Ten is good; twenty is likely to tax an interviewee's patience.
- List your questions numerically, and leave space between each question for the interviewee to insert the answer.
- Include a final "open" question (e.g., "Is there anything else you'd like to say on this subject that hasn't been covered above?") that will enable the interviewee to add information or ideas that weren't covered by your script.
- Let the interviewee know how soon you need the answers. If you need to follow up on a late interview, be polite. Remember that the interviewee is doing you a favor and is under no obligation to comply with your request or meet your deadline.

E-mail interviews don't work for everyone or in every circumstance. They may not be appropriate, for example, if your interviewee is uncomfortable with written questions (they may look too much like a test) or doesn't enjoy expressing ideas in writing. Under the right conditions, however, e-mail can add an extra level of convenience to an interview—and give you a written record of the conversation.

E-MAIL SURVEYS

Another way to gather information via e-mail is to conduct a survey. Once again, the Internet offers an unparalleled opportunity: You can send a list of questions to hundreds of potential respondents at no cost to you.

At the same time, caution is in order. Some respondents may regard a survey as a form of spam. Your e-mail should state the nature and purpose of the survey as quickly, succinctly, and courteously as possible. Assure respondents of privacy, and guarantee that you won't cite anyone by name or organization without permission. If you're soliciting comments as well as statistics, ask respondents to indicate whether or not they may be quoted and how they should be cited.

Like interview questions, survey questions should be short, clear, well organized, and limited in number. Unlike interview questions, however, survey questions should encourage "yes/no" or multiple-choice options. Respondents are also more likely to answer a short questionnaire than a long one.

An easy format is to follow each question with the answer options (e.g., "Yes" or "No") on a separate line or lines. Place a set of parentheses in front of each option, with space for a response:

1. Do you accept e-mail queries?
   ( ) Yes
   ( ) No

2. How do you prefer to receive manuscripts?
   ( ) Hard copy (printed)
   ( ) On diskette
   ( ) By e-mail, in the body of the e-mail message
   ( ) As an e-mail attachment

This enables the respondent to simply insert an "x" in the appropriate space and mail the form back as a reply. If you are offering a multiple-choice question that could have more than one answer, indicate whether you want the respondent to "check only one" or "check all that apply."

To ensure your respondents' privacy, place all the survey addresses in the "BCC" (blind copy) field of your header. If you have a large number of addressees, send the survey in several batches rather than all at once.

When you mail your survey, several may bounce back immediately as undeliverable. Keep track of these bounces so that you know exactly how many surveys went out. This will enable you to calculate the correct percentage of responses. For example, if you send out one hundred surveys, get ten back as undeliverable, and receive fifty responses, you have a 55 percent response rate.

The bulk of your responses will typically arrive in a flood within the first two or three days of your mailing. After that, the flow will taper to a trickle. At some point, you'll have to decide when it's time to cut off the survey and tally the results, even if you're still getting an occasional response. It's also helpful to set up a separate e-mail folder to store your responses until you're ready to tally them.

Once you've completed the survey, make a list of the respondents and send them a thank-you note for participating. If respondents are interested in the results of your survey, let them know when and where the article will appear.

CITING ELECTRONIC REFERENCES

ONCE YOU'VE LOCATED INFORMATION online, how do you reference it? While several sites offer "official" guides to referencing electronic information (see Resources), there do not seem to be any hard-and-fast guidelines that everyone chooses to follow.

Here are some basic tips on referencing online materials:

- Most publications prefer that the "http://" prefix be omitted from URLs that begin with "www." If, however, the URL does not begin with "www" and might be unclear, the "http://" should be retained (e.g., "*www.mysite.com*" versus "*http://mysite.com*").
- While there was a move to include online references in angle brackets (<reference>), this seems to have been dropped in most consumer publications; parentheses are generally preferred.
- When citing a Web site in a footnote or bibliography, follow the same guidelines as for citing an article: author's name, title of article or site (or both), and URL. If a date is available, provide it. Otherwise, you can list the date upon which you accessed the material. For example:

    Allen, Moira. "Getting the Most from Online Classes," Writing-World.com, *www.writing-world.com/basics/classes.html, 2001.*

- When citing e-mail, list the author's name, the date of the e-mail, and the general subject—e.g., "Personal e-mail from John Smith on how to reference URLs, May 3, 2002."
- When citing newsgroup messages, include the author's name if available, the date of the posting, the subject, and the name and e-mail address of the newsgroup.

PULLING IT ALL TOGETHER

ONCE YOU'VE FOUND WHAT you're looking for, what do you do with it? Here are some tips on managing the information you locate online.

BOOKMARK USEFUL SITES

Add a bookmark to any site you're using for a current project, that you expect to visit in the future, or that you want to be able to return to easily after exploring other links. Don't rely on your "back" button to take you back to a useful site; it's too easy to lose that type of navigational information. If, for example, you use the "Go to" or "History" function to jump back several sites, you may lose subsequent site information—and you'll lose all your navigation information if your browser crashes.

Organize, file, and purge your bookmarks periodically. Rename bookmarks that don't describe their destination. Bookmarks pick up the name that the site owner has given to the site. If no name is given, you'll get the first characters of the site by default, and these may not be useful in helping you relocate important sites. File bookmarks by project or category, and update them if the URLs change.

PRINT OR SAVE IMPORTANT MATERIAL

Forget the myth of the paperless office. The Internet is an unreliable, ephemeral medium: A site may be here today, gone tomorrow. Don't count on being able to go back a month later, or even a day later, to do more research on an important site. Get what you need now.

Include the page location on your printouts. You'll find this option under "Page Setup" on most browsers. Some offer the option of printing the date the site was accessed, which can also be important when referencing a site. By printing out the page location, you'll always be able to relocate a site even if you haven't bookmarked it, and you'll be able to reference it properly.

Another option is to save a page directly to your hard drive. When you select the "save as" command in Internet Explorer, you'll be given the format options of saving the page as a Web Archive, HTML source, or text. Under "Web Archive," you'll also be given the option of saving the images, links, and other subordinate files associated with the page; the more items you select, the more memory each archived page will consume. The "save as text" option requires the least memory, but also tends to produce pages on which all the text is run together in a single huge block, making the material difficult to reference later.

You can also copy and paste the pertinent content of a Web page directly into a Word document, thus preserving most of the format of the page but omitting unwanted graphics, ads, etc. If you choose this method to archive research materials, be sure to copy the URL of the page as well, as it will not be captured automatically. In addition, you will not have access to any links that may have been in the material unless the URL is actually displayed on the original Web page; hotlinks will be lost.

If you lose a site, or can't find a site as listed, try truncating the URL to relocate it. Sometimes site owners move pages within a site, and sometimes a link may be misprinted. If you can't find your destination page, peel back the URL section by section (starting at the end and moving back toward the domain name), until you reach a home page or index that can redirect you to the page's new location. You'll be amazed at how often this works.

KNOW WHEN TO QUIT

When conducting research online, you may find the lure of "just one more site" hard to resist. It's tempting to check just one more link, visit one more database, do one more variation on your search. How do you know when enough is enough? Some possible stopping points include:

- When you've scanned twenty or thirty search results without finding a useful site; this indicates that you should redefine your keyword search—or conclude that the information may not be available.
- When you've found the answer to your question, and further research is unnecessary, even though it might be interesting.
- When information becomes redundant—every page you find tells you the same thing.
- When links start taking you back to sites you've already visited.
- When you find less than one good hit per ten search results.
- When you reach an arbitrary limit on search results (e.g., "I will screen no more than one hundred hits").
- When your printer runs out of paper—or when your browser crashes and you don't care.

Research online can be addictive. It can also be seductive: It feels like working, but you may find that you're spending more time looking for information (including information that you don't really need) than actually writing. Sometimes, knowing how to stop researching can be more important than knowing how to start.

RESOURCES

SEARCH ENGINES

Alta Vista
www.altavista.com
In addition to basic search functions, Alta Vista offers a number of special-ized search options, such as the ability to search in different languages and to search for illustrations. It also has a translation facility, allowing you to translate a Web site or short sections of text.

Google
www.google.com
Google is perhaps the top-rated search engine; one of its advantages is that it does not offer "paid positioning" (i.e., moving sites to the "top" of the list for a fee). Google is also used by Yahoo! for Web searching.

Yahoo!
www.yahoo.com
Yahoo! itself is actually a directory rather than a search engine. Its entries are archived in a complex hierarchy of cate-gories. A search on Yahoo! will turn up Yahoo! directory entries first, then "Web results," which are found through Google.

META/MULTI SEARCH ENGINES

Dogpile
www.dogpile.com

Easysearcher
www.easysearcher.com
Links to more than three hundred search engines and tools.

MetaCrawler
www.metacrawler.com

INTERNATIONAL SEARCH ENGINES AND DIRECTORIES

Foreign Language Internet Search Engines
www.bizforms.com/search.htm
A good source, but many links don't work.

Search Engine Colossus
www.searchenginecolossus.com
Lists 1,500 search engines from 149 countries, in various languages.

USING SEARCH ENGINES EFFECTIVELY

Internet Tools for the Advanced Searcher
www.philb.com/adint.htm
An overview of advanced search strate-gies and tips, plus excellent links. This site also offers comparison tables of the functions, features, and performance of major search engines and meta/multi search engines.

Major Search Engines
http://searchenginewatch.internet.com/facts/major.html
The Search Engine Watch site offers a wealth of information on how search engines work; overviews of search engines, directories, and hybrids; com-parison tables of major search engine features; and information on how to design your site for better indexing by search engines (including the use of meta tags and other features).

DIRECTORIES AND DATABASES

Assignment Editor
www.assignmenteditor.com
Links to a vast array of resources, including newspapers, TV news sites, wires, news

archives, business magazines, comic strips, medical news, government directories, weather, photos, research and reference guides, maps, time zones, entertainment, media, travel, "cop stuff," and more.

Association of Research Libraries/Copyright and Intellectual Property
www.arl.org/info/frn/copy/copytoc.html
Information and legal documents regarding copyright, fair use, and other rights information.

Calculators On-Line Center
*www-sci.lib.uci.edu/HSG/
RefCalculators.html*
Calculators on just about every imaginable subject (and more): Besides the basics of numbers and slide rules, this offers calculators on such topics as "galaxies and black holes" (coordinates and radiation), pets, religious topics (calculate the date of Easter for any year), sailing, music, navigation, and hundreds of other topics.

Directories
www.nwu.org/links/lnkdirs.htm
Links to various types of reference directories, such as yellow and white pages, address finders, Web site directories, lists, and guides.

direct search
www.freepint.com/gary/direct.htm
"A compilation of links to the search engines of resources ... not easily searchable or accessible from general search tools," including databases and other resources.

GovSpot
www.govspot.com
Links to a variety of U.S. government Web sites and resources.

Historic Events and Birth-Dates
www.scopesys.com/today
Find out what happened and who was born on any day of the year; fascinating historical "date" research source.

History/Social Studies For K–12 Teachers
http://my.execpc.com/~dboals
You don't have to be a K–12 teacher to appreciate this huge assortment of links to research and reference information on almost anything imaginable. Lots of links to primary sources and documents.

ibiblio: the public's library
www.ibiblio.org/collection
Links to a huge range of directories, databases, resources, information pages, and so forth.

Infomine: Scholarly Internet Resource Collections
http://infomine.ucr.edu
Hosted by the University of California, Infomine allows you to search multiple databases, find electronic journals, look for government information, use maps, and locate Internet "enabling" tools (e.g., HTML, etc.).

Labyrinth, The
http://labyrinth.georgetown.edu
Georgetown University's massive database of everything medieval.

Library of Congress/American Memory: Historical Collections for the National Digital Library
*http://memory.loc.gov/ammem/
ammemhome.html*
A collection of oral histories (transcribed) and other U.S. historical and first-person accounts.

LibrarySpot
www.libraryspot.com
Links to a wide range of research tools and sites.

Multnomah Cty. Library Electronic Resources
www.multcolib.org/ref/quick.html
An excellent selection of online data bases and other reference sites of particular value to writers (such as quotes, authors, associations, statistics, and more).

My Virtual Reference Desk
www.refdesk.com
A huge directory of databases, encyclopedias, fact books, databases, and resource sites. Updated regularly; check "new listings" for fascinating sites.

NASA
www.nasa.gov

Online Books Page, The
http://digital.library.upenn.edu/books
Links to more than 18,000 free e-books and texts, plus news archives and links to other resources.

Project Gutenberg
http://gutenberg.net
A source of copyright-free e-texts, from classics to primary historical documents.

Research and Facts
www.nwu.org/links/lnkfacts.htm
Links to a variety of research sources and directories.

ResearchBuzz
www.researchbuzz.com
This newsletter on the latest research and search engine news offers a great deal of useful information for the writer or researcher. To subscribe, send a blank message to
join-researchbuzz@lists.lyris.net.

Search.com
www.search.com
A wide selection of directories, data bases, and subject-specific search tools and engines that provide access information not retrievable by regular search engines.

Topic Specific Directories
http://jlunz.databack.com/netresources/ topic_specific_directories.htm
Links to online directories for medicine and health, education, shopping, contests, and images.

EVALUATING WEB SITES

Evaluating Internet Research Sources
www.virtualsalt.com/evalu8it.htm

Evaluating Web Pages
www.lib.duke.edu/libguide/ evaluating_web.htm

Evaluating Web Sites
http://servercc.oakton.edu/~wittman/find/ eval.htm

FINDING EXPERTS

Pitsco's Ask an Expert
www.askanexpert.com
A source of free advice from experts on a wide range of topics; search the experts' Web sites or submit a query.

ProfNet
www2.profnet.com
"Your direct link to news officers at colleges and universities, corporations, think tanks, national labs, medical centers, non-profits, and PR agencies." Allows you to send information queries directly to the experts.

Sources and Experts

*http://metalab.unc.edu/slanews/internet/
experts.html*

Links to guides, directories, universities, institutions, and other "clearinghouses" of expert sources.

Top 101 Experts

www.bookmarket.com/101exp.html

A list of "expert" sites—places where you can get answers to a variety of questions, generally for free.

SEARCHING NEWSGROUPS

Google Groups

http://groups.google.com

This site archives newsgroup messages virtually "from the beginning"; you can find a record of just about any topic ever discussed in a newsgroup here.

<< CHAPTER 4 >>

NETWORKING ONLINE: JOINING THE WRITING COMMUNITY

THE INTERNET HAS BEEN DESCRIBED as an "electronic community." This community includes a number of "writing neighborhoods," in the form of e-mail discussion groups, newsgroups, chat rooms, and critique groups. These are places where writers meet to discuss topics of mutual interest, share information, and provide mutual support. You can also improve your skills and network with other writers through online classes, which often provide the opportunity for discussion and even mentoring.

DISCUSSION GROUPS

DISCUSSION GROUPS ARE EXCELLENT SOURCES of information, not only on writing but on a host of other topics. They also provide valuable opportunities for networking. Many top-name authors and editors participate in writing newsgroups and lists. These opportunities are not limited to writing discussion groups. Among the thousands of special-interest discussion groups online, you're bound to find one that covers your favorite topic, whether that topic is Arthurian lore or auto mechanics.

Like any community, discussion groups have certain rules and social customs. Some of these are spelled out in the "welcome" message you'll receive when you join, while others remain unspoken until broken. To get the most from a group, you need to know how such groups work, what to expect from them, and what they will expect from you.

Discussion groups come in four basic formats: e-mail discussion lists, newsgroups, forums, and chat. Each involves a slightly different technology and ground rules.

E-MAIL DISCUSSION LISTS

These are simplicity itself: Members post messages to a central e-mail address, and those messages are then forwarded to everyone on the list. You can opt to receive your messages individually or in a digest format (a single daily message that incorporates that day's mail traffic).

Free list-management sites like YAHOO! GROUPS and TOPICA offer thousands of lists on every imaginable topic. Some have hundreds of members; others have fewer than ten. Most groups offer a Web site that provides membership details and subscription instructions. To subscribe, you'll need to send an e-mail to the group's "subscription" address (which processes subscriptions only; any other type of message will simply bounce). Once your subscription has been received, you should receive a "welcome" message that explains some of the commands you can use on the list, including how to unsubscribe. The welcome message may also spell out some of the purposes and rules of the group itself. Be sure to keep a copy of this message for future reference; discussion lists are annoyed by folks who pester the list with questions like "How do I unsubscribe?"

NEWSGROUPS

Newsgroups function as electronic bulletin boards and are hosted on Usenet; they can be accessed through your browser. Not all are open to the public. Many are also moderated, which means that messages are screened before being posted. Messages to moderated newsgroups must often be sent to an e-mail address for screening rather than posted directly on Usenet. You can also visit and post to newsgroups through the Internet via such sites as GOOGLE GROUPS. Messages are posted chronologically (from newest to oldest) and hierarchically by "thread" (subject heading).

Newsgroups are divided into eight subject categories, including Comp (computer topics), News (Internet news), Rec (hobbies, recreation, sports, arts, etc.), Sci (science, sociology, culture, etc.), Talk (debate), Misc (topics not easily categorized elsewhere), and Alt (groups that have chosen to bypass the other categories; this category includes many controversial groups but also many that are simply hard to categorize). Writing groups are usually found in the "Rec" category. Support groups often meet under the "Alt" heading, making this a good place to search for personal experiences and anecdotes.

FORUMS

While these are organized much like newsgroups, they are hosted on Web sites rather than on the Usenet. Many writing sites contain discussion forums. Some sites offer unrestricted read-only access to their forums, but require that you register and choose a user name to post messages. Others require registration before you can read messages. Forums are often used as an alternative to real-time chat (in fact, some sites mislabel their forums as chat rooms).

CHAT

"Real-time" conversation on the Internet can take many forms. Most chats are available directly from the host's Web site; you won't need any additional software to access a chat room or participate in a discussion. (Chats offered through services such as AOL are generally open only to AOL members.) Many sites host chats with well-known authors or experts. (See chapter 11 for tips on how to promote your books through author chats.)

Another form of "chat" is "instant messaging," which enables you to "talk" to another person (or a group) online in real time. Instant messaging requires special software, such as AOL INSTANT MESSENGER or ICQ; however, these can be downloaded free. (A word of warning: If you want to concentrate on a writing project, turn off your instant messaging software, or you will be subject to constant interruptions.)

BLOGS

In its simplest form, a "blog" (short for "Web log") is a means for a person to publish the equivalent of a diary, journal, or running commentary online. However, groups can establish blogs to enable members to talk to each other online. In this form, a blog is similar to a forum, but access tends to be more restricted. Members will need passwords to access and post to the blog. Generally, an internal "group" blog of this nature will not be accessible to the "public." Blogs are hosted by a variety of "blog" sites (see Resources), which can either run your blog on their own Web page or provide software to host it through your site or server.

ADVANTAGES OF ONLINE "TALK"

The benefits of discussion groups include information, networking, writing advice, marketing tips, diversity, and encouragement.

- **Information.** Both writing and special-interest groups are excellent sources of research and background information. You never know what sort of experience group members have. A simple question like "Does anyone know ... ?" can bring rich results. A writing list to which I subscribe, for example, recently covered such topics as wound management (with information contributed by a former U.S. Navy field corpsman) and what really happens to the human body in the vacuum of space (with information contributed by a vacuum physicist). When list members don't have firsthand information on a topic, they can often provide references and URLs. Special-interest groups are the place to look for in-depth information on a specific topic. A cat-lovers' discussion group, for example, is the place to turn for information on a particular feline malady, whether you want technical information or personal anecdotes.
- **Networking.** One of the benefits of joining a discussion group is getting to know people in your field and letting them get to know you. While some writing groups are primarily for amateurs, others are frequented by well-known authors and editors and expect a correspondingly high degree of professionalism from all participants. If you've posted useful, worthwhile, professional comments or critiques, chances are that an editor will remember your name.
- **Writing Advice.** Writing groups provide opportunities to get advice on style, technique, plot, character development, and a host of other writing skills from

experienced writers and editors. Some groups focus entirely on discussions of technique, including such issues as how to develop a novel synopsis or an agent query. While some groups welcome amateur inquiries, others don't.

- **Marketing Tips.** Writing groups are good sources of marketing information, including announcements of new markets, market changes, contests, markets to avoid, and more. A word of warning, however: Groups can also be hotbeds of rumor, so be sure to verify information.

- **Diversity.** Online discussion groups boast a membership roster that can never be equaled by a local group. You may find yourself discussing character viewpoints with a writer from Singapore, or examining issues of social violence with a writer from Sweden. Such diversity can only help expand your own view of the world, and consequently, your ability to write about that world effectively.

- **Encouragement.** Some groups go beyond "neighborhood" to become the equivalent of "extended family." In such groups, you'll find people who genuinely understand what it means to be a writer: how it feels to be rejected, to be accepted, to be afraid to send your work to market, to experience writer's block, or to work for months on a story that just won't come together. You'll find support for your efforts, applause for your successes, sympathy for your failures, and perhaps a well-needed boot to the rear if you're having trouble putting your work in the mailbox. You may even find yourself building some genuine friendships.

THE DOWNSIDE OF DISCUSSION

Discussion groups have disadvantages as well as benefits. Disagreements can escalate into flame wars, and "chatter" can fill a member's mailbox with useless messages. A sad side effect of such problems is that they tend to drive professional writers off the lists; I've seen many "pros" leave discussion groups because they don't have time for the chatter, or the patience to deal with other members' immaturity. Some of the most common disadvantages include the following:

- **Mailbox clutter**. When you sign on to a discussion list, you may find your mailbox flooded with e-mails that don't relate to the purpose of the list. These generally fall into two categories: "off-topic chatter" and "fluff." Off-topic chatter is anything not directly related to the stated purpose of the list. For example, if the list is about "writing science fiction and fantasy," a discussion of the movie *Titanic* would generally be considered "off-topic" (though a discussion of *The Lord of the Rings* or *The Matrix* might be acceptable, until it veers into a comparison of the cuteness of the male leads). Many groups prohibit the posting of jokes, inspirational stories, and news items as being "off-topic."

  The other type of clutter, which I describe as "fluff," is the tendency to clutter a list with personal posts: thanks, congratulations, personal wishes, "got your message" messages, and so forth. Most lists encourage members to take this type of exchange off-list, but members rarely do.

- **Flamers and Flame Wars.** The most destructive problem on any type of discussion list is the proliferation of antagonistic, hostile, or offensive messages, called "flames." Flamers (people who write flames) often attack not only the opinions being expressed by an individual, but the individual as well. "Flame wars" arise when the attacked person (or others) respond to the original flame—and escalate when other list members jump in on one side or the other. Flamers and flame wars create a hostile environment and reduce the opportunity for serious discussion. Some groups act quickly to extinguish such wars, but others allow them to rage unchecked.

One question to ask before joining a discussion group is whether it is moderated or unmoderated. A moderated group has a human host who either monitors message traffic (and screens out inappropriate messages) and who can be contacted by group members if a problem arises. A moderator can take action against offenders either by issuing a warning or by removing an offender from the group. Unmoderated lists have no such "higher power" to deal with problems such as flamers or off-topic chatter.

TWENTY TIPS ON EFFECTIVE DISCUSSION

While every discussion group has its own guidelines, the following strategies will help you make the most of a group and its resources:

1. **Lurk for a period of time before becoming an active participant.** This will give you a chance to determine the tone, style, and content of the group.
2. **Read everything:** FAQs, instructions, and other information provided by the list or newsgroup. This will prevent you from annoying the group with questions like "How do I unsubscribe?" or "How do I receive messages in digest format?" Some FAQs also include "content" information that a member is expected to be familiar with. For example, a newsgroup on science fiction might include a definition of science fiction in its FAQ and would expect a new member to read this definition rather than posting a question such as "Say, what is science fiction anyway?"
3. **Introduce yourself.** When you decide to participate, introduce yourself with a brief description of your background, as it relates to the group.
4. **Compose your messages with care.** Remember that messages posted to newsgroups can be publicly accessed forever (e.g., through Google Groups), while e-mail lists generally keep archives. Think before you hit that "send" button. It's easy to send off a hasty reply without thinking about how others may interpret your message.
5. **Check the address you're e-mailing to!** More than one list member has been embarrassed to discover that a message that was meant to be private was accidentally sent to the entire group.
6. **Be courteous at all times,** even when others are not courteous to you.
7. **Use text-only in e-mail messages.** Turn off any special formatting programs, including programs that convert e-mail into HTML format. Otherwise, such messages may come across in HTML code (or not at all). Don't use font colors

or background colors (I know one individual who sends everything in pale yellow).

8. **Avoid special characters.** Don't use characters that require a keyboard combination, such as an em dash (use a double hyphen instead) and smart quotes. These rarely translate properly and usually come across as distracting symbols. (For information on how to avoid "e-mail hieroglyphs," see Turning Off the Gibberish in chapter 6.)

9. **Don't type messages in ALL CAPS.** This is considered shouting. Use asterisks and underscore characters to indicate *boldface* and _italics or underlining_.

10. **Use emoticons to indicate your tone or emotion,** especially if your wording might be misinterpreted otherwise. But use them sparingly!

11. **Try to keep messages short.** Not everyone has inexpensive or free e-mail, especially recipients in other countries.

12. **Cut and Snip**. When replying to a message, include only those passages of the original message that you are actually responding to and "snip" the rest. A common complaint on e-mail lists is the continual and unnecessary forwarding of lengthy messages.

13. **Never send attachments.** With the concerns about viruses these days, attachments irritate just about everyone. If there's something you'd like to share, such as a cute image file, e-mail the group and ask anyone who would like to receive it to contact you off-list.

14. **Use appropriate subject headings.** If you change a topic, change the subject heading.

15. **Don't post or e-mail copies of Web pages**. Instead, cite the complete URL, and include the "http://" part of the address (otherwise, the link won't necessarily be "clickable").

16. **Don't advertise.** If you have a Web site or product that you believe would be of interest to the group, list it in a discreet signature block at the end of your message. Posting advertisements to a group is considered spamming.

17. **Sign your e-mails, or use a signature block.** That way, if your original e-mail attribution is lost through replies or forwarding, people will still know who wrote the original message.

18. **Get permission before cross-posting messages.** Do not forward messages from one group to another or send them to someone outside the group without the original author's permission.

19. **Attribute material.** When posting material such as jokes, anecdotes, humor, etc., to a group or mailing list, provide an attribution or source (including copyright information) whenever possible.

20. **Stay out of flame wars.** Many people launch "flame wars" simply to get attention—and all too often, they succeed. The best way to banish a flamer is to ignore him or her rather than responding. Resist the temptation to jump in or take sides. Often, when a flame war gets out of hand, a moderator will respond by kicking *everyone* who is participating off the list, regardless of who started it or who is "right."

CRITIQUE GROUPS

ONLINE CRITIQUE GROUPS OR WORKSHOPS give writers the chance to submit their work for review while reviewing the work of others. Most groups work like discussion lists, handling submissions and critiques by e-mail; others post material and critiques to a Web site. Critique groups are not places for "talk"; off-topic chatter is strongly discouraged, and some groups don't even permit members to enter into a discussion of a critique. If you want to discuss a critique or submission with another member, you will often be asked to do so off-list.

To find the group that is right for you, you'll need to make three important decisions:

1. **Subject or genre.** Some critique groups are open to any submissions, including fiction and nonfiction, short stories, and ongoing novels. Most, however, are more specialized, open only to materials within a specific genre or field. Fiction groups are far more common than nonfiction groups. In some cases, a single sponsor will host critique groups in a variety of genres.
2. **Experience requirements.** Some groups accept members of any level of experience; others require members to be of a specific level of expertise. The latter will ask for a writing sample and an outline of your writing history before accepting you as a member. Each has its advantages and disadvantages. In a group where members share similar levels of expertise, your work will be critiqued by someone at your own level of writing ability—which can be an advantage if you are an experienced writer looking for feedback from peers, but a disadvantage if you are a new writer looking for feedback from more experienced pros. Both types of groups generally give you an opportunity to mentor and to be mentored.
3. **Participation requirements.** Most groups have participation requirements, some more intense than others. Members may be expected to critique (or "crit") a certain number of submissions per week or month. You will usually be expected to critique a certain number of submissions before you can post your own work to the group, and you may also be expected to maintain a "crit-to-sub" ratio (e.g., three crits for every submission). Some groups are very strict about these requirements and may suspend you from active membership, or eventually drop you from the list entirely, if you don't meet your quota. If you join such a group and are unable to critique for a time for any reason (e.g., going on vacation), inform the list moderator so that you won't be penalized for nonparticipation.

ADVANTAGES OF ONLINE CRITIQUING

Like real-world writing groups, online critique groups are not created equal. Some are considered highly effective; others aren't as well reviewed. The effectiveness of a group can also be a matter of personal taste. Online groups offer certain advantages over real-world groups—as well as some unique disadvantages that arise from the electronic environment. Advantages include:

- **No cost.** Perhaps the greatest advantage of this type of feedback is that you don't have to pay for it. It's far cheaper than hiring a tutor, a book doctor, or a personal editor to review your work. You don't have to pay dues to cover room rental and refreshments, or worry about who's bringing the doughnuts. Nor do you have to make copies of your manuscript to hand out.
- **Convenience.** Online groups fit easily into one's writing schedule. You can read submissions on your own schedule and in the comfort of your own home.
- **Broad membership base.** Members of your group aren't limited to your local community. Instead, they may come from around the world. This brings an amazing diversity of backgrounds, cultures, educational levels, and interests to the group—which in turn leads to an amazing diversity of perspectives and viewpoints. It can also provide a much broader range of feedback—don't be surprised if your big fight scene is critiqued by someone with actual weapons training or medical expertise.
- **Rapid feedback.** In a real-world group, you hand out your material at one meeting and wait until the next for feedback. If your material is part of an ongoing project, or if you have a deadline, this can be frustrating—you may not receive feedback for an entire month. Online, however, you may see responses to your submissions within hours, and if you're on an active list, you'll rarely have to wait longer than a day.
- **Individual attention.** Most real-world critique groups try to give a few minutes of time to everyone at each meeting. The larger the group, therefore, the less actual feedback you're likely to receive. In an online group, however, each submission is handled individually, so the critiquer can spend as much time as necessary to give you feedback.
- **Multiple points of view.** In a real-world group, there is often a tendency to move toward a consensus—and less confident members may not speak up if their opinions differ from the majority, or from those of the most outspoken members. In an online group, members may not even see the critiques of other members, and so are less likely to be influenced by the opinions of the rest of the group. No single voice will be drowned out by disagreement or silenced by lack of time.
- **Multiple submissions.** Some groups allow you to submit new material as often as once a week (or as often as you meet the crit-to-sub ratio). This enables you to get feedback on more of your work more quickly.
- **Anonymity.** If you're shy about sharing your work, the facelessness of an online group may make you feel more at ease. You don't have to sit squirming in your chair as critiquers tear your prose to shreds. In many cases, no one else will even see the feedback you receive, and no one will ever see your blushes. You can also be sure that critiquers are responding to your work, and not to you as a person.

DISADVANTAGES OF ONLINE CRITIQUING

While online critiquing offers many benefits over the old-fashioned "photocopy and pass it around" approach of real-world groups, it also shares all the *disadvantages* of real-world groups and more. Any critique group will encounter "personality problems"; online, these can be magnified by the anonymity of e-mail. Typical online critique group problems include:

- **Amateur feedback.** While some groups accept only experienced writers, others are open to all. That means you may receive feedback from someone who knows little or nothing about the actual craft of writing or who may be unfamiliar with the type of material or genre you're submitting. You may receive feedback from someone who lacks your vocabulary, and therefore who considers the material "too hard to understand," or who inaccurately attempts to correct your grammar. You may receive feedback from someone with no knowledge of the markets you're writing for, and who therefore cannot give you any useful feedback on whether your material is suitable for those markets. Finally, you may receive feedback that says little more than "Gee, I really liked this piece" or "Gee, sorry, I didn't."
- **Amateur submissions.** Any open group will have its share of amateur, unskilled writers whose material is riddled with grammatical errors, misspellings, and structural and conceptual flaws. You may find it difficult to critique such material in a constructive fashion. The best approach is usually to find something that works at least moderately well ("good story idea" or "interesting characters") and work from there.
- **Anonymity.** While the facelessness of an online group can be comforting to a shy author, it can create as many problems as it solves. It may, for example, bolster the courage of the "hypercritter" who confuses critiquing with shredding—and whose feedback ranges from a sarcastically dismissive paragraph to a line-by-line vivisection of your work. It may also encourage the "hypersensitive submitter"—the author who responds to negative feedback by lashing out in anger or whining about ill-treatment. Fortunately, most groups take a strong stance against problematic members and will either reprimand or, if necessary, remove a member who refuses to play by the rules.
- **Submission overload.** Some groups impose a queue system that limits the number of submissions to the list; others allow unlimited posts. While you may feel tempted, or even obligated, to reply to every submission, doing so can often cut significantly into your own writing time. As you become more familiar with the group, you may find it easier to determine which submissions you will review and which you would prefer to pass.
- **Fear of theft.** Many writers are concerned about posting their material online for fear that it will be copied or stolen. Thus far, this has not proven a peril for online groups. Most groups have firm guidelines on issues of plagiarism, copying, or distributing materials in any form without permission. Perhaps more importantly, participants in such groups tend to be serious, if sometimes inexperienced, writers who are more interested in receiving feedback on their own work than in trying to pick up a story from someone else. When you post a story to a critique group, it is viewed by a large number of people, all of whom could later verify your authorship if a question of theft or copying actually arose.

Many groups also archive messages, which provides a permanent record not only of your authorship, but of the date of your submission. Thus, any issue of theft could quickly and easily be resolved in your favor by a variety of mechanisms.

FIVE TIPS ON SUBMITTING

To endear yourself to fellow members of your group, and to improve your chances of positive feedback, observe the following submission guidelines:

1. **Submit your best work.** Polish your material as carefully as if you were submitting it for publication. Never submit something you would consider a rough draft (i.e., a story that still has holes to be filled or problems to be resolved). It's perfectly acceptable to ask, "Does this work?" but not, "What do you think my character should do here?" Also, be sure that your work meets the content guidelines of the group. If your group specifies "romance only," for example, don't submit a horror story or a sample of your science fiction novel. (Writers who complain about a harsh crit with the defense, "Gee, I thought you realized it was only a *draft!*" receive little sympathy.)
2. **Spellcheck and proofread.** Many of the errors I've seen on submissions could have been caught by a basic spellcheck. Remember that spellchecking won't catch grammatical and punctuation errors, so give your material a thorough proofreading as well. If you post material that contains numerous spelling or grammatical errors, you risk alienating your critiquers, who will either take you to task for every single error or advise you (sometimes harshly) to review the basics before submitting more work.
3. **Observe length restrictions.** Some groups specify a maximum number of words per submission. If your submission is longer, ask the moderator for permission before submitting. It's usually wise to divide longer submissions into two parts. Be sure to specify how many parts are being sent, and in what order—e.g., "Part 1 of 2, Part 2 of 2."
4. **Don't submit revised work without permission.** Most groups prefer not to see the same material twice, especially if you've made only minor grammatical revisions. If you would like a specific reviewer to take another look at your work, contact that reviewer directly and ask if he or she would look at the revised piece off-list.
5. **Always thank your critiquers—and don't argue with them.** Even if you don't agree with a critique, thank everyone who took the time to review your work. (This is generally best done off-list, unless you wish to thank several people at once.) Don't argue with a reviewer's comments, or try to point out why the reviewer is wrong. If you develop a reputation for reacting negatively or rudely to critiques, people will quickly cease reviewing your material, and you may be dropped from the list. If, on the other hand, you receive a review that seems unduly negative, hostile, or rude, don't respond angrily to the critiquer. If the problem continues, discuss it with the list moderator; you may not be the only person having troubles with this critiquer. Many lists will reprimand and ultimately remove a member who submits inappropriate critiques.

Since material submitted for critique is often composed in a word-processing program and then cut-and-pasted into e-mail, it is especially prone to "special-character hieroglyphs"—the odd characters that result from using smart quotes, em dashes, and word-processing formatting commands such as bold or italic text. Just as they can muddle messages sent to discussion groups, these "hieroglyphs" can make your story literally unreadable, so be sure to check for them (see Turning Off the Gibberish in chapter 6 for more information).

TEN TIPS ON CRITIQUING

While every group has its own guidelines for critiquing, all share certain basic expectations. The first rule, of course, is to behave courteously and professionally at all times and under all circumstances. Beyond that, a good critiquer should:

1. **Be specific.** Critiques should say more than "I liked it" or "I didn't like it." Members want to know why you liked a piece and, more specifically, what sections you liked and what sections you didn't. Let the author know what works and what doesn't. On the positive side, are the characters believable? If so, can you list specific details or incidents that make a character believable? On the negative side, does the author skimp on description? Can you point to a paragraph where added detail would have helped the reader "see" the scene or setting? Point out sections that seem unclear or confusing, that contradict one another, or that are rough or hard to read. Many critiquers use the "reply" function to go through a submission paragraph by paragraph, noting parts that work and parts that seem awkward.

2. **Be constructive.** It's often easier to point out the flaws in a piece than its positive qualities. Even if a piece is badly written, it's important to find some element to praise. Try focusing on areas that could use more development, and describe those areas in a positive tone: "I really liked the character of Zelda and would have liked to see more of her in the story. Perhaps you could give her a few more scenes or some additional dialogue." Or, "You have a talent for imagery, and your piece is loaded with vivid descriptions. A few times, however, I found that the descriptions got in the way of the story, as in the paragraph where ... "

3. **Suggest "fixes" when appropriate.** If you have factual information that could help an author correct a scene, by all means provide it—most authors will thank you for it. If you can suggest a way to make a passage run more smoothly, perhaps by varying sentence structure or changing punctuation, don't hesitate to do so. If a scene could benefit from more (or less) description, provide suggestions on what to cut or what to add. Often, an author may recognize that a scene has problems, but may have run out of ideas on how to make changes. Your suggestion may be just what the author needs to look at the scene from a new direction or perspective. Just remember that the author is under no obligation to actually use your suggestions!

4. **Be sensitive.** Even experienced authors can have thin skins, and beginning authors can have extremely fragile egos. When dealing with a new author,

remember that while this person may be writing truly appalling material now, she may improve with practice. A badly timed shot can discourage a budding author from seeking feedback in the future. Try to take into account an author's level of experience when critiquing. Encourage an amateur author's strengths, and choose no more than one or two problem areas to focus on— e.g., point-of-view errors or faulty dialogue tags.

5. **Be unbiased.** Members of your group may write about ideas, subjects, themes, or viewpoints that you disagree with—perhaps passionately. The purpose of a critique, however, is not to argue the merit of an idea, but to assess how well that idea is presented. If you find that you can't deal objectively with certain themes, simply refrain from critiquing those materials.

6. **Focus on presentation, not plot.** You may not like a particular type of story, plot, or theme; however, it's never appropriate to respond with a negative critique based purely on personal taste ("I thought this was a boring story, like all *Star Trek* stories."). Instead, focus on specifics: Does the story start in the right place? Is the conflict effective? Are the characters well developed? Is the dialogue believable? Is the resolution appropriate? Address the manner in which the story is written, rather than the story itself.

7. **Avoid nitpicking on grammar.** Some groups welcome grammatical corrections, especially if you can explain the rule behind the correction. Others don't. It's a good idea to lurk for a while and see how others handle this issue before plunging in with the electronic equivalent of the red pen. When you do comment on grammar, don't undertake to proofread an entire submission. Instead, focus on specific problem areas—for example, a writer who consistently confuses "its" and "it's," or who misuses dialogue tags. Point out consistent spelling errors, but don't quibble over mistakes that might well have been typos (though if you see a lot of those, you could politely recommend that the writer spellcheck material before submitting).

8. **"Snip" whenever possible.** Don't simply hit "reply" and send the entire submission back to the submitter. Instead, "snip" (delete) those paragraphs that you aren't responding to.

9. **Don't read other critiques before submitting your own.** Reviewing what other people have said about a piece can sometimes influence your own thinking—you may not approach the piece with a fresh outlook. It may also cause you to omit certain comments because they have already been made by others—but it can be precisely this sort of repetition that convinces an author that a problem actually exists.

10. **Respect the author's confidentiality.** Besides the obvious rule of no plagiarism, most groups also have rules against sharing submissions with anyone outside the group. If an author shares personal information with you, perhaps to clarify events in a story, don't pass that information along to the group (e.g., by inadvertently mentioning it in your critique). Respect the author's privacy at all times.

It's also important to remember that no matter how experienced your critiquers may be, or how urgently they advise you to make changes, you are the final judge of your own work. You are not required to agree with anyone else's opinion or follow anyone else's suggestions. A good critique group can offer you valuable tips on improving your writing, but it is up to you to determine how (or whether) to apply those tips.

STARTING YOUR OWN GROUP

WITH FREE GROUP-HOSTING SERVICES like Yahoo! and Topica, it's easy to launch your own discussion group or critique group for writers. And writers are doing just that, by the score. If you perceive a niche that needs to be filled, you might want to launch your own "mini-community" to talk about it.

Before you do, however, ask yourself whether you are ready to take on the challenge of being "in charge." If you decide to run a group, all the problems that arise in that group—from simple questions about how to unsubscribe to major flame wars—will be on your shoulders. You'll be tasked with the chore of keeping order, of laying down and enforcing the rules, of reprimanding (and perhaps banishing) members who won't obey those rules, of solving problems, of answering questions, and of trying to manage the list so that it works smoothly for everyone. If you're up to the challenge, here are some tips to help you make your group a success:

- **Establish a clear purpose for the group**. What is it designed to discuss? What is the general subject, and what topics are included (and excluded) by that subject? For example, if you want to run a group covering "how to write romance," what types of topics would be acceptable? Do you want the discussion to be limited to how-to topics, or are you willing to include discussions of published romance novels? Make sure everyone knows what the group is supposed to be talking about (even if it occasionally talks about something else).
- **Determine your membership requirements**. Should members be actively involved in the subject area (e.g., active romance writers), or is the group open to anyone who simply has an *interest* in the topic? Do you wish to limit the group to professionals, or open it to writers of any level of experience? (This is an especially important question if you're launching a critique group.) How will you enforce those membership requirements?
- **Establish the method by which the list will function**. This includes basic "mechanics" issues—one group to which I belonged became embroiled in a lengthy dispute over how one should reply to the group. (Some wanted the list set up so that the default "reply" function went to the individual who sent a message rather than the group, while others wanted it to go to the entire group.) Some groups like to use specific subject headers to indicate what type of topic is being discussed. (For example, a writing group might have headers like "Tips" or "Markets.")
- **Determine what type of talk, if any, is prohibited**. Some groups ban any "off-topic" discussion, including personal chat, "congratulations," sharing of jokes and stories from other sources, etc. If you choose to set specific guidelines about what members can and can't discuss, be ready to enforce them.

- **Keep an eye on the list, even if you're not actively moderating it**. You can choose to have a fully "moderated" list, in which all messages must be screened (by you) before being posted. Or, you can simply step back and let anyone post whatever they like—while keeping a watchful eye out for problems. If you are not actively involved in the list yourself, be sure that members will know how to contact you off-list if a problem does arise.
- **Be prepared to take action against offenders**. Every group will have its occasional "problem member" (and some have more than one). Unfortunately, it will be your responsibility to enforce order and discipline (and manners) within your group. If a person begins to cause problems (by inciting or launching arguments or flames), be prepared to "speak" to that person privately, and if necessary, remove the person from the list. Your group will function much more smoothly if members can be confident that "bad behavior" won't be tolerated.
- **Spell out the group's rules, expectations, and "list commands" in your "welcome" message**. Your welcome message should explain the purpose of the group, provide any necessary introductory information, and spell out what is accepted and what is not. It should also provide a basic list of commands that the user needs to know (such as how to subscribe and unsubscribe, how to receive messages in "digest" format, how to receive copies of his/her own messages, etc.). These commands will be available from your list server.

Running your own group can be fun, but it is not a challenge to undertake lightly. It's not just about talk—it's also about control. The most effective groups are those in which the members know that mature, polite behavior is expected—and, if necessary, enforced.

ONLINE EDUCATION

A MORE INTENSIVE APPROACH to improving your writing skills is to take a class online. On the Internet, you can find courses to help you build skills in your current field or to teach you how to write in a totally new field or genre.

Online classes (also referred to as "distance education") offer a number of benefits to the busy writer. You don't have to live near a major city or university to have access to high-quality courses and reputable instructors (and many universities now offer online "extensions"). You don't have to leave your home or sit in a smelly classroom. You can fit lectures and homework into *your* schedule. Often, you can receive one-on-one feedback from the instructor. And you don't have to feel shy about asking a question in front of the rest of the class—it's just between you and the prof.

Of course, there are disadvantages as well. Besides the fact that courses may vary widely in quality, there is no class participation. You can't sit with a group, interact with other writers, make friends, and hear the questions and discussions raised by other class members (which may cover issues you wouldn't have thought of).

Writing courses are available from a number of sources, including major universities, private companies, and writing sites. Costs vary on an equally wide scale. While a class at COFFEEHOUSE FOR WRITERS or WRITING-WORLD.COM might cost $40 to $125, a course from UCLA might cost as much as $550. With such a range of prices, it's important to know what to look for while shopping for a class and what to expect when you find one.

HOW ONLINE CLASSES (GENERALLY) WORK

Some online courses include Web elements—e.g., lectures posted on a Web site, discussions held through a forum or "blog" (which works like a private newsgroup), and even scheduled meetings in a chat room. However, the primary benefit of an online course is the ability of a student to participate on his or her own schedule (and in private), so such courses are moving increasingly to the "pure e-mail" model.

In this type of class, instructors e-mail lectures directly to students, and students "turn in" homework and receive feedback by e-mail as well. In some cases, classes will include an e-mail discussion list that enables the instructor and students to interact as a group (and, in some cases, share material for group critiquing); in others, each student interacts one on one with the instructor but not with the rest of the class.

Most online courses include the following elements:

- **Lectures**. Instructors "lecture" via e-mail or by posting their lecture on a Web site. While some courses offer fairly short lectures, others are considerably more substantial.
- **Readings**. An instructor may post materials on a Web site for students to read or, more typically, direct students to specific URLs for reading materials. (Using URLs also helps instructors avoid copyright issues.)
- **Discussion**. Some courses attempt to bring the entire class together in a chat room for real-time discussions. Most, however, recognize that much of the benefit of an online course is the freedom from any preset schedule, so any "discussion" is conducted via e-mail or a Web site forum or "blog." Students and instructors post questions and comments, but don't "talk" in real-time.
- **Homework**. A good writing course should ask you to write. One of the advantages of learning online is the ease and speed with which you can submit your homework to the instructor and have it evaluated and returned. Generally, assignments are handled by e-mail. Some courses also ask students to post or share their homework assignments for class critiquing.
- **Individual feedback**. Your instructor should provide detailed comments on your homework assignments and also be available to answer your questions by e-mail. If you raise a question that would benefit the rest of the class, the instructor may ask your permission to share the question and answer in the public discussion.

QUESTIONS TO ASK WHEN CHOOSING A CLASS

Not all writing courses are created equal. Since virtually anyone can host a course by e-mail, you should check out a course carefully before signing up. Be sure you can answer the following questions:

- **Does the topic match my needs?** If you're looking for a course on screenwriting, for example, don't just jump at the first screenwriting course you see. Review the course description and the syllabus for the course (which should be posted online). Remember that you're not limited by geography to the courses offered by your local college; you can pick and choose, finding the one that is right for you.
- **How advanced is the course?** Make sure the course matches your level of expertise. Is it described as beginning, intermediate, or advanced—and what do those terms actually mean? Are there prerequisites for the course, such as previous courses or a demonstrated level of writing ability? Is the course part of a series?
- **Who is the instructor?** Have you ever heard of this person? What credentials are listed? How much experience has this instructor had in the actual subject area of the class? For example, if the instructor is offering a class on "Writing for Magazines," how many articles has he sold? An instructor who has sold two hundred articles can probably share more market tips than one who has sold two, or even twenty.
- **Who is the sponsoring organization?** In some cases, this may be of little importance. Many writing sites now offer hosting services for instructors, which enable any qualified writer to offer a class by using the site's resources. Still, it won't hurt to ask around in newsgroups or mailing lists to find out whether anyone has had an especially positive (or negative) experience with a particular organization.
- **What are the requirements of the class?** How long (and comprehensive) are the lectures? How much reading material will you be expected to review? Will you be expected to write? Again, review the syllabus carefully—and find out if you can review sample lectures or assignments from previous classes.
- **Does the class offer credit toward a degree program?** Many colleges offer online courses as part of the requirements for an MFA (Master of Fine Arts). These courses are usually more expensive than ordinary writing classes (which are often the online equivalent of a continuing education course), but may offer more instruction and add specific education credentials to your résumé.
- **Can I get my money back?** Find out whether the sponsoring organization has a drop option that enables you to reclaim your tuition (or a prorated portion of your tuition) if you find that the course is not what you expected or that you can't participate for some reason.

One of the primary advantages of the Internet is that it has ended the legendary "isolation" of the writer. Even if you're not the sort of writer who doesn't normally care to join real-world groups, you can find stress-free, supportive networking opportunities online. And while you may find it difficult to find a local group of writers who share your interests or skills, you'll be able to find such a group online, where participation is based on commonality rather than locality.

Another good reason to join a group today is the importance of shared information in what is becoming, for writers, an increasingly hostile environment. As the writing market shrinks and contracts become increasingly demanding, a writer's group can help writers fight back by sharing information. By joining a group, you can be kept up-to-date on alerts about publications that renege on payments or that have recently imposed unfriendly contracts. You can also find out about the predators and perils that face writers—including scams that may look like an easy way to get published but that simply serve as a way to separate writers from their money (see chapter 10). The publishing world is becoming an increasingly "writer-unfriendly" place—but by networking with other writers and staying informed, you can protect yourself against some of its pitfalls while gaining valuable support and feedback.

RESOURCES

DISCUSSION LISTS

CataList, the Official Catalog of LISTSERV Lists
www.lsoft.com/lists/listref.html
This list produced the best results for discussion groups on the subject of "writer" or "writing."

DiscussionLists.com
http://discussionlists.com
Directory of discussion lists on a wide range of topics.

Everything E-mail/E-mail Discussion Groups and Newsletters
http://everythingemail.net/ email_discussion.html
Everything you need to know to start your own discussion group or participate in online discussions; plus links to directories of discussion lists.

Google Groups
http://groups.google.com
Search for discussion lists by subject, or search for topics that have been discussed.

Misc. Writing Mailing Lists
www.scalar.com/mw/pages/ mwmlist.shtml

Publicly Accessible Mailing Lists
http://paml.alastra.com
Check the topic directory for an idea of the types of lists available online.

Tile.Net
http://tile.net
A site that can be searched for types of discussion groups or specific discussion topics.

Topica
www.topica.com
Search by keyword for writing-related lists. (Consider using more specific keywords, such as "mystery," "science fiction," "romance," etc.)

Writers' Groups
www.writers.com/groups.htm
A selection of writing groups and classes; includes a helpful participation FAQ.

Yahoo! Groups
http://groups.yahoo.com
Hosts hundreds of small (and large) writing discussion lists, critique groups, and newsletters; search by keyword.

CHAT SOFTWARE

AOL Instant Messenger
www.aim.com/index.adp
Free downloadable program that enables you to "talk" with others online.

ICQ
www.icq.com
Another free "talk" program.

BLOGS

Blogger
www.blogger.com
Perhaps the best-known "blog" host, with plenty of information on how to start your own blog.

Blogphiles Webring
www.blogphiles.com/webring.shtml

A place to link your blog with other "bloggers."

Blogspot
www.blogspot.com
Another blog-hosting service.

Blogstyles
http://blogstyles.com
A site where you can obtain templates to change or improve the appearance of your blog (including columns, fonts, etc.).

CRITIQUE GROUPS

Awesome Writers
www.topica.com/lists/AwesomeWriters
A mailing list for writers of all genres to post their writing and request critiques.

Coffeehouse for Writers/Our Critique Community
www.coffeehouseforwriters.com/groups.html
Offers a variety of critique groups, along with writing workshops, chat, a newsletter, and a monthly contest.

Critters Workshop
http://brain-of-pooh.tech-soft.com/users/critters
This highly recommended workshop focuses primarily on speculative fiction (though it offers other workshops as well). The site offers sample critiques, tips on critiquing and participating in a group, and market information (including the "Black Hole" page that lists response times for speculative fiction markets). Considered a high-intensity group with high workload demands.

Internet Writing Workshop
www.manistee.com/~lkraus/workshop

A workshop open to all styles and genres of writing, including fiction and nonfiction, long and short works. Must remain an active member to stay enrolled.

My Writer Buddy
www.writerbuddy.com
Look for a mentor, a critique partner, a collaborator, a research assistant, or just another writer to chat with, on this unique site. It includes classifieds where you can post a "buddy wanted" ad, chat rooms, forums, and more.

Noveldoc.com
www.noveldoc.com
A workshop for serious authors who have completed a novel of 60,000 words or more. Guidelines for participation are strict; this is not for "would-be" novelists.

Online Writing Workshop for Romance
http://romance.onlinewritingworkshop.com
A fee-supported workshop hosted online (not by e-mail). First month membership is free.

Online Writing Workshop for Science Fiction, Fantasy and Horror
http://sff.onlinewritingworkshop.com
Formerly hosted by Del Rey, this online critique workshop for science fiction and fantasy is now independent and charges an annual membership fee.

Preditors and Editors/Writing Workshops
http://anotherealm.com/prededitors/pubwork.htm

Quixotics
www.quixotics.com
A critique and discussion group with fairly stringent participation requirements.

SF Novelist
www.sfnovelist.com/index.htm
A critique group for writers of "hard science" sci-fi novels.

SFWA/Workshops
www.sfwa.org/links/workshops.htm
Links to speculative fiction critique groups and workshops.

Writer's List
http://web.mit.edu/mbarker/www/writers.html
A writing sample is required to establish skill level.

Writers Write: Writers' Groups Online
www.writerswrite.com/groups.htm
A list of critique, support, and chat groups for writers.

Writing-World.com/Critique Groups
www.writing-world.com/links/critique.shtml
Links to a variety of critique and discussion groups.

Young Writers' Clubhouse
www.realkids.com/critique.htm
Critique group for young writers.

ARTICLES ON CRITIQUING

Critiquing Others' Work
www.geocities.com/Area51/Labyrinth/6977/writing11.html
A short article offering some good examples of "right" and "wrong" critiquing methods.

Fiction Critiquing 101
www.cyberus.ca/~alette/Critique.htm
Tips on how to benefit from a critique group, and how to become an effective critiquer.

Hardcore Critique Advice
www.crayne.com/download/casiltip.txt

An excellent, detailed article by Amy Sterling Casil on how to write an effective critique.

How to Critique Fiction
www.crayne.com/howcrit.html
Most critique groups recommend this article by Victory Crayne as the reference to review before undertaking a critique, as well as to help you interpret critiques of your own work. The rest of the site also has a number of useful critique and writing resources.

CLASSES

Coffeehouse for Writers/Workshops
www.coffeehouseforwriters.com/courses.html

Fear of Writing Online Courses
www.fearofwriting.com/course/index1.htm

Freelance Success Institute
www.freelancesuccess.com

MagazineWriting.com
www.MagazineWriting.com
"Online study for aspiring magazine writers," featuring beginning and advanced classes.

School for Champions
www.school-for-champions.com/writing.htm
Courses on writing methods, technical writing, and fiction writing.

trAce Online Writing School
http://trace.ntu.ac.uk/school/index.htm

UCLA Extension
www.onlinelearning.net/CommunitiesofStudy
Click on "Writing" to find out more about this program.

Worldcrafter's Guild
www.simegen.com/school/index.html
Chat-based courses on a variety of topics.

WritersCollege.com
www.WritersCollege.com
Offers almost sixty online courses in a variety of genres and fields.

Writers.com
www.writers.com/writing-classes.htm

Writer's Village University
http://4-writers.com

Writers Workshops
www.nwu.org/links/lnkwks.htm
A list of online and offline workshops, seminars, writers' groups, and discussion lists.

WritingClasses.com
www.writingclasses.com

This is an excellent place to acquaint yourself with how online classes work: It offers a "sample" class that enables one to explore a syllabus, posted lectures, student forums, homework assignments, etc.

WritingSchool.com
www.WritingSchool.com

Writing-World.com/Classes
www.writing-world.com/classes/index.shtml
This site offers a variety of classes by experienced writers and editors (including courses taught by the author).

Writing-World.com/Class Links
www.writing-world.com/links/classes.shtml
Links to a variety of online writing courses.

CHAPTER 5

FINDING MARKETS ONLINE

THE MAJORITY OF U.S. MAGAZINES now offer Web sites, and many (though by no means all) post their guidelines online. More guidelines are available through various guideline databases. Thousands of newspapers are also online, giving writers access to contact information for feature editors, managing editors, and departments. While fewer non–U.S. magazines have established Web sites, you can still find a wealth of international market information on the Web— and contacting an editor on the opposite side of the world can be as easy as tapping the "send" button. The Internet also offers its own market opportunities in the form of e-zines, e-mail newsletters, content sites, and more.

"New media" doesn't necessarily mean "new rules," however. While terms like "hypertext" and "online journalism" gave writers the impression that writing for the Web would be vastly different from writing for print publications, in reality very little has changed. Online publications feature a wide range of approaches and styles, and the rule for breaking in remains the same: Study the market! Fortunately, the Internet makes that easy. Here are some places to start your search.

PRINT MARKETS

TRADITIONAL PRINT DIRECTORIES SUCH AS *The Writer's Market* are still helpful tools for locating new market information—but they are rarely up to date. Nor do they cover more than a fraction of the magazines that are actually available and open to freelance contributions. To find more (and more current) information, try these resources:

ELECTRONIC NEWSSTANDS

Although compiled primarily as a means of attracting subscribers, electronic newsstands like NEWSDIRECTORY.COM are gold mines for writers. Search by subject area, and you're bound to find magazines you never heard of before (and probably couldn't find anywhere else). For example, a search under "pets" reveals that the leading publisher of pet magazines, Fancy Publications, actually offers more than thirty pet publications, instead of the half-dozen listed in *The Writer's Market*.

You can search a newsstand for a particular title, or by subject area, or by country. Most offer links to English-language magazines around the world. Most will also give you a direct link to the magazine's Web site, and in some cases an e-mail address (though most often this will be to the subscription department). To find the editor's e-mail address, you'll generally need to visit the site itself.

GUIDELINE DATABASES

One of the market resources that has changed significantly in the past four years is "guideline databases." On the bright side, more such databases (and more comprehensive databases) are now available to writers. On the not-so-bright side, most of these databases (including the WRITER'S MARKET Web site) charge a fee, which can range from around $50 to over $100 for a one-year "subscription." A few free databases do exist (such as *WRITING FOR DOLLARS!*), but these are often not updated regularly; many are simply compilations of markets that have been featured over time in a newsletter.

Most guideline databases can be searched by subject or magazine title, and some can be searched by region and pay range. Some link directly to a magazine's Web site, while others post the guidelines within the database; still others compile summaries of the publication's terms and requirements rather than posting the actual guidelines. WOODEN HORSE PUBLISHING provides publications' editorial calendars as well as their guidelines. Some databases are kept "clean" and up to date, but others have their share of dead links and outdated guidelines (including links to magazines that have folded years ago).

MARKET NEWSLETTERS

There are now several excellent electronic newsletters that offer market information for writers. Some, such as *WritersWeekly, Writing for DOLLARS!,* and *Writing World,* include articles, columns, and other resources. Some, such as *Freelancing4Money* and *WriteMarket Reports*, focus exclusively on market information, and are available only by paid subscription.

A certain camaraderie exists between the different online writing newsletters—most of the editors know and help one another, even though, to a certain extent, the newsletters are also competing with one another. Consequently, most of the newsletters try to carve out their own territory when it comes to featuring markets. Thus, while you will sometimes find the same markets listed in different publications, you may want to do a sampling of writing and market newsletters before deciding where to subscribe.

PUBLICATION WEB SITES

Though some magazines offer Web sites that are little more than animated subscription ads, many offer elaborate mirrors of their print editions. Some post articles or excerpts from the current issue, while others archive some or all of their back issues. Some also offer material and resources that don't appear in their print issues. (In some cases, this extra information is available only to magazine subscribers; in other cases, a magazine may require one to "sign up" for access to the extra online material, even though the material is free.)

Such Web sites provide a handy, inexpensive way to study a market and determine whether it is appropriate for your writing. While an article archive won't give you the "feel" of the magazine itself (you won't see most of the illustrations, the advertising, or the quality of the layout and production), you will be able to determine the type of content the publication prefers. If the magazine publishes full-length features on its site, you'll be able to study the publication's style, slant, and depth of reporting—as well as the type of material that catches the editor's eye. Even if the publication offers nothing more than an index of the contents of back issues, you'll be able to determine what topics have been published in the past, and the type of topic that is most commonly covered.

Tracking down a publication's submission guidelines can be a challenge. Though many publications post an obvious link to their "contributor's guidelines" or "writers guidelines," many do not. If you don't see a link for submissions, check under such categories as "About Us" or "Contact Us." The "Contact Us" section is also where you're most likely to find up-to-date information on the editorial staff, including e-mail addresses for editors, managing editors, and department editors. If you still can't find the magazine's guidelines, send an e-mail to the managing editor and request them.

NEWSPAPERS

There are now anywhere from three thousand to five thousand U.S. newspapers online, ranging from the smallest of local monthlies to the largest national publications. Of these, only the nationals—e.g., *New York Times, Los Angeles Times, Wall Street Journal*—tend to charge for access, and most of those offer free access to current issues, charging only for material that is archived (usually after a week). Of the smaller papers, some offer archives, but most post only their current issue online. You won't find "writers guidelines" for a newspaper, but you can generally find current contact information, including managing editors and department editors (such as sports, travel, lifestyle, cooking, etc.).

You'll find links to these newspapers through any of more than a dozen "news-stands"—which also feature links to English-language newspapers around the world. Some also offer links to non-English papers, though this is less common.

INTERNATIONAL MARKETS

Remember when submitting material to overseas publications meant standing in line at the post office, buying International Reply Coupons, and then waiting and wondering whether your material had ever arrived at its destination? Thanks to the

Internet, those days are over. Many of the electronic newsstands offer extensive links to English-language periodicals around the world, and other sites, such as WORLDWIDE FREELANCE WRITER, offer up-to-date market information and tips.

Many overseas editors are happy to do business with U.S. writers via e-mail. You can often conduct an entire transaction—from the initial query to the electronic deposit of your fee—without ever leaving your computer. The one complication is still "getting paid"—while some international publications are able to do business through PayPal, you're still likely to end up paying a transaction fee for international payments.

While many international magazines do have Web sites, the percentage is lower than in the United States, and many do not post guidelines. If you can't locate submission information, send a polite e-mail to the editor asking whether, as an overseas author, you can submit a query or article by e-mail. When dealing with international publications, it's very likely that your negotiations will take place by e-mail as well; non-U.S. periodicals tend to be much less formal about contracts than those in the United States. Most likely, you'll receive a letter outlining when the material will run, how much you'll be paid, and when. If you don't feel comfortable without a formal contract, ask the editor to fax or snail-mail an agreement for signature. Keep in mind that payment will generally be provided in the currency of the publisher's country, so use an online currency converter to determine what you'll be paid in dollars.

Some writers worry about collecting payment if an editor in another country reneges on a contract. While this could certainly prove difficult, it is equally difficult to collect from domestic editors! This, therefore, should not be a deciding factor in approaching international markets.

International publications can be an excellent market for reprints. If you've sold one-time rights or FNASR (First North American Serial Rights) to your material, you can still offer "First European Rights," "First International Rights," first rights in the language of the publication, and a host of other rights subdivided by regional and other definitions. Some publications pay less for reprints, but others treat them as new material. If you are adept at another language (or know a good translator), this opens up still more markets for your reprints. Do not, however, attempt to run your article through an online translation program—the results may prove humorous, but certainly not salable!

BOOK PUBLISHERS

While many of the rules for submitting books or book proposals to publishers haven't changed, you can still learn a great deal more about your prospective market online than you could have learned through print directories. Most major book publishers have Web sites that offer detailed information on submission policies, manuscript preparation guidelines, and editorial contacts. Such Web sites usually offer a catalog of recent titles, which can help you determine what types of books the company is looking for or whether they've recently published a book on your topic. A Web site is the place to find the latest information on house policies and changes. You may find, for example, that a publisher has recently closed its doors to unagented or unsolicited submissions, or that it is no longer accepting a particular type of manuscript.

Some publishers also offer free e-mail newsletters that can give you an even better idea of what is in style at a particular house. Subscribing to a publisher's newsletter in your genre can also help keep you up-to-date on the latest publications of other authors in your field, as well as on the titles being accepted from newcomers. Some also offer free chapters—or entire free books—on their Web sites.

Some nonfiction publishers are willing to discuss the preliminary stages of a book proposal online. For example, it's sometimes possible to pitch a handful of proposal ideas by e-mail. After determining which topics actually interest the publisher, you can submit a more detailed proposal by snail mail. This helps ensure that you don't waste time submitting proposals that won't be of interest to the publisher and that your proposal doesn't languish in the slush pile. E-mail can also be used to negotiate a book contract. The publisher simply e-mails a copy of the contract, and then the writer (or agent) can select the clauses that require further negotiation and discuss terms online. Once the contract is finalized, a hard copy can be mailed for signature.

ELECTRONIC MARKETS

THOUSANDS OF ELECTRONIC PUBLICATIONS HAVE emerged over the past few years, but most, unfortunately, offer no pay to contributors. In addition, the number of actual paying markets has been slowly but steadily decreasing, eroded by economic factors such as the failure of the "dot.com boom" and the difficulty in finding an effective source of revenues. Advertisers are less and less willing to pay high prices for ads based on "eyeballs" (the number of visitors to a site), while subscribers are unwilling to pay a subscription fee for online publications. However, even a nonpaying market can offer a writer increased visibility that he or she might not be able to obtain from a print market.

Electronic markets include e-zines, e-mail newsletters, online editions of print publications, "content" sites, and other less traditional venues.

E-ZINES

E-zines, or "electronic magazines," are simply Web sites that are updated on a regular basis (e.g., monthly). They are available on nearly any subject you can imagine, and on a few that you probably wouldn't have imagined. Their editorial content can take one of several forms:

- **Traditional.** Many Web publications offer standard, linear articles and stories that are really no different from those you would find in a print publication. Such material is generally presented on a single "page" (unless it is unusually long), and may include graphics, sidebars, or hyperlinks to related materials.
- **Interactive.** Some Web material is divided into several stand-alone, hyperlinked sections that allow the reader to "choose a path" through the material. Sometimes the path is predefined (by "next" and "previous" buttons), and

sometimes the reader is given a menu of choices of what to read next. While such a text may have an introduction, there may be no "linear" connection between subsequent sections.

- **Multimedia.** Some publications offer elements that can't be incorporated into a print publication, such as sound clips, video, or animation. For example, a written interview might include a sound clip of the actual spoken interview; an article on Peruvian music might include a clip of that music. While multimedia was once touted as the "future" of Internet publishing, however, it has proven cumbersome. Most writers, editors, and publishers lack the programming skill to incorporate such elements, and sites that *do* include multimedia elements are often slow to download, or may require additional software (or may simply cause one's browser to crash). In general, as a writer, you will not be asked to produce multimedia elements or effects.

E-zines cover both fiction and nonfiction. Fiction e-zines generally tend to pay less than their print counterparts (with a few significant exceptions). Payment from nonfiction e-zines can range anywhere from $25 to $500; however, you'll rarely find an online market that pays $1 a word or more unless it is associated with an offline organization, such as a print publication (e.g., *Reader's Digest*) or television network (e.g., Discovery.com).

Approaching an e-zine is much the same as approaching a print publication. You will generally be able to find the e-zine's submission guidelines and contact information on the Web site. Most e-zine editors prefer (or insist upon) e-mail queries and submissions (which will be discussed in more detail in chapter 6). Beyond that, however, the basic rules of "studying the market and sending an appropriate query" apply.

E-MAIL NEWSLETTERS

E-mail newsletters are proliferating on a wide range of topics. Unfortunately, the majority are produced by individuals, and do not pay for contributions. However, there *are* paying e-newsletters, and these can be a way to get your work in front of a wide audience.

E-mail newsletters are a strictly text-only medium. Consequently, they use only traditional, linear articles. Most (but not all) prefer shorter material, seeking articles that do not exceed one thousand words. Most also don't pay a great deal—rates range from $10 to $50 per article. Some also accept reprints of material that has appeared in print, online, or in another (noncompeting) newsletter. Most include all articles within the newsletter itself, but some provide only teasers and hyperlinks to a Web site, where the reader can find the entire article.

While you won't get rich writing for e-mail newsletters, you can achieve a high level of visibility, especially if you write for one of the more respected publications. Since such newsletters are often more current than print publications in the same field, they are widely read by the editors of those print publications—who may then recognize your name from the newsletter when you drop by with a query.

Editors may also contact you. E-mail newsletters are distributed worldwide. Don't be surprised if an editor from New Zealand or South Africa contacts you for permission to reprint one of your articles—or even to offer you an assignment.

"ONLINE" EDITIONS

Many newspapers and some magazines host a separate online edition that features articles and other materials that aren't included in the print edition. You will also find online editions of broadcast media, such as the Discovery Channel and the History Channel. Some online editions, such as *Reader's Digest* and *National Geographic,* provide expanded versions of print articles or supporting materials and links to outside sources.

Other publications post selected articles from their print editions online. Some pay extra to the writer if the material is used electronically; *The Writer* magazine, for example, offers an additional 25 percent if they post an article on their Web site. Others seek to acquire the option to use material electronically without paying extra.

Since "online editions" are sponsored by publications or organizations whose primary audience and market is "offline" (e.g., a print publication or television network), these organizations don't need to rely on online revenue sources for their funding. Consequently, they can be more lucrative markets for writers.

"CONTENT" SITES

Many sites use content as a way to attract readers to their product or advertising. The now-defunct Pets.com, for example, posted hundreds of pet-related articles on its Web site, in an effort to build a "community" that would attract customers. Myria.com, a site covering pregnancy and parenthood, publishes articles and newsletters and is supported by advertising. No matter what your interest, chances are that you can find a catalog site that addresses it, which might be interested in articles and columns. Again, as these sites are supported by other types of revenues (e.g., sales), they tend to offer higher payments to contributors than most e-zines. The downside is that many ask for all rights, or at least all electronic rights, to your material.

ONLINE JOURNALISM

A few years ago, many predicted that the Internet would prove to be the death of traditional print journalism. After all, paper was costly, ink stains the hands, and who would want to read a bulky print paper when one could easily surf the headlines online, picking and choosing articles of interest and skipping the rest?

These predictions were a bit over-optimistic. In a 2001 survey by Insight Express, 73 percent of those polled said that they preferred paper to online editions of magazines and newspapers. Banners and pop-up ads have turned out to be far more annoying than print ads, and the ability of online publications to deliver "instant" news hasn't made up for the problems of eye-strain in trying to read that news.

While "online journalism" still exists, therefore, it does not appear at this time to be a separate market category for freelance writers. Though thousands of U.S. and international newspapers have online editions, the majority are simply mirrors of the print editions; only a few of the larger metropolitan papers offer additional information online (such as background details or extra coverage of a print story). That extra information is generally provided by the papers' staffs, rather than freelancers.

NONTRADITIONAL MARKETS

MOST OF THE ELECTRONIC MARKETS listed above look for much the same type of material that you might submit to a traditional print publication. There are, however, other types of online markets that use freelance material as well.

WEB GUIDES

In the previous edition of this book, I provided information about the two major "Web guide" sites—SUITE101.COM and ABOUT.COM (then known as The Mining Co.). At that time, both sites paid freelance writers to "host" a "guide" site on a particular topic. Web guides were expected to contribute regular articles of their own and provide extensive links to other online resources; some also sponsored chats or forums and put out regular e-mail newsletters.

Unfortunately, as of December 2001, Suite101.com ceased paying its contributors. About.com, which was purchased by Primedia in 2001, still pays its guides a percentage of ad revenues based on a guide's visitor count. About.com provides a base stipend of $100 or more, plus a share in ad revenues, based on site traffic: The more visitors one brings in, the higher one's share. One respondent stated that she typically earns $700 per month. However, in the past year the site has dropped several hundred of its topics and editors, and as of this writing it is being sued by several of its contributors for nonpayment and other issues.

Another site that promised its hosts shares of ad revenues was Webseed.com, which offered personal domains and an attractive template. Unfortunately, the anticipated revenue sources never materialized, and Webseed ceased to exist as a "content network" in the summer of 2002.

Despite the problems with payments, however, many writers pointed out that they had other reasons besides money for acting as Web guides or hosts. "Do it because you love what you are writing about, because you have always wanted a Web site on a specific topic but have not had the ability or money to launch one yourself, or because you want to promote your writing services—but don't do it for money. You will almost assuredly be disappointed in the results," says Wen Zienteck-Sico, former host of *www.holidaycrafter.com* on the now-defunct Webseed. Cynthia Polanski, host of the boxer dogs site on Suite101, says that she "loved the idea of writing on a regular basis about a topic near to my heart. Not many publications would afford this kind of opportunity. The freedom to write whatever I want ... I don't have to worry about using a particular voice or targeting an esoteric readership. It's liberating to be the sole editor of my work." Sam Vaknin, editor of *www.balkanlands.com*, notes that "It is a very effective promotional tool. It allows me to be in touch with potential customers for my niche-targeted titles."

Another issue to consider is rights. Suite101.com requires exclusive electronic and print rights for ninety days, followed by nonexclusive electronic rights. About.com requires the license to use a writer's work "on the Internet," meaning that it may sell the writer's work elsewhere—in which case it will split revenues 50/50 with the writer.

To become a guide, you'll be asked to submit a proposal describing your chosen topic, your expertise, and the type of information you'd provide on your site. If accepted, you'll receive training and site templates (which belong to the host site and cannot be transferred to a personal site). Your host site will also provide editing services and other assistance.

DISTANCE EDUCATION

Another place for writers to turn their talents into cash online is through online classes. Several independent writing sites host or sponsor writing classes and are always on the lookout for experienced writers who can effectively pass their expertise on to others. Though it can be helpful to have some prior teaching experience, this isn't always necessary. What you'll need most are good communication skills and appropriate writing credentials.

Teaching online offers a flexibility you'll never find in a traditional continuing education program. Though some classes include real-time chat sessions, most have no formal schedule (other than the scheduled delivery of lectures and, in some cases, deadlines for assignments). Instructors prepare and deliver lectures, review homework, and discuss questions with students at their own convenience.

Rates for online writing courses depend on the sponsoring site, the reputation of the instructor, and whether the course is part of a degree or accreditation program. Some sites have fixed rates; others allow instructors to set their own fees. Fees can range from $50 to $350, depending on the site. Of those fees, the instructor may receive anywhere from 60 to 85 percent. (Classes on Writing-World.com, for example, generally cost between $75 and $125, and the instructor receives 75 percent of the total.)

When you teach an online course, you'll generally be expected to provide the following elements:

- **Course syllabus**. Besides the basic title and content of your course (e.g., "Freelancing Basics"), your syllabus should include a description of what students will learn from the course (e.g., "how to market, outline, query, and develop an article") and what the outcome of the course will be (e.g., "students will complete a marketable feature article by the end of the course"). The syllabus may also list lecture topics, homework assignments, and sources (or URLs) of additional readings.
- **Lectures**. Some sites offer a password-restricted Web site where the instructor posts course lectures. In most classes, however, the instructor e-mails

lectures directly to the students. Since the lecture tends to be the instructor's primary contact with students, this is generally the most important aspect of the course; think of each lecture as being an article in itself.

- **Readings**. The Internet makes reading assignments simple: Just direct students to relevant URLs. You may want to compile a list of useful URLs that you can recommend to individual students for specific problems, such as grammar sites. Using Web sites for readings also helps avoid the potential copyright problems involved in transmitting "readings" by e-mail.
- **Homework**. Since many writing courses are specifically designed to help students develop or improve their skills, you'll generally be expected to assign (and review) homework exercises. Independent courses usually don't involve grades, but students may expect editorial comments to guide them. Homework is usually submitted and returned via e-mail.
- **Individual feedback**. In addition to answering discussion questions, you'll also be expected to provide a certain amount of one-on-one guidance to individual students. Students will expect to be able to contact you with questions and will also expect feedback on their homework assignments.

Some classes also provide an option for discussion, either through a chat room (which involves meeting at a scheduled time), or through a discussion list that enables students to interact with each other and the instructor via e-mail. Most courses, however, do not include a discussion component.

Most of us became writers because of our passion for the written word. Teaching others how to write effectively is a rewarding way to share that passion and to give back some of the lessons and insights we've gathered along the way. It can also bring in a decent paycheck!

HANDHELD CONTENT

Not surprisingly, the market for material that can be read on handheld devices, such as a PalmPilot (or even a cell phone), is growing steadily. Sites like PALM DIGITAL MEDIA (formerly known as Peanut Press) and FICTIONWISE offer "handheld" formats for previously published material—e.g., novels and short stories that were originally published in print. (Neither of these sites is open to unpublished freelance submissions; Fictionwise, however, will review reprints of stories, particularly speculative fiction, that have appeared in reputable print journals.) Other sites, such as THE PHONE BOOK and HANDHELD CRIME, seek very short material that is suitable for handhelds and cellphones. HandHeld Crime, for example, seeks stories of no more than 1,200 words; The Phone Book seeks stories of no more than 150 words. Given the length of the material involved, these markets actually pay quite well—though many writers find it more difficult to write "short" than to write longer fiction!

ELECTRONIC GREETING CARDS

You've probably received them in your e-mail—and you can make money writing for electronic greeting cards as well. According to greeting card writer Nadia Ali, electronic greeting card companies seek short, humorous punch-line material. The turnover time between sending in an idea and receiving a response tends to be short; however, such companies rarely offer bylines. Ali notes that many companies also have a pool of in-house talent, and only use freelancers when "in need." Pay also tends to be low, around $10 per punch line as opposed to $75 or higher for print cards.

"Before you can submit any ideas, you have to be an accepted writer by the online greeting card market," says Ali. "This means that you will be given access to the developers' area where you have your own password and login name. Once you gain access to this area you can submit card ideas on a preloaded descriptive area, which permits the use of four scenes to make an animated or interactive card, giving graphic descriptions of your idea to the graphic artist who will make it into a fully operative animated card."

Ali also notes that "The online card service is built on immediate trends. For instance, if there is a big news headline or event, they can automatically cash in on its popularity, as was seen online by the various cards for the 2000 USA elections with Bush and Gore. Also because they can monitor which cards are sent, you can see from their daily top ten sent cards whether your card is very popular or not."

To break in, Ali suggests watching the online greeting card sites, as some have "job" areas (usually in the "about us" section). Or, simply query a company to find out if any work is available.

TO MARKET, TO MARKET—TODAY

MARKETS FOR WRITERS ARE IN a constant state of change. Editors move, addresses change, publications go out of business—and writers may be none the wiser until their manuscripts come back stamped "undeliverable." Print directories are often months out of date before they even come off the press.

The greatest advantage of conducting market research on the Internet is perhaps its ability to keep writers current with market changes and developments. If your editor leaves your favorite magazine, or a periodical stops accepting e-mail queries, or a book publisher closes its doors to unagented submissions, that information is likely to turn up online within days of the change—which means that you'll be able to find out before you waste time and money on an unsuitable submission. You'll also be able to check a publication's guidelines or sample articles when you first conceive of an idea for that publication, rather than having to wait weeks or months for guidelines and a sample copy to show up in your mailbox.

This means, however, that keeping current is more important than ever. Editors will expect their writers to be aware of the latest changes in editorial guidelines, submission policies, or editorial transitions, because those changes are posted online for anyone to find. Writers who don't bother to check this information risk appearing unprofessional and out of touch. So even if you still crank out manuscripts on your Underwood portable, be sure to log on before you try to send those same manuscripts to market!

RESOURCES

GUIDELINE DATABASES AND LISTS

AcqWeb
www.library.vanderbilt.edu/law/acqs/email-ad.html
AcqWeb offers an "international directory of e-mail addresses of publishers, vendors and related professional associations, organizations and services." A good place to look for markets.

Children's Writers Marketplace
http://write4kids.com/wmarket/index.html
Margaret Shauers' Children's Writers Marketplace, formerly hosted on Inkspot, is back online at Write4Kids.com.

Colossal Directory of Children's Publishers Online, The
http://childrenspublishers.signaleader.com
Comprehensive, alphabetical listings of children's magazines and book publishers, including links to submission guidelines and Web sites. Plus articles which focus on the submission process, not the writing process.

FreelanceWriting.com/Magazine Guidelines Database
www.freelancewriting.com/guidelines/pages

Jacqui Bennett Writers Bureau/UK Markets
www.jbwb.co.uk/markets.html
A huge selection of U.K. markets for fiction and nonfiction.

Market List, The
www.marketlist.com
Covers speculative fiction markets (e.g., sci-fi, fantasy, horror).

Markets for Writers
www.chebucto.ns.ca/Culture/WFNS/periodicals.html
This list focuses primarily on Canadian markets, with some U.S. magazines as well.

Spicy Green Iguana
www.spicygreeniguana.com
More than two hundred links to sci-fi, fantasy, and horror magazine publications.

Wooden Horse Publishing
www.woodenhorsepub.com
Though the markets database on this site costs $149 per year, the site is also packed with loads of free stuff, including extensive coverage of magazine industry changes (new magazines, shut-downs, editorial changes, etc.).

Working List of Speculative Fiction Markets
http://home.att.net/~p.fleming/Sfmarket.html
Lengthy text listing of speculative fiction markets, with Web sites and e-mail addresses. (Not hot-linked.)

Writer's Market
www.writersmarket.com
Paid membership.

WritersWeekly.com Markets & Jobs
www.writersweekly.com/markets/markets.html
A listing of paying markets, updated daily, from the publisher of *The Write Markets Report*.

WritersWeekly Warnings Reports
www.writersweekly.com/warnings/warnings.html
This is a great place to check on Web sites and publishers that (a) have a reputation for slow or nonpayment, or (b) are going out of business or are rumored to be having troubles.

Writers Write: Writer's Guidelines Directory
www.writerswrite.com/guidelines
Offers an extensive list of paying markets, as well as a number of nonpaying markets. Can be searched by category, keyword, paying vs. nonpaying, and by markets that accept fiction, nonfiction, or poetry.

Writing for DOLLARS!/Guidelines Database
www.writingfordollars.com/Guidelines.cfm
Offers nearly 1,200 listings, drawn from past issues of *Writing for DOLLARS!* This means that while the listing collection is extensive, it may not be absolutely up to date—but it's worth reviewing.

PUBLICATIONS WITH MARKET LISTINGS

Children's Book Insider
www.write4kids.com/aboutcbi.html
Monthly print newsletter for children's writers, offering writing tips and new markets (paid subscription).

Fiction Factor: The Online Magazine for Writers
www.fictionfactor.com
You'll find a host of interesting features and markets on this site, including author interviews, book reviews, alerts, and more.

Freelancing4Money
www.freelancing4money.com
Weekly e-mail markets newsletter (paid subscription).

Worldwide Freelance Writer
www.worldwidefreelance.com
Articles and information on international markets.

Write Markets Report, The
www.writersweekly.com/shop/ forwriters.html#4

Monthly electronic (PDF format) markets newsletter, usually offering at least fifty markets per issue; paid subscription.

Writer, The
www.writermag.com
Monthly print magazine, with an extensive market section.

Writer's Digest
www.writersdigest.com
Monthly print magazine, with Web site.

Writers Weekly
www.writersweekly.com
A weekly e-mail newsletter listing markets and jobs for writers, plus links to online articles and columns.

Writing for DOLLARS!
www.writingfordollars.com
A monthly newsletter offering tips and markets.

Writing World
www.writing-world.com/newsletter/ index.shtml
A free biweekly e-mail newsletter. The markets section primarily covers new "calls for submissions" (for anthologies and publications) and electronic markets.

E-ZINE DIRECTORIES

Electronic Journal Miner
http://ejournal.coalliance.org

eZINESearch
www.refer-me.com/members/ e-zine-master/
A searchable list of more than three thousand e-zines.

Ezine-Universe.com
http://Ezine-Universe.com

Well-organized lists of e-zines and newsletters.

Flying Inkpot's Zine Scene
www.inkpot.com/zines

NewJour/New Journals and Newsletters on the Internet
http://gort.ucsd.edu/newjour/New JourWel.html

Newsletter Directory
www.newsletter-directory.com
This site offers an extensive directory of online publications on a variety of subjects.

WebScout Lists
www.webscoutlists.com
Easy-to-search directory of e-zines and newsletters; newsletters are archived under appropriate categories.

ELECTRONIC NEWSSTANDS, MAGAZINE DIRECTORIES, AND INTERNATIONAL MARKET RESOURCES

Council of Literary Magazines and Presses
www.clmp.org
If you'd like to find a literary magazine or a small literary press, check here first; this site offers an extensive member directory, and also offers a larger directory for sale.

Magazines of Europe
www.travelconnections.com/Magazines/Europeindex.htm
For magazines from other parts of the world, go to www.travelconnections.com/Magazines.

MagoMania: Canada's Magazine Search Engine
www.magomania.com/english

NewsDirectory.com
www.newsdirectory.com
A worldwide database of magazines.

WebWombat/Magazines
www.webwombat.com.au/magazines
An Australian search engine that offers extensive listings of magazine homepages around the world, including many non-English publications.

Yahoo! Australia and NZ Directory
http://au.dir.yahoo.com/news_and_media/magazines
Links to Australian and New Zealand publications.

Yahoo! Directory/News and Media
http://d1.dir.dcx.yahoo.com/News_and_Media/Magazines/By_Region
Search for newspapers and online media by region.

NEWSPAPER DIRECTORIES

ABYZ News Links
www.abyznewslinks.com
Links to more than 16,800 newspapers and other news sources from around the world; regularly cleaned and updated.

Fleet Street Online
www.fleet-street.com/top.htm
Links to U.K. newspapers.

International News Links
www.inkpot.com/news
Links to newspapers with an online presence around the world.

JournalismNet
www.journalismnet.com/papers/index.htm
Lists publications by region.

Media UK
www.mediauk.com
Find U.K. newspapers and other media.

Mercator
www.aber.ac.uk/~merwww/allang.htm
This is a fascinating site that links to resources related to "minority languages in the European Union." Look here for links to newspapers, media, newsgroups, and more, for such languages as Asturian, Basque, Ladin, Occitan, etc. The page is offered in English, Welsh, and French.

NewspaperLinks.com
www.newspaperlinks.com/home.cfm
Links to U.S. dailies and weeklies, Canadian and international papers, press associations, and other newspaper-related sites.

Newspapers.com
www.newspapers.com
Links to newspapers around the world.

Paperboy, The
www.thepaperboy.com/welcome.cfm
A site that enables you to search for international newspapers and international news topics.

PPPP.Net/Ultimate Collection of News Links
http://pppp.net/links/news
Another major collection of newspaper links.

US Newspaper Links.com
www.usnpl.com
A huge collection of links to U.S. news-papers and radio stations, searchable by state.

BOOK PUBLISHERS

Association of American University Presses
http://aaupnet.org

Includes a member directory of university presses.

Audio Publishers Association
http://audiopub.org
Industry resources for audiobooks.

BookWire/Book Publisher Index
www.bookwire.com/bookwire/publishers/publishers.html
In addition to a general listing of book publishers, this site offers both general and genre- or topic-specific listings. Check here for lists of children's publishers, mystery publishers, religious publishers, sci-fi/fantasy publishes, travel publishers, publishers of non-English books, and more.

Children's Publishers
http://susettewilliams.com/
A list of children's book and magazine publishers. *(Click link at top of page.)*

Colossal Directory of Children's Publishers
http://childrenspublishers.signaleader.com

Midwest Book Review/Publishers
www.midwestbookreview.com/links/publish.htm
This page offers a huge array of publisher links, including children's book publishers, trade publishers, scholarly and academic publishers, computer and software book publishers, e-book publishers and dealers, and more. It will keep you busy.

Mysterious Home Page/Publishers
www.cluelass.com/MystHome/Publishers.html
List of mystery publishers, including several international publishers.

Overbooked Book Links: Mystery, Suspense, Thrillers, Crime Fiction Publishers
http://freenet.vcu.edu/education/ literature/mystpub.html
Extensive collection of links to book publishers, including international and small press publishers.

Publishers' Catalogues Home Page
www.lights.com/publisher
A search tool enabling one to look up publishers by name, location, subject, or type of material published.

Publishers Online
www.peak.org/~bonwritr/pub.htm
Links to a variety of resources, including small presses, the British book industry, greeting card markets, Canadian publishers, computer books, and more.

Publishers on the Internet
www.faxon.com/title/pl_am.htm
Though focusing primarily on academic and technical publishers, this list offers many links to mainstream publishers as well.

Romance Publishers
www.rwanational.com/pub_links.stm
A list of romance publishers (some with links, some without) from Romance Writers of America.

World Publishing Industry
http://publishing-industry.net/Publishers
A directory/search engine for the publishing industry; offers extensive listings in various publishing categories.

Writers' Information Network/Publishers
www.bluejaypub.com/win/publishers.htm
Extensive list of links to Christian book publishers.

WriteLinks/Commercial Book Publishers
www.writelinks.com/Creative/Links/Book Publishers/crea06_02.htm
A comprehensive listing of book publishers in every category, including genre, address, Web site, and e-mail.

WritersMind, The
www.thewritersmind.com
A site that allows agents and publishers to post listings. Well-categorized.

CLASSES

(See Resources for chapter 4)

WEB GUIDES

About.com
http://beaguide.about.com/index.htm

Suite101
www.suite101.com/editorapp/member.cfm

MARKETS FOR HANDHELD CONTENT

Fictionwise/Information for Authors
www.fictionwise.com/authorinfo.htm
Accepts reprints of previously published short stories and novels from established writers; does not accept unsolicited original material.

HandHeld Crime
www.handheldcrime.com
Publishes very short mystery stories (under 1,200 words).

Phone Book, The
www.the-phone-book.com
Publishes "short short" stories (150 words or less) on a range of topics for viewing on a cell phone.

ELECTRONIC GREETING CARDS

Regards.com
www.regards.com
See "about us" for freelance opportunities.

WickedMoon.com
www.wickedmoon.com
Send résumé to *jason@wickedmoon.co.uk*.

WritersWrite: Greeting Cards
www.writerswrite.com/greetingcards/ecards.htm
List of online greeting card companies.

Yahoo! Directory/Virtual Cards
http://d1.dir.dcx.yahoo.com/Entertainment/Virtual_Cards
Lists e-card companies alphabetically and by category (e.g., holiday, adult, animals, etc.), as well as a list of the most popular e-card companies.

<< **CHAPTER 6** >>

E-MAIL QUERIES AND SUBMISSIONS

OF ALL THE ADVANTAGES OF being connected to the Internet, e-mail is perhaps the greatest. It offers the most significant savings to writers in terms of time and money, enabling a writer to contact an editor anywhere in the world, submit a proposal, and deliver a manuscript—all without licking a stamp. It also enables writers to conduct interviews at the convenience of both parties and conduct surveys that would otherwise involve hundreds of dollars in mailing costs (see chapter 3).

While e-mail won't replace every form of correspondence, it offers the following advantages, not only to writers but to editors and publishers as well:

- **It saves postage.** When you send a query or manuscript by e-mail, or a request for information or a response to such a request, you're saving at least one stamp and usually two. On manuscripts, you may save several dollars.
- **It saves paper.** E-mail may not be the ultimate act of recycling, but it certainly helps! Each time you submit a manuscript by e-mail, you've saved the paper needed to print the piece and the envelope required to mail it. You also save paper at the other end by enabling an editor to reply to your e-mail rather than having to compose and mail a formal response.
- **It saves time.** E-mail transmissions usually arrive instantly. That means you can send a query or an article to an editor anywhere in the world without wondering whether it will arrive or when. This makes manuscript tracking easier, as you no longer have to factor delivery time into your estimate of response time. It also means that you can add precious days to your deadline, because you can transmit material literally on the day it is due.
- **It encourages an immediate response.** The ability to simply type a line or two and hit the "reply" button encourages many editors to reply to e-mail queries

more quickly than to traditional mail. E-mail eliminates the need to draft a formal response, type a letter, find a reply form, locate your SASE, or type an envelope. Consequently, you may receive a reply to an e-mail query within days, or even hours, rather than having to wait weeks or months. E-mail also provides a good way to follow up on a query or submission.

- **It provides a convenient means of exchanging information.** Do you have a question for your editor? Does your editor have a question for you? With e-mail, you can exchange information without having to play telephone tag, send a fax, or compose a letter. Information exchanges are usually informal. The question and the answer may be little more than a line or two apiece.
- **It streamlines negotiations.** E-mail makes it possible to conduct an entire contract negotiation in days rather than weeks. The original contract can be transmitted by e-mail, whereupon both parties can "snip" clauses that require further discussion or change and send their comments back and forth until a final agreement is reached. Once the contract has been finalized, a paper copy should be drafted and faxed, or snail-mailed—e-mail as yet offers no legally accepted way to transmit a binding signature.
- **It enables editors to download documents.** With e-mail, you don't have to worry about translating your documents into a program your editor's computer can read. (This is especially good news for Mac users in a PC world!) No more sending disks back and forth; e-mailed material can be copied directly into your editor's word-processing or formatting program.
- **It opens doors to international markets.** No one likes dealing with International Reply Coupons (IRCs). Writers have to visit the post office to buy them; editors have to go to the post office to redeem them. Consequently, international publications are often more than happy to bypass this hassle and do business electronically. Many U.S. publications will accept e-mail submissions from non-U.S. authors, even if they don't accept them from domestic writers.

E-MAIL QUERIES

AMAZINGLY, SOME BOOKS AND ARTICLES still warn writers not to submit queries by e-mail. While it is true that some publications still don't accept material via e-mail, hundreds of others do. In 1998, I surveyed 720 consumer magazines that listed e-mail addresses in the *1999 Writer's Market*. Of the 360 editors who responded, 88 percent were willing to accept e-mail queries, while 87 percent accepted assigned manuscripts by e-mail. Today, the majority of the 2,000-plus magazines listed in *The Writer's Market* accept e-mail queries and submissions. If a market listing doesn't indicate whether e-mail queries are accepted, send a polite e-mail to ask. If you don't receive a response, assume the answer is "no."

Besides saving paper and postage, e-mail queries save time. You don't have to wonder when, or whether, your query was received; you know that it reached the editor's "desk" within seconds of leaving your own. If it did not, you should receive a "bounce back" notification of undeliverable mail within a few minutes.

In addition, many editors tend to answer e-mail queries more quickly than traditional queries. It only takes an instant to type a response to an e-mail—whether a rejection, an acceptance, or a request for more information. Editors that you work with regularly are likely to respond even more quickly, and you don't have to wait for them to dig your envelope out of a pile of snail mail. (It's important to remember, however, that e-mail doesn't *obligate* an editor to respond quickly—and no editor appreciates being nagged about whether they've reviewed the query or article you e-mailed to them five minutes ago.)

E-QUERY FORMAT

Just because an editor can respond quickly and informally to an e-query doesn't mean that the query itself should be hasty or informal. When you're approaching an editor for the first time, the primary difference between an e-query and a traditional query is the mode of transmission. The content should be composed as carefully as that of any paper query.

An electronic query letter involves three basic sections: the header, the body, and your signature.

THE HEADER

The header of your e-query includes such information as the editor's e-mail address, your return address, the date sent, and the subject of the e-mail. Some of these fields are automatic; others must be filled in. As the header contains the first information an editor will see, it's important that every aspect of this section (including the automatic fields) reflect your professionalism. Pay special attention to the following fields:

- **To**: Besides inserting the e-mail address of the editor, you can personalize this field by adding the editor's name and title. Type the name and title first, without commas (use colons or dashes for punctuation or this information will be treated as part of the address), followed by the e-mail address in angle brackets:

  ```
  To: John Smith: Editor -- GREAT MAGAZINE
  <jsmith@greatmag.com>
  ```

- **From**: If you use an e-mail alias, it will appear in this field, so be sure your alias is appropriate for a query letter. Calling yourself "Studmuffin" or "Firesinger Dragonheart" is fine among friends, but will not endear you to an editor! Also, if your alias is uninformative (e.g., MQW@isp.com), consider entering your full name in the "reply" option of your e-mail settings:

  ```
  From: "Mary Q. Writer" <mqw@isp.com>
  ```

- **Subject**: Make sure the editor knows this is a query and what it is about:

  ```
  Subject: QUERY: Feline Heart Disease
  ```

- **CC**: Send yourself a copy of the query, both as a record for your files and to retransmit if the first transmission doesn't succeed. (To save time and typos, make yourself a mailing "nickname" such as "Me," or set your e-mail program to automatically save a copy of all outgoing mail.)
- **Attachments**: Never send attachments without permission. Due to the fear of viruses, most editors will delete unsolicited attachments unread (and may delete the e-mail that sent them as well). Never attach electronic "clips" or any other information to an unsolicited query letter.

THE BODY

The body of your query begins with the salutation and should proceed like any traditional query. It's perfectly acceptable to write your query just as you would if you were mailing it the traditional way. However, many editors find that they prefer shorter (and less formal) queries by e-mail, partly because they prefer not to have to scroll through a lengthy letter onscreen. Thus, more writers are turning to brief, one- to three-paragraph queries, dispensing with such elements as the "hook" paragraph and moving straight to the point. Here's an example of a query I received from a regular contributor to my e-zine:

Hello! I promised you a query, so here you go.

"Flash What?" is an exploration of the (at-first-glance) strange medium of flash fiction. The article does not attempt to define the form, as flash is virtually undefinable, but it does identify the many styles of flash, and its many names. I cite such writers as Lila Guzman and Pamelyn Casto and their thoughts on the form. Following this, I segue into a general how-to segment on writing flash, listing three essential questions every flash writer must ask. Once that's finished, I close out with market listings and other resources.

With flash fiction becoming more and more prevalent in the literary community, especially the online publishing world (whole zines are devoted to the medium), I think that this piece is very useful to Inkspot's many readers who double as fiction writers. "Flash What?" is about 1220 words long. I'll be happy to send along the full piece if you are interested.

Thanks! Looking forward to your reply.[1]

When crafting an e-mail query, therefore, give serious thought to ways that you can "condense" your information into a compact summary that the editor can view

[1]Yes, I accepted the query; you can read the article at *www.writing-world.com/fiction/flash.shtml*.

on a single screen. Just be sure that your summary actually covers all the salient points that you wish to make!

CREDENTIALS AND CLIPS

It's perfectly acceptable to list your credentials in an e-mail query just as you would in a traditional query. Many writers also use this opportunity to provide a link to a Web site where editors can learn more about the writer's qualifications, or perhaps view writing samples. Some editors will check the sites you list; some won't. It's wise, therefore, to state your credentials explicitly, and offer Web sites only as a backup. Never send "clips" in an attachment.

THE SIGNATURE

If you use a signature block, make sure it is appropriate for this type of correspondence. Don't include a block that lists the names of your nine cats, your favorite *Star Wars* quote, or your "Firesinger Dragonheart" alias. Sign your query with your full name. Include your snail mail address, a telephone number, and a fax number.

E-MAIL SUBMISSIONS

IF THERE IS A SINGLE rule about e-mail submissions, it is this: Never send an unsolicited manuscript by e-mail! No editor wants twenty unsolicited pages in her inbox—or worse, an attachment that takes five minutes to download. And with today's fears about viruses, many editors will delete unsolicited attachments unread—along with the e-mail that sent them.

Many editors welcome assigned manuscripts by e-mail, however, and often prefer them to hard copies or disks. An e-mail submission generally allows an editor to download a manuscript file directly, without having to worry about compatible word-processing programs or platforms (especially if the submission is within the body of the e-mail). Such submissions also enable writers to turn in manuscripts at literally the last minute.

Always include all sections of the manuscript (including sidebars and any other information) in a single document. Place a brief cover memo at the beginning of the document to provide any necessary information to the editor, including the word count of the submission.

Some editors prefer to receive manuscripts within the text of the e-mail; others prefer attachments (most commonly MS Word). Be sure to determine the correct or preferred format before sending your manuscript.

TURNING OFF THE GIBBERISH

SENDING A QUERY OR MANUSCRIPT electronically isn't simply a matter of copying your material from a word-processing file (such as MS Word) and pasting it into an e-mail. All too often, a straight cut-and-paste results in a message that looks something like this:

    %Please don‚t reject my manuscript‚@ the author cried,
    pleading ? but to no avail, as the editor wasn&t in
    the mood for such %gibberish@!

Even a single line of this can be annoying; having to wade through an entire query—or worse, a manuscript—of this nature is beyond the patience of most editors. Kind-hearted editors will send such a submission back and ask you to fix it; less-understanding editors will simply send a rejection.

Gibberish and "nonsense symbols" are the result of transferring a word-processed document directly to e-mail without "undoing" many of the special characters and commands that such a program (like Word) automatically embeds in your file. Unless instructed otherwise, for example, Microsoft Word will auto-matically convert dashes (--) into a special dash-symbol (—), turn all apostrophes and quotes into "smart quotes," transform ellipses (...) into yet another special character, and superscript the ending of words like "1st" or "7th."

These special characters look nice on the printed page, but are the result of hidden codes in your electronic file that do not "translate" when copied into an e-mail document. Instead, those codes are converted into various symbols and odd characters. Any formatting codes in your document (e.g., bold, underline, italic) will be similarly transformed. Converting your document to .rtf format, or even .txt, does not always remove all embedded codes.

To prevent these and other e-mail problems in your submissions, be sure to take the following steps before submitting a query or manuscript electronically:

- **Turn off all special-character commands.** In MS Word, you can do this by going into the "AutoCorrect" menu under "Tools." In the "Autoformat as You Type" and "Autoformat" menus, uncheck everything under "Replace as You Type." In the "Autocorrect" submenu, look at the list of automatic corrections, and delete the correction that replaces an ellipsis with a special character. In particular, turn off the command to convert quotes and apostrophes to "smart" quotes.
- **Replace special-character commands in existing documents.** If you're submitting a document that you prepared *before* turning off these "replace" commands, you'll need to do a search-and-replace on the problem characters. For smart quotes, simply enter a single quote in the "Find and Replace" box and do a "Replace All"; this will correct all apostrophes and single quotes. Do the same for double quotes. To replace an en dash, use the keyboard combination [Option + hyphen on a Mac or Ctrl + hyphen on a PC, using the hyphen on the numerical pad, not the main keyboard] to enter the dash in the "Find" box; replace it with a hyphen surrounded by spaces. To replace an em dash, use the keyboard combination [Shift + Option + hyphen on a Mac or Ctrl + Alt + hyphen on a PC, again using the hyphen on the numerical pad, not the main keyboard] to enter the em dash in the "Find" box; replace it with a pair of hyphens and a space on either side. To replace ellipses, use the keyboard combination [Option + ;] on a Mac or [Ctrl + Alt + .] on a PC in the "Find" box, and replace with [...].

- **Double-space between paragraphs.** E-mail wipes out tabs, which means that a manuscript that relies on tabs to indicate new paragraphs will end up as a nearly solid block of text. If you don't want to double-space manually, simply do a search-and-replace on the "paragraph" character, replacing one paragraph character with two. (In Word, click on "More" in the "Find and Replace" menu. The paragraph command is the first item under "Special"—hit this option once for the "Find" box and twice for the "Replace" box.)

Editors will be even happier with your electronic submissions if you follow these guidelines:

- *Don't* use HTML formatting in your e-mail. Turn off any commands that automatically convert your e-mail to an HTML document.
- *Don't* use colors. Just as you wouldn't type a query in yellow ink, don't send an e-mail query in any font color other than black.
- *Do* use a large, readable font. Sometimes I feel the urge to send a query back simply because it seems to be written in micro-print. Make sure your font size is set to "normal"—or to a minimum of 12 points.
- *Don't* send any "automatic" attachments. If your e-mail program is set up to send a "vcard" attachment, turn off that option.
- *Do* keep a copy of all correspondence with editors. This will make it much easier for you to send a copy of your original query if you need to follow up. One way to handle this is to create a folder in your e-mail directory for "queries and submissions" that are still awaiting response, and another for queries and submissions that have received a reply. By checking your "awaiting response" file, you can easily determine, by the dates of your e-mails, when a submission should be followed up.

The ability to contact editors electronically has made life much easier for writers around the world. To retain this ability, however, we must make sure that we make life as easy as possible for our editors as well!

OBSERVING PROPER NETIQUETTE

PERHAPS MORE THAN ANY OTHER electronic invention, e-mail has changed the way writers and editors do business. Like any technology, however, e-mail can easily be abused. Its simplicity often fosters an inappropriate attitude of informality, an inattention to detail. Traditional mail contains a number of steps (composing, typing, proofreading, mailing) that act as safety buffers, offering the opportunity for second thoughts about tone or content. E-mail, with its type-and-send capability, removes those buffers, making it easier to send an ill-considered or poorly edited message.

Because e-mail costs virtually nothing, it can also be overused. Editors have no more wish to be bombarded with e-mail messages than with phone calls.

And absolutely no one appreciates unsolicited writing samples—especially when sent as attachments!

Simple courtesy and professionalism, however, can eliminate most of the negatives from e-mail communication and will go far toward keeping open those lines of communication between writers and editors. For both, the negatives are generally far outweighed by the positives!

RESOURCES

A Beginner's Guide to Effective E-mail/ Acronyms and Jargon
www.webfoot.com/advice/
email.jargon.html?Email

A Beginner's Guide to Effective E-mail/ Domain Names
www.webfoot.com/advice/
email.domain.html?Email
A guide to help you determine where an e-mail comes from, based on the domain suffix.

A Beginner's Guide to Effective Email/ Greetings and Signatures
www.webfoot.com/advice/
email.sig.html?Email
Offers some good tips on "netiquette" for different situations, including international e-mail correspondence.

Coolsig—E-mail Signature Files
www.coolsig.com
Quotes and jokes that can be included in signature files.

E-Mail Attachments: Your Questions Answered
http://everythingemail.net/attach_help.html

E-mail File Attachments
http://telacommunications.com/nutshell/
email.htm
"In a nutshell," why e-mail attachments often fail to work. (Yes, it's "tela.")

Everything E-mail
http://everythingemail.net/index.html
A site addressing a host of e-mail-related topics, including software, netiquette, handling mailing lists and discussions, news, and more.

Internet Smileys
http://members.aol.com/bearpage/
smileys.htm
A list of common emoticons or "smileys" ;)

Preparing E-mail Queries, by Moira Allen
www.writing-world.com/basics/email.shtml

Siglets
www.siglets.com
Jokes and ASCII "pictures" that can be included in a signature block.

<< CHAPTER 7 >>

THE SCREENWRITER'S WEB

BY LENORE WRIGHT[1]

MARKETING A SPEC SCRIPT THROUGH a powerful Hollywood packaging agency increases your chances of a sale—no doubt about it. But what if you don't have an agent—let alone a Hollywood heavyweight—to promote your script and help you to get it read by the right people? What if you don't even live in Hollywood?

You can still get your scripts read by people who can help you market them. The Web provides a wealth of insider information and marketing opportunities for screenwriters—if you know where to look.

WHERE TO SUBMIT YOUR SCRIPTS

HERE ARE SOME STEPS YOU can take to target your script submissions more effectively.

STEP 1: GATHER INSIDER INFORMATION ON RECENT SCRIPT SALES

You can find out (instantly!) which stories and scripts have sold, who sold them and who bought them. Log on to HOLLYWOODLITSALES.COM or DONE DEAL (click on the section titled "Script Sales"). These free sites provide an overview of the scripts currently in development and which stars and producers have studio deals. They also offer more detailed insider information by subscription.

---

[1]Copyright © 2002 by Lenore Wright. All rights reserved. This chapter was originally published as a series of articles in Inscriptions.

For a small subscription, you can have access to WHO'S BUYING WHAT: THE FILM SCRIPT MARKETPLACE from MOVIEBYTES—a terrific online source for screenwriting markets and recent deals agents have brokered.

Agents use this insider information to target their script submissions—so can you! You might even do a better job of targeting because you know your material better than any agent ever will.

STEP 2: IDENTIFY THE RIGHT PRODUCER FOR YOUR PROJECT

Use the script sales sites above to figure out which independent producers have current deals. Find out what scripts they've bought in the past, their successful produced credits, and which stars they have already worked with. This will help you customize your query pitch specifically for them.

These sites provide great lists of active independent producers:

- RX4SCRIPTS
- FILM STEW
- FILM INDUSTRY CENTRAL

Film Stew and Film Industry Central offer very complete listings for film professionals, but Tracy Keenan Wynn's RX4Scripts site is more accessible because he includes personal comments from his own recent screenwriting experiences. He's an award-winning writer with decades of Hollywood experience, and also a respected script coach if you need professional feedback before marketing your script.

STEP 3: TARGET STARS' PRODUCTION COMPANIES

It's never easy to get your script read by a popular movie star, but if you do the script sales research mentioned above, you will increase your chances. Two suggestions: Only target stars who are appropriate for your material, and target stars who have a film or television production company of their own—there are dozens of film and TV stars who develop their own projects.

Querying a star's agent directly rarely works because of conflict of interest. Packaging agents usually try to guide their star clients to in-house film scripts, that is, screenplays written by writers already represented by the agency.

To find the contact information for a star's production company, look them up in one of the free online talent databases. The three I like to use are:

- CELEBHOO.COM: YOUR GATEWAY TO CELEBRITIES
- WHOREPRESENTS?.COM
- MOVIEPARTNERS.COM (click the "Cool Pages" tab, then on "Stars and Agents")

Once you know the contact info, write a sharp, enticing query letter. Keep the query to one page. It should serve as a dynamic trailer for your movie, not a plot synopsis.

Don't expect the star to answer your query personally. Your goal is to convince the star's assistant, reader, or story editor to agree to take a look at your script.

If the script impresses them, they will pass it on up the food chain—that's part of their job.

STEP 4: CHECK THE CREDENTIALS OF FILM PROFESSIONALS *BEFORE* SENDING THEM YOUR SCREENPLAY

The two best places I've found for investigating film credentials are:

- THE INTERNET MOVIE DATABASE (free!)
- THE HOLLYDEX DIRECTORY

The Hollydex Directory is part of the INTERNET HOLLYWOOD NETWORK, an essential mega-site for film professionals (by subscription).

Two free services which offer fairly complete directories of film pros:

- MANDY'S
- THE PROFESSIONAL DIRECTORY

When a star or a producer commits to your script, they will spend a year or two, probably more, trying to set up the script at a production house and getting the movie made. That's a big commitment. Before they will agree to read that great script you've written, you have to convince them it's worth it. The power of the Web can give you the insider's edge you need.

WHERE AGENTS HIDE OUT

CAN'T FIND AN AGENT? Once you know where to look, you'll discover they're hiding in plain sight. The trick is to sift through the information with an insider's eye.

AGENTS THE PROS USE

The best list of agents for the American film market resides on the WRITERS GUILD OF AMERICA Web site.

Don't click on that link just yet! To derive the most benefit from the Guild's list, you have to know how to process the information the Guild gives you.

Why is their list the best? Because (1) they target agents who specialize in film and television writers; (2) they list agents geographically; and (3) the WGA staff vets each agency for criteria vital to aspiring screenwriters. Those criteria include the following:

- **Is the agency a Guild Signatory?** Guild Signatories are members of the Association of Authors' Representatives. They have agreed to abide by the Guild's regulations and uphold the WGA's Minimum Basic Agreement. This is *important*. These agents cannot charge you a fee for reading your script; nor can they encourage you to accept a non-Guild contract.

- **Will the agency consider new writers?** The WGA list puts an asterisk (*) by those agencies that will consider new writers and an (L) by those agencies that require query letters from writers *before* submitting a script. Agencies marked with two asterisks (**) will *only* consider writers with endorsements from film industry professionals they know personally. Unless this applies to you (lucky you!), do not waste your time pursuing the (**) agencies.

Pay attention to these vital details and you will save yourself work and heartache. More importantly, you will give yourself the best chance of finding a reputable agent who can help you achieve your Hollywood dreams.

OUTSIDE THE HOLLYWOOD LOOP

Should you consider pursuing agents beyond the Hollywood loop? Yes; however, most agents representing screenwriters working in the American market reside in California or New York.

THE WRITERS' GUILD OF GREAT BRITAIN, THE AUSTRALIAN WRITERS' GUILD and the WRITERS GUILD OF CANADA share many of the same ideals and goals for writers as the WGA; however these sites do not post local agent lists. Don't worry, I found some helpful lists elsewhere.

If you live in the United Kingdom, AUTHOR-NETWORK.COM offers several helpful pages, including a list of agents and an article titled "What an Agent Can Do for You."

Another U.K. site, READMYWRITING.COM, offers an agent list with details on their special interests and areas of expertise. If you reside in Australia or New Zealand, try OZLIT. In Canada, the CANADIAN AUTHORS' ASSOCIATION suggests aspiring writers use their publication, *The Canadian Writer's Guide*, to research agents.

Selling a new writer's work is difficult. Only a small percentage of agencies want to hear from new writers—10 percent of the agencies on the WGA list. Don't be discouraged, some agents hide out under other names like Manager or Entertainment Lawyer.

MANAGERS AND ENTERTAINMENT LAWYERS

Managers and entertainment lawyers often submit scripts to film industry pros on the behalf of screenwriters. Established managers or lawyers with active film clients—directors, stars, producers, and studio contacts—will have access to the talent you need to get your script read by the right people.

SCRIPT REP offers an extensive list of Managers and Entertainment Lawyers. Click on the "Industry Info" tab to get a menu listing separate pages for Managers and Entertainment Attorneys.

The *Script Sales Agency List*, compiled from the HOLLYWOOD CREATIVE DIRECTORY, includes many managers.

DEEP AGENTING

Once you've found an appropriate agency to target, you might want to pursue an individual agent for particular projects or if your career needs special handling.

Finding detailed information on individual agents will help you choose the best ones to query. These sites offer the juicy details you need.

- AUTHORLINK. The agency list from Authorlink targets book agents primarily, but many indicate they handle screenwriters as well. Look under "Writers Resources" on their homepage and click on "Agency Directory." Some listings reveal helpful details: the writers or books they've represented, what they've sold recently, what they like and what makes them cranky.
- MOVIEBYTES offers a service called "Who's Buying What." For a modest subscription fee, you can access a database that pairs up agents with the deals they've brokered. You can search for information about a particular agent or a particular script sale.

Some aspiring screenwriters attract an agent who helps open doors for them; others attract serious interest in their scripts without using an agent and later employ an agent or lawyer to negotiate the contract. Most ambitious screenwriters try both these tactics. If you decide to pursue agents, don't just spin your wheels, get where you're going!

SCRIPT CONTESTS: DON'T GET BURNED!

HUNDREDS OF WRITING CONTESTS TEMPT screenwriters with the lure of prize money, instant film industry contacts and personal feedback from film professionals. But contests can be costly, so screenwriters should choose intelligently.

Before you write that check, research and evaluate the contests that interest you. Narrow down your choices to the best contests for you personally and the best ones for your scripts. These guidelines might help.

TIPS FOR RESEARCHING CONTESTS

- **Check out their Web site.** Nearly all contests have an online page with guidelines and other vital details. I know it's tempting to salivate over the prize list and ignore the other features available on the site. Don't let the promised goodies distract you (e.g., $10,000 and a trip to Hollywood to meet the film industry movers and shakers you dream of impressing). You're on a mission. You need to find out if the contest has preferences regarding the subject matter of the script, the ethnicity/gender of the author, or the area where the writer resides. At the very least read the FAQ page and note the submission deadline.
- **Rely on peer reports.** If you belong to any online screenwriting discussion lists (and you should!), post a query about the contests you're considering. Learn from the experiences of others. MovieBytes offers a very useful feature to help you: THE CONTEST REPORT CARD. Writers evaluate contests they've entered and post their comments. Take advantage of this wonderful resource.

- **Feedback, feedback, feedback.** Unproduced writers need professional feedback. Some contests offer feedback on your script as part of the package. Even if you don't win, you've received some extra value for your money. If the source of the "professional feedback" is not listed on the site, send an e-mail requesting this information. It's important—pin them down!
- **Script readings.** Some contests offer a staged reading of the winning script (or the scripts of all the finalists) as part of the prize. Script readings can be a great tool to help you polish your script as well as good industry exposure. Film festival script competitions in particular seem to offer script-reading opportunities to their finalists.

TIPS FOR EVALUATING CONTESTS

- **Who are the sponsors?** The people or companies sponsoring the contest should identify themselves and should have film industry credentials. Some contests feature a well-known director, actor, or producer as a nominal sponsor, implying that this person will read the final scripts or at least the winning one. If that is so, it should be stated in their guidelines or on their Web site—don't just assume it's true.
- **Who are the judges?** Some contests post their judges' names and credentials. I find this reassuring; however, many legitimate contests don't make this information available for various reasons, not necessarily because they're hiding something shady. A general guideline: The less information the contest makes available, the more aggressively you should query the contest contacts before your write them a check.
- **Do they provide press releases?** You want to win a contest that makes an effort to publicize their winners. When you come across the press releases of contests that tout their finalists or winners, resist pitching a rant at your agent; instead, swallow your envy and jot down the contest details so you can enter the next time around.
- **Do they provide paid ads announcing winners?** The most helpful form of publicity for contest winners are paid ads in the film industry trade papers. This species is rare; but when you come across it, make a note to at least research the contests that promote their winners in *Variety, Hollywood Reporter,* and the major film magazines.
- **Do they provide industry contacts?** Many contests promise that the winners and/or finalists will be exposed to important film industry contacts. Vague promises or innuendoes don't count. The legitimate contests are specific about what they mean by exposure. Exposure could mean a phone conversation with an agent, a script submission to a studio slush pile, a professional pitching session, or an all-expense-paid trip to Hollywood or New York City. Find out.
- **Will they produce your script?** Some contests promise that the winning script or scripts will be produced. Yippee! But do they back up this promise with

results? Find out—call their bluff. Tip for cynics: Request a contact e-mail for a previous winner or finalist.

I hope these guidelines help you find a contest that works for you and your script. Be choosy—it's your money, your script, and your career.

GLOBAL SCREENPLAY MARKETING: USING SCRIPT REGISTRIES

ASPIRING SCREENWRITERS KNOW THE IMPORTANCE of that first script sale. Yet few of us are prepared for how difficult it is to get that first script read by the right people and sold. How can we beat the odds?

A new marketing tool—online script registries—can increase our chances by putting our scripts into the hands of a receptive audience.

HOW REGISTRIES WORK

Writers post a logline and synopsis of their script in an online database. Industry professionals—publishers, movie producers, film executives, and agents— subscribe to the registry. If a post interests them, they request to see the script.

Since most unproduced screenwriters must market their own material until their careers are well established, a marketing tool like this can prove useful.

POPULAR REGISTRIES

Most registries charge for each script posted; but the fees are generally modest. Some registries charge for other services but allow writers to post for free.

- FILM TRACKER. In addition to a script registry service, this helpful portal for film professionals offers industry news, box office stats, networking opportunities, and promotion services for writers and filmmakers.
- HOLLYWOOD SCRIPT READERS DIGEST. This free registry accepts film synopses and television proposals. In addition to their online database, they distribute a print edition, *Hollywood Script Readers Digest*, to 1,200 film and TV production companies.
- NEVER HEARD OF THEM. A U.K. talent directory for writers and performers. Currently, writers can post up to five pages of their work for free. Listing pages are ad-free.
- RIGHTS SHOWCASE. Authorlink.com currently showcases eight hundred manuscripts and screenplays online. The Authorlink staff reviews all material. There is no fee for the staff review, but they do charge to post to The Author Showcase. Authorlink.com sends several direct mailings a year to producers and publishers promoting the work of their writers.
- THE SCREENPLAYERS. Sam Quo Vadis founded The Screenplayers, a serious group of experienced screenwriters who joined this alliance to market their work. The Web site features their writers' accomplishments as well as their

posted work. They don't post every script submitted; each script must be nominated and accepted.

- The SCREENWRITERS MARKET. The Screenwriters Market is a free script registry. They offer a bulletin board for independent producers to post job queries and a message board for screenwriters to share marketing experiences.
- SCREENWRITERS UTOPIA. This great site offers a free script registry along with other helpful features for screenwriters who market their scripts from outside the Hollywood loop. Their subscription service offers lots of premium features that will give you even more of an insider's edge.
- SCRIPTIVERSE SPEC SCRIPT MARKETPLACE. Dan Garcia's site promises to "save the universe one script at a time." Screenwriters post free for the first six months.
- UNMOVIES. This boffo Web site by screenwriter Daniel Knauf includes a script registry. There is a fee for coverage because he wants to filter the scripts for quality, but if the reader recommends the script then the posting is free.
- WRITERS SCRIPT NETWORK. Since Jerrol LeBaron founded this registry, Writers Script Network has amassed a huge database of quality scripts. They post their marketing success stories regularly online and offer an e-mail newsletter with marketing information. In addition to the script database, Jerrol sends a bimonthly printed newsletter (*Players Marketplace*) to five thousand producers and agents promoting his writers and their scripts.

HOW TO PROTECT YOUR SCRIPT

Some writers fear this type of global exposure will tempt unscrupulous producers or writers to steal their ideas, characters, and situations. Protect your original material from pilferage with these precautions:

ESTABLISH THE DATE OF CREATION

You establish yourself as the copyrighted author when you put your story on paper; but it's important to establish *when* you wrote your story. Two ways to establish the date of creation:

- Apply to the Library of Congress (*www.loc.gov/copyright*) for the copyright to your work.
- Register your material with the WRITERS GUILD OF AMERICA. You don't have to be a Guild member. If a dispute develops over who wrote the material or when it was written, the Guild has your script or story on file and they will back you up.

KEEP DETAILED RECORDS

Choose a registry that keeps track of who looks at your synopsis. Many registries require that the interested buyer e-mail you for permission to read the script. Keep track of all correspondence.

SURE THING OR CYBER–SLUSH PILE?

Some writers believe that floating their loglines in cyberspace will prove ineffectual. It's too new to be a sure thing.

Marketing a spec script is a proactive endeavor. Writers need to create their own advantages whenever they can, if they want to build a career in creative writing. Tools that facilitate global-style marketing help creative writers worldwide find a home for their original material.

RESORCES

SCRIPT SALE INFORMATION

Done Deal
http://Scriptsales.com

Film Stew
www.filmstew.com

HollywoodLitSales.com
http://Hollywoodlitsales.com

RX4Scripts
www.Rx4scripts.com

Who's Buying What?
www.moviebytes.com/wbw/wbwfaq.cfm?

CONTACT INFORMATION AND DIRECTORIES

Celebhoo.com/Your Gateway to Celebrities
www.Celebhoo.com

Film Industry Central
www.IndustryCentral.net

Hollydex Directory
www.hollywoodnet.com/search

Internet Hollywood Network
www.hollywoodnet.com/indexmain.html

Internet Movie Database
http://imdb.com

Mandy's
http://mandy.com

MoviePartners.com
http://filmpartners.com

Professional Directory
http://filmindustry.com

MovieBytes
http://moviebytes.com

whoRepresents?com
www.WhoRepresents.com

AGENTS

Authorlink
www.authorlink.com

Author-Network.com/Agents
www.author-network.com/agents.html

Author-Network.com/What an Agent Can Do for You
www.author-network.com/litagent.html

Canadian Authors' Association/Canadian Writer's Guide
www.canauthors.org/pubs.html

Hollywood Creative Directory
www.hcdonline.com
Source of the Script Sales Agency List.

OzLit
http://home.vicnet.net.au/~ozlit/agents.html

Readmywriting.com
www.writersworld.tv/authors/ukireliteraryagents.htm

Writers Guild of America
www.wga.org

Writers Guild of America/Guild Signatory Agents and Agencies
www.wga.org/agency.html

SCRIPT REGISTRIES

Film Tracker
www.filmtracker.com

Hollywood Script Readers Digest
www.screenscripts.com

Never Heard of Them
www.neverheardofthem.co.uk

Rights Showcase
www.authorlink.com

Screenplayers, The
www.screenplayers.net

Screenwriters Market, The
www.screenwritersmarket.com

Screenwriters Utopia
www.screenwritersutopia.com

Scriptiverse Spec Script Marketplace
www.scriptiverse.com

Unmovies
www.unmovies.com

Writers Script Network
www.writerscriptnetwork.com

ADDITIONAL RESOURCES

Australian Writers' Guild
www.awg.com.au

The Contest Report Card
http://moviebytes.com/ReportCard.cfm

Creative Screenwriting
www.creativescreenwriting.com
Magazine offering interviews with screenwriters, plus other resources.

From FADE IN through FADE OUT
http://members.aol.com/anniraff/
contents.htm
The complete text of a book on screenwriting, available free.

How to Write a Screenplay
www.visualwriter.com/descript.htm
A free downloadable e-book discussing
how to write a screenplay "from planning an idea through developing a
plot to finishing the play." For
Windows only.

Inside Film Magazine Online/Screenwriting
www.insidefilm.com/screenwriting.html

A list of conferences and other events for
screenwriters.

Online Communicator
www.online-communicator.com/writvid.html
Links to a variety of screenwriting
resources.

Screenwriter's Master Chart
http://members.aol.com/maryjs/scrnrite.htm
"What's Supposed to Happen—When?
A Summary of Various Script Breakdowns
and Systems." This interesting chart lets
you know that in a 120-page script,
"Point of No Return" should occur by
page 60.

Screenwriters Web
http://breakingin.net
Lenore Wright's site, including tutorials,
articles, market news, columns, interviews, and other resources, plus a free
newsletter.

Screenwriting
http://screenwriting.miningco.com
Links, articles, chat, script templates,
contacts, dialogue sound files, legal
issues, supplies, and research resources.

Screenwriting Contests Directory
http://moviebytes.com/directory.cfm

Scriptapalooza
www.scriptapalooza.com
A variety of resources and links, including
screenwriting contests.

SCRNWRiT
www.panam.edu/scrnwrit
This site is a "companion" to the
SCRNWRiT mailing list, and offers a
range of information on screenwriting,

including an extensive FAQ, a list of contests and fellowships (may be outdated), links, and a glossary.

Writers Guild of America
www.wga.org
"The official Web site of the WGA, with valuable advice and information on the art and craft of professional screenwriting for film, television, and interactive projects." The site includes many resources for nonmembers, including interviews, profiles, research sources, a free newsletter, and articles from back issues of its publication *Written By.*

Writers Guild of Canada
www.writersguildofcanada.com

Writers' Guild of Great Britain
www.writersguild.org.uk

<< CHAPTER 8 >>

PROTECTING YOUR ELECTRONIC RIGHTS

THE ABILITY TO PUBLISH WORK on the Internet has opened up a new dimension in rights issues for writers. Electronic rights have become a hot commodity—so before you venture into the electronic marketplace, you need to know the types of rights you'll be selling and the pitfalls that await the unwary.

WRITING FOR ELECTRONIC PUBLICATIONS

AS ELECTRONIC PUBLICATIONS BEGAN TO proliferate in the latter half of the 1990s, editors began to realize that they needed new terminology for the transfer of rights between authors and publishers. Terms like "First North American Serial Rights" (FNASR) had little meaning on the Web, where a publication might be read by visitors around the world, and remain online indefinitely.

The term "electronic rights" originally applied to any form of electronic media (and, in particular, to publication on CD-ROM or some other tangible format). As the market has evolved, however, this term has come to refer more commonly to publication on the Web—either on a Web site publication (e.g., an e-zine) or in an e-mail newsletter. Generally, if a publication intends to include CD-ROMs or similar uses, they will specify that in an electronic rights clause.

Here are some of the common types of rights sought by electronic publications.

FIRST OR ONE-TIME USE

The majority of online publications ask either for "first" or "one-time" electronic rights. If a publication requests "first electronic rights," this generally means that the material must not have appeared in any other online publication—but it's generally okay for the piece to have appeared in print. If the publication requests "one-time electronic rights," then it doesn't matter if the piece has been published online, or if it is still online in another publication.

While each issue of a print magazine is "gone" once it is off the shelf, every issue of an electronic publication can remain online virtually forever. Thus, many publications specify not only "first" or "one-time" rights, but also a time period for the use of those rights. A monthly e-zine, for example, might specify the use of first rights for a period of thirty days. A site that keeps material active for a longer time might ask for a ninety-day grant of "first rights."[1]

Some electronic publications specify "exclusive" and "nonexclusive" rights, rather than "first" or "one-time." If an electronic publication wants exclusive electronic rights, this means that the material cannot appear elsewhere in electronic form during the period for which the rights are requested (e.g., thirty days, ninety days, etc.). If the publication asks for nonexclusive rights, the material can appear elsewhere online at the same time. Again, most electronic publications don't care if the material appears in print at the same time that it appears online—so exclusive electronic rights don't preclude you from selling the same piece to a print publication at the same time.

Most electronic publications don't consider a personal Web site to be "another publication," and so may not object if you post an article or story on your own site. Some, however, *do* preclude the use of your work on your own site during their period of exclusivity, so if you have any doubts, check first before posting.

Another controversial issue that has arisen regarding "first" rights is whether posting material on your own Web site *before* you publish it elsewhere constitutes a use of first rights. It's important to realize that rights aren't simply something you sell or license to another publication; they are also something that you can "use up" yourself. The question of whether personal Web site use constitutes "first" use is still being debated by authors and editors. To be on the safe side, however, it's generally wiser to get your material published somewhere else *first,* and then post it on your site as a reprint (assuming that you've retained the right to do so!).

ARCHIVAL RIGHTS

In addition to "first" or "exclusive" electronic rights, many electronic publications also ask for the right to archive your material. Some ask for the right to do this "indefinitely," meaning that the archives may be retained as long as the publication remains in existence. Others ask for archival rights for a limited period, most commonly one year. Most publications ask for nonexclusive archival rights, meaning that you have the right to sell the piece to another online publication. Typically, an electronic publication will ask for a combination of rights—e.g., "exclusive first electronic rights for thirty days, plus the nonexclusive right to archive the material for one year thereafter."

Keep in mind that if your material is archived on one site, you can't sell exclusive electronic rights to another. Thus, when granting archival rights, be sure to determine whether you can request to have your material *removed* from the

[1]See a sample contract at the end of chapter 14.

publication's archive at a later date if you should happen to sell it somewhere else. Many editors are willing to remove archived material on request. The exception is archives of electronic newsletters, which are usually stored "in their entirety" (just like the back issues of a print publication). However, publications that seek exclusive electronic rights generally aren't concerned about whether your article appears in this form of archive.

ALL RIGHTS OR ALL ELECTRONIC RIGHTS

The number of electronic publications and "content" sites that ask for all rights or all electronic rights is still relatively small—but it is growing. You're more likely to see this request from a site run by a major company than from a smaller e-zine. As more content sites are purchased by corporations interested primarily in squeezing money from the Web, the demand for "all rights" to online content is growing.

If you sell all electronic rights to a publication (whether electronic or print), you will not be able to use it in any other electronic format. Most publications that want all electronic rights also frown on the use of your material on your personal Web site—and, technically, you no longer retain the rights to use that material yourself. If you sell *all* rights to a piece, you won't be able to sell it *anywhere* else—whether the publication is print or electronic.

E-RIGHTS FOR PRINT PUBLICATIONS

Ironically, print publications are far more demanding of rights than most electronic publications. While many electronic publications make no claims upon your print rights (and don't care if material is previously or simultaneously published in print), the reverse is not true. Many print publications won't accept material that has previously appeared online, or will treat it as a reprint even if "first print rights" have not actually been sold. Further, as many print publications have Web sites (which often offer selected articles from each edition of the publication), such publications will usually claim some (or all) of your electronic rights to a piece, whether they actually mean to use those rights or not.

Many print publications make the claim that electronic rights are "included" in a transfer of First North American Serial Rights. Legally, this is not the case; the 1996 *Tasini* ruling (see sidebar on page 113) stated that a publication could not claim that "first" rights meant "first in every media." Unfortunately, many publishers ignore this.

When you get a contract from a print publication, check it carefully. Does the publication offer any extra compensation if your work is published on the magazine's Web site? If the magazine claims the right to archive your work, can you ever have it removed from the archive? Watch out for publications that seek exclusive electronic rights; this means that you won't be able to sell reprints to either (a) electronic publications or (b) any *other* print publication that seeks to use your work electronically.

THE "ELECTRONIC DISTRIBUTION" CLAUSE

Some publications have sneaky clauses that don't sound harmful, but that can cost you. One of these is the "electronic distribution" clause. Watch out for a contract that asks you to grant a publication the "nonexclusive right to *distribute* the material electronically." This means that the publication can resell your work to electronic databases, which then market it to researchers and readers—all without ever giving you another penny of profit. It also means that the publication could resell your material to any other electronic venue and pocket the proceeds. For example, when hundreds of writers suddenly discovered in 2000 that their work was being offered for sale on the now-defunct Contentville Web site, many could do nothing about it—because they had given their publisher the right to "distribute" their work electronically.

PROTECTING BOOK RIGHTS

IN RECENT YEARS, BOOK PUBLISHERS have also become increasingly likely to demand electronic rights, not only for online or CD-ROM use, but in any future medium "yet to be developed." A lawsuit filed by Random House against the electronic publisher RosettaBooks has thrown this issue into the spotlight.

In brief, Random House sued RosettaBooks for publishing electronic editions of titles that had originally been published in print by Random House. The titles in question had been published decades earlier, before the concept of "e-books" even existed—and the contracts for those books did not include a specific reference to electronic rights. They did, however, specify that Random House had the right to publish the manuscripts "in book form"—and the lawsuit hinged on the question of what, exactly, that meant. Lawyers for RosettaBooks contended that, in the context of when those contracts were issued, "book form" referred to a bound and printed book, not to an electronic edition that had no physical existence. Random House contended that it referred to any form of publication, physical or ephemeral.

In July 2001, Random House lost its attempt to obtain a preliminary injunction to block RosettaBooks from publishing and selling the contested titles. Federal judge Sidney Stein declared that the term "book" in a book contract did not automatically include e-books, and that publishers who did not have explicit electronic rights clauses in their contracts (which includes most contracts issued more than fifteen years ago) could not claim that their contracts covered electronic editions of books previously published in print. Stein cited Random House's own Webster's Unabridged Dictionary definition of "book" as "a written or printed work of fiction or nonfiction, usually on sheets of paper fastened or bound together within covers." Electronic digital editions, he ruled, are a different medium and therefore must be treated separately in a contract.

In March 2002, the United States Court of Appeals upheld this decision, and in December 2002, Random House and RosettaBooks announced that they had reached a settlement agreement whereby RosettaBooks could continue to publish the disputed titles, and would collaborate with Random House on future titles. Under the agreement, RosettaBooks would be able to obtain a renewable three-year license to publish selected Random House titles electronically, and would pay an advance and royalties not only to the original authors, but also to Random House, for each title so published.

While this is good news for writers who negotiated a print-publishing contract more than fifteen years ago, today it means that book publishers are simply going to be more aggressive in securing *all* potentially useful rights to a book manuscript. Following are some key issues to be aware of when negotiating a book contract.

ELECTRONIC EDITIONS AND E-READERS

In the past, electronic rights were usually lumped under "subsidiary rights" (e.g., translation rights, movie rights, etc.). Publishers rarely used those rights directly, but often sold them to third parties—and authors usually received a 50 percent share of the proceeds of such sales.

The development of electronic editions designed for use with handheld "e-readers" has changed all that. Today, many publishers claim that electronic editions are simply another form of "distribution" of the print edition, and are offering authors nothing more than standard print royalties (often 10 percent or less) for electronic rights. Publishers claim that because of the heavy discounts demanded by e-reader companies, profits are too low to offer authors a higher share. (For example, NuvoMedia, which distributes e-books through Barnes & Noble, demands a 60 percent "distribution fee" from publishers, and offers no advance for authors.) However, as publishers typically offer bookstores a discount of anywhere from 40 to 60 percent, such costs are already built into a book's pricing structure—and since the remaining production costs (which are also built into the price of a print book) are still dramatically lower, authors are justified in asking why they aren't being offered a larger percentage of revenues.

REVERSION OF RIGHTS

Traditionally, authors could reclaim their rights to a manuscript if the publisher allowed it to go out of print (i.e., did not make it available for sale for six months or longer). This, too, is changing. More and more commercial publishers are exploring the option of printing "books on demand," a technology that enables publishers to print single copies of books rather than huge quantities.

Authors' groups fear that when books can be printed "on demand" whenever a customer places an order, this will prevent books from officially going "out of print"—and authors from reclaiming their rights—even if a book is selling no more than a single copy a year. According to an article in *Publishers Weekly,* at least one publisher claims that a book is "in print" as long as it is "displayed for sale" in any format, regardless of how many copies are actually being sold. Others are adopting clauses that specify the number of copies that must be sold per year (e.g., three hundred) to qualify as "in print." Still others leave contract language vague unless the author insists on a well-defined rights-reversion clause.[2]

Authors who do regain their rights to out-of-print titles face another electronic dilemma: whether to have their books reprinted by a "print-on-demand" firm. The Author's Guild has already partnered with one such firm to reprint its members'

[2]Steven M. Zeitchik, "The Great Ether Grab," *Publishers Weekly,* June 14, 1999, *http://publishersweekly.reviewsnews.com/index.asp?layout = articleArchive&articleId = CA166973.*

out-of-print titles. Other agencies offer similar services. Such reprinting, however, is usually handled on a "subsidy" basis, meaning that you pay a fee for publication and are primarily responsible for marketing your book. As with any subsidy arrangement, you should read the contract carefully before making a decision.

ELECTRONIC BOOKS

Commercial e-publishing contracts tend to be more author-friendly than contracts from traditional print publishers. Most ask only for the rights they intend to use, and make no claims on print rights (unless offering a print-on-demand service) or subsidiary rights such as movie or translation rights. Reputable e-publishers also tend to offer higher royalties (40 percent is becoming the industry standard), usually paid quarterly.

E-publishers also avoid the "reversion of rights" issue by offering time-limited contracts, which are generally effective for a period of one to three years. This enables either the author or the publisher to opt out at the end of the contract period, and also offers the author the chance to test a book's marketability in the electronic marketplace while still pursuing print publication. Some e-publishing contracts have a clause enabling either party to terminate the contract at any time with thirty to ninety days' notice.

Ironically, electronic subsidy contracts tend to be less author-friendly than those of commercial e-publishers. Many offer lower royalties (15 to 20 percent) even though you are paying a fee for the publication to begin with. Many also ask for a larger number of subsidiary rights, even though the publisher is unlikely to use them. (If, however, *you* use one of those rights—e.g., you sell the work in audio format—the subsidy publisher may then claim a percentage of your royalties from that sale, even though the publisher had nothing to do with the sale.)

When considering an electronic subsidy publisher (or print-on-demand publisher), read the contract carefully. Some contain rather sneaky clauses. One well-known print-on-demand publisher, for example, claims the right to use portions of your manuscript in its own collective works, without your prior permission, offering a "pro-rata" share of royalties. That means that if, say, you published a collection of poetry, the publisher could select some of the poems from your work and include them in its own poetry anthology. This same publisher also offers an interesting termination clause: While the author can terminate the publishing agreement, the publisher still claims the nonexclusive right to continue distributing the work for one year after the author has cancelled the contract.[3]

At least this publisher posts its contracts online. Many subsidy publishers do not, or omit vital clauses. (I found one contract online that contained the phrase, "This clause deliberately omitted." Another noted that the posted "sample contract" was not complete, to protect the publisher's "intellectual property.") Make sure that you are able to review a *complete* contract before you choose a subsidy publisher (or any publisher). See chapter 16 for more information on electronic subsidy publishing.

[3]"Writers Club Publishing Agreement for New Manuscripts," *www.iuniverse.com/publish/wcpressagr.html.*

ELECTRONIC RIGHTS AND YOUR WEB SITE

HOW MUCH OF YOUR WEB SITE do you actually own? The answer depends, literally, on what you put into it. A Web site is not a discrete entity, but the sum of several components that may each involve separate rights issues.

DESIGN

Web site design can be defined as the layout of the site as expressed through its coding. That design may include the arrangement of elements on each individual page, the navigational pathways within and between pages, the design and structure of the navigational menu, and the arrangement of frames (if any). It also includes such elements as special fonts, logos, background patterns or textures, navigation icons, and graphic elements.

Copyright of a Web site design belongs to the designer. If you designed the site yourself (i.e., wrote the code), you can be fairly confident that you "own" it. This may also be true if you use a Web site design software package, but still create your own design rather than using a template provided with the package. If you do use such a template, the design will usually belong to the software company rather than to you, unless it is specified as "copyright-free," in which case it is in the public domain and doesn't belong to either of you. Similarly, you can't claim "ownership" of a site that uses a template provided by a host (such as HOMESTEAD)—though you do own the content. Finally, if you hired a designer, that individual owns the copyright to the design, and you may not be able to modify it without permission.

Fortunately, the copyright to a Web site can be transferred just like any other copyright. To do so, you must negotiate a valid, written agreement with your designer, specifying the rights and terms involved. Ideally, you should do this before your site is designed. Later, you may have to pay an additional fee to regain those rights. For more information on design ownership, see attorney Ivan Hoffman's article, "WHO OWNS THE COPYRIGHT IN YOUR WEB SITE?"

CONTENT

If you run a personal Web site, you will generally be the copyright owner of any material you write specifically for that site, such as a column, article, FAQs, etc. Similarly, you own any previously unpublished material, such as a short story or poem, that you choose to post on your site, even if you didn't write it specifically for the site. Be aware, however, that such a posting is generally considered a "first use," which means that you may not be able to sell such material as "new" thereafter.

You may also post previously published material on your site, if you own the necessary rights. You cannot post material to which you have sold all rights, all or exclusive electronic rights (with no reversion or duration limit), or which you wrote as "work-for-hire." Since most book contracts include an electronic rights clause, you will usually have to obtain permission from your publisher to post a book excerpt.

If you post material written by someone else, it's wise to create a written agreement specifying the rights involved. Even if your agreement is nothing more than an e-mail or a letter, it will help prevent misunderstandings.

Be extremely cautious about posting unattributed material on your site, such as the many supposedly "anonymous" stories, jokes, anecdotes, or poems that are circulated on the Internet. Just because no author has been cited doesn't mean the material is in the public domain. Copyright information is often lost when these snippets are forwarded from one person to another.

GRAPHICS

You can claim copyright only to those graphic elements that you have actually created, such as your own photos or drawings. You don't own the copyright to publicity photos taken by a professional photographer or studio (though you may have the license to use such images), and you don't own the copyright to your book's cover image (unless you designed it yourself). Nor do you own any public-domain images that you've downloaded from a Web site or software package. You simply have the license to use them. Since some people assume that any images posted online are copyright-free, it's wise to post a copyright notice on any images that you do own.

LINKS

While links (URLs) are information and cannot be individually copyrighted, a list of URLs in a "resource directory" can be considered sufficiently "creative" to qualify for copyright protection. This means that you can't simply copy someone else's list of links directly to your site, or vice versa—but you can use the information on that list as the basis for developing your own resource guide.

LOGOS

Many sites provide official logos and images for various promotional reasons—e.g., a partnership or associate arrangement, as an award, as a hotlink icon, or as part of a Webring. If you display a logo belonging to another Web site, be aware that it does not "belong" to you—although you can usually transfer it along with the rest of your site.

SCRIPTS

Many Web sites include CGI or Java scripts that enable a visitor to sign a guestbook, complete a form, search the site, or send a form message. Many such scripts are in the public domain, but others may be offered by a site's service provider. If you are looking for a script, it's better to find one on a site that provides free CGI scripts than to borrow one from another site. In any event, unless you wrote the script yourself, you don't own that part of your Web site code. If the script was provided by your service provider (e.g., a hit counter), you may have to replace it when you change providers.

BELLS AND WHISTLES

Beware of posting music clips, videos, animation, etc., that aren't specifically authorized or listed as public domain. Don't be tempted to download a clip of your favorite Enya CD as a sample of "music I write by" or to provide ambiance. Audio-visual companies tend to be strict about such infringements.

DOMAIN NAMES

While a domain name can, under certain circumstances, be trademarked, it can't be copyrighted. Thus, while your domain name will be unique on the Internet, there is nothing to prevent someone from using that name in another context (e.g., as a title).

POSTING COPYRIGHT NOTICES

To protect the material on your Web site from inadvertent piracy (i.e., from people who simply don't know better), it's wise to post a copyright notice not only on your home page, but on every individual page that you wish to protect. Remember that not all visitors reach your page through the "front door." Search engines and off-site links may lead visitors directly to specific "content" pages on your site, bypassing the home page entirely.

Your copyright should include the title of the site or page being protected, the copyright symbol, the date the material was placed under copyright, your name, and the phrase "All Rights Reserved." If your material was previously published elsewhere, it's a good idea to cite that publication as well.

Copyright Notice
"Great Writing Site" Copyright © 2002 by Ima Good Author[4]

All rights reserved on all material on all pages in this site, plus the copy-right on compilations and design, graphics, and logos. For information on reprinting material from this site, please contact ImaAuthor@myISP.com.

USING UNPUBLISHED MATERIAL ON YOUR WEB SITE

One question that pops up again and again is whether posting an article, story, poem, or novel on your own Web site constitutes a use (or loss) of rights. Unfortunately, the growing consensus is that, indeed, you *can* forfeit "first rights" by using up those rights on your own site—as this is considered a form of "self-publication." Many publications will treat previously posted material as a reprint (and pay you reprint rates), and some won't consider it at all. Posting a novel online is particularly risky, as it could jeopardize your chances of selling it to a publisher. The thing to keep in mind is that you don't have to *sell* a right to *lose* that right—you can "use up" a right (such as a "first publication right") by posting or publishing your own material online.

Showcasing your unpublished works on a Web site is poor policy for other reasons as well. The main reason is that it can make you appear to be an amateur—someone who can't "get published" any other way. Contrary to the

[4]If you write your own HTML, use the code "©" to create a copyright symbol.

hopeful opinions bandied about in some writing circles, editors do *not* surf the Web looking for promising material on personal Web sites, and posting your unpublished material online is *not* an effective way to get it "picked up" by a publisher. Nor are editors interested in queries that invite them to read your available articles online—first, they don't have time, and second, such a query makes it clear that you are offering generic articles rather than material tailored specifically to their publication.

It's much better to post previously *published* material on your site, if you retain the reprint rights. (If you've sold all rights to a piece, you won't be able to do this.) Once you've sold an article or story, you can post it on your site with a notice as to where it was previously published, and use this as an online "clip." This can be a useful promotional tool, for it shows that you are a *published* writer—not just a hopeful wannabe.

ELECTRONIC RIGHTS AND E-MAIL

PERHAPS NOWHERE ELSE ON THE Internet are copyrights violated as routinely as through e-mail. You've probably seen numerous postings or "forwardings" of stories, anecdotes, jokes, or poems that may have no accompanying attribution or source information—but that are, in fact, covered by copyright.

It has been argued that passing along such materials doesn't really harm the author and may even be helpful by making an author's works more widely known. This argument is plausible only if the author's name and copyright information are actually included with the work—and still does not alter the fact that the author has not specifically authorized such distribution. It has also been argued that forwarding material by e-mail or posting it to a newsgroup isn't really a copyright infringement, because it doesn't constitute publication but is only a public display of the material. This argument is also on shaky ground, particularly as many people incorrectly assume that any material posted without attribution is in the public domain.

The same dangers apply to anything you send by e-mail as well. E-mail messages never die. Many become part of permanent archives that may be publicly accessible. Even when you send a message to a private individual, you cannot always be certain that it won't be forwarded without your permission. If you send a private e-mail to an individual at a company address, be aware that your message may become part of that company's e-mail archives and will almost certainly be considered "company property." Never assume that your messages will remain private or protected.

The following precautions can help you protect your copyright, and that of others:

- Don't post anything to a newsgroup or mailing list that you wouldn't want strangers to read. Once posted, such messages usually become part of an online archive, which may be publicly accessible through such sites as GOOGLE GROUPS. In addition, you never know who will pick up and pass along your message.

- Don't forward e-mail without the author's permission. Most newsgroups and mailing lists ask members to refrain from forwarding posts to outsiders.
- Don't post material from a Web site to an individual or group (unless the Web site specifically authorizes such use). Instead, pass along the URL.
- Don't forward e-mail newsletters (or excerpts of newsletters) to individuals or groups unless the newsletter provides written permission. Many newsletters *do* permit such posting, but others prefer to keep track of their subscription numbers (and one should *never* forward a newsletter that is available only by paid subscription). Instead, provide the URL or subscription information for the newsletter. If a newsletter seems particularly appropriate for a mailing list, ask the editor (and your list moderator) for permission to forward it to the list.
- Don't post or forward anecdotes, jokes, stories, poems, or similar materials if you're unsure of their source or copyright status. While many of these materials are publicly available, many others are actually copyrighted, but have been stripped of identifying information. Remember that many less-informed users often assume that such material is in the public domain if they receive it by e-mail.
- Be cautious about posting or submitting your own work. Most critique groups have strict rules about copyright protection and forbid members from passing material along to others. Posting material to a critique group is generally not considered publication—but make sure that the group's archives, if any, are not publicly accessible.
- If you wish to share your own work with friends or a mailing list, include a copyright notice.

Finally, if you receive material by e-mail (or find it in a newsletter or other source) that you know came from a copyrighted source, (a) do not pass it along; (b) notify the sender or publisher (e.g., of the newsletter or site on which the material appeared) that the material is copyrighted, and advise the sender of the source; and (c) notify other recipients (e.g., the mailing list to which the material was posted) of the copyright information, and advise members not to pass the material along.

RECENT DEVELOPMENTS IN ELECTRONIC RIGHTS

ARGUMENTS OVER RIGHTS IN CYBERSPACE have wandered into extremes of silliness on both sides—from the assertion that temporarily downloading a copy of a Web page onto your browser constitutes a copyright violation, to the claim that "information wants to be free." The trouble is, silliness can sometimes become legislation.

In the past few years, many bills and proposals have been put forward to regulate—or deregulate—the exchange of information and material on the Internet. A good place to track this legislation, and the ensuing arguments, is the ASSOCIATION OF RESEARCH LIBRARIES (ARL) Web site, which offers links to texts of proposed legislation, summaries, analyses, and formal arguments and testimonies for and against each bill.

In an effort to address some of the copyright issues raised or affected by today's "digitally networked environment," Congress passed the Digital Millennium Copyright Act (DMCA) on October 12, 1998. Among other things, this Act:

- **Prohibits circumvention of copyright protection systems.** The DMCA prohibits "gaining unauthorized access to a work by circumventing a technological protection put in place by the copyright owner where such protection measure otherwise effectively controls access to a copyrighted work."[5] This means it will be illegal to remove any digitally encoded copyright identification associated with your material, including coding that limits or controls the use or transfer of that material.
- **Prohibits the design, manufacture, and marketing of devices** specifically developed to circumvent copyright protection systems. This prohibition takes place immediately, but contains a number of exceptions and exemptions.
- **Prohibits tampering with "copyright management information,"** which can be loosely defined as any encoded information that identifies the author, source, title, or other copyright information related to a work. It is not clear whether this prohibition applies to "omitting" copyright or source information on material that is transmitted by e-mail or to "innocently" passing along such material that has been stripped of attribution.
- **Protects online service providers (OSPs) from copyright infringement liability** related to material posted or distributed by a client or user. Essentially, this means that OSPs are not liable for copyright-infringing materials posted or transmitted by clients, provided the OSP is not aware of the infringement. This frees the OSP from being responsible for material it "caches" for a user (e.g., by hosting a Web site), and also ensures that OSPs will not have to police Web sites or invade a client's privacy. OSPs are responsible for taking appropriate action, however, if they are informed of a copyright violation. This provision also has a host of conditions, exceptions, and exemptions.

Issues of electronic rights will undoubtedly be debated and contested for years to come. The one certainty is that policies and decisions made by publishers in this arena are rarely going to be favorable to writers. Writers are already facing a steady erosion of their rights to keep and reuse material, or choose how it is published—and they are also facing increased efforts by publishers to gain more rights for less compensation. The writer's only recourse is to remain informed, so that a contractual "rights grab" won't slip by undetected.

[5]Band, Jonathan, "The Digital Millennium Copyright Act," *www.arl.org/info/frn/copy/band.html.*

The _Tasini_ Decision

ON JUNE 25, 2001, THE Supreme Court ruled 7 to 2 that newspapers and magazines could not sell freelance contributions to electronic databases without the permission of the writers. This ruling supported the U.S. appeals court decision of 1999, which overturned a previous ruling in favor of the publishers.

First, a bit of history. In 1993, Jonathan Tasini (president of the National Writers Union) and six other writers launched a suit against several major publishers, including the New York Times Company, Newsday, and Time Inc. The suit alleged that the publishers had sold the authors' articles to electronic databases such as LEXIS/NEXIS without the authors' permission (and without any compensation), and that this was an infringement of the authors' copyright. In most cases, no actual contracts existed between the publishers and authors, so the authors claimed that all the publishers could assume they had acquired was First North American Serial Rights, and _not_ any electronic rights.

The publishers claimed that the use of the articles in such databases constituted a "revision" of the editions of the publications in which the articles originally appeared. Section 201(c) of the Copyright Code grants holders of "collective copyright" (e.g., the publisher who holds the copyright to a publication such as a magazine or newspaper, but _not_ to the individual articles therein) are entitled to issue revisions of that work without obtaining additional permissions. The publishers argued that use of the articles in a database was no different from, say, issuing a microfilm or microfiche copy of the newspaper.

In 1997, a federal judge ruled in favor of the publishers, agreeing with their interpretation of Section 201(c). That ruling _did_ have a few benefits for writers—it established, for example, that:

- "First rights" did not mean that a publication had first rights in _every_ medium, but only in a single medium. I.e., a purchase of first print rights would not automatically confer first electronic rights.
- A stamp on the back of a check indicating that signing or depositing the check constitutes a "transfer of rights" is _not_ a legal contract, as a contract must be issued _before_ the transaction is completed, not after.

In 1999, a U.S. appeals court overturned the 1997 decision, and in 2001, the case went to the Supreme Court. The Supreme Court's decision upheld the 1999 decision, in favor of the authors.

NOT A REVISION

The key issue in the decision was the definition of the term "revision." The court rejected the publishers' assertion that a database was simply a "revision" of an edition of a magazine or newspaper. In the majority decision, the judges noted that:

> Here, the three Databases present articles to users clear of the context provided by either the original periodical editions or by any revision of those editions ... When the user conducts a search, each article appears as a separate item ... An article appears to the user without the graphics, formatting, or other articles with which it was initially published ... That each article bears marks of its origin in a particular periodical suggests that the article was *previously* part of that periodical, not that the article is *currently* reproduced or distributed as part of the periodical.

The judges' decision also confirmed the rights that a publication could assume it owned in the absence of a contract, noting that Section 201(c) of the Copyright Code states that:

> In the absence of an express transfer of the copyright or of any rights under it, the owner of copyright in the collective work is presumed to have acquired *only* the privilege of reproducing and distributing the contribution as part of that particular collective work, any revision of that collective work, and any later collective work in the same series. (Emphasis added by the court.)

WHAT DOES IT MEAN FOR WRITERS?

While the decision was touted by Tasini et al. as a "victory" for writers, its actual effect on writers in general, and the business of freelance writing, is far from clear. The *Tasini* suit itself was not a class action lawsuit, so the damages that may be received by the plaintiffs will not be shared by writers at large. (At the time of this writing, those damages have not yet been settled.) Still pending at the time of this writing is another case in Manhattan involving three consolidated class action suits against fourteen electronic databases; the outcome of those suits will have a greater impact on the "relief" that freelance writers in general may be eligible for, though that relief is likely to be limited.

Richard Marini, vice president of contracts for the American Society of Journalists and Authors (ASJA), felt that the positive impact on writers was likely to be minimal. "I don't think this is going to change much day-to-day in the fight for freelance rights," he noted in a public statement. "Many publishers will continue to write contracts in such a way as to deprive writers of their copyright. . . . This is not going to end the fight."

Indeed, that seemed to be the primary result of the original *Tasini* suit: As early as 1993, publishers began the rush to all-rights and work-for-hire contracts, assuring that they would thus retain any and all rights they might wish to use in the future (whether they would actually use them or not), without the need to give any additional compensation to writers. "As a result of *Tasini,* publishers increasingly are attempting to pay writers the same—or even lower—rates for all rights than they traditionally have paid for first print rights," noted Jim Morrison, president of ASJA. The New York Times Company has required freelancers to sign away such rights since 1995, and informed the court that "given its superior bargaining power," it has not had to pay freelancers extra for those rights. Since freelancers generally lack that bargaining power, it is likely that the push toward "all rights" contracts as an "industry standard" will continue.

So—was this truly a "victory for creators and consumers," as the National Writers Union declared? In principle, perhaps. The decision legally established that publications can't use writers' contributions in ways that exceed the terms of a contract without obtaining permission (and, perhaps, without providing additional compensation). But if the end result is simply to encourage more publications to demand all rights from writers from the beginning, robbing writers not only of the right to ask for additional compensation from the original publication but also of the right to resell that material elsewhere, that victory may be hollow.

COPYRIGHT: GENERAL INFORMATION

Association of Research Libraries/Copyright and Intellectual Property
www.arl.org/info/frn/copy/copytoc.html

Copyright Basics
www.copyright.gov/circs/circ1.html
An easy-to-follow summary of copyright issues and questions from the U.S. Copyright Office.

Copyright Code, The
www.loc.gov/copyright/title17
The entire text of the U.S. Copyright Code.

Copyright Terms and Expirations
www.authorslawyer.com/c-term.shtml
When does a copyright expire? It depends—and this chart explains what it depends upon.

Digital Millennium Copyright Act (summary)
www.arl.org/info/frn/copy/band.html

Digital Millennium Copyright Act (overview)
www.gseis.ucla.edu/iclp/dmca1.htm
Includes a link to the full text of the DMCA.

Do We Need to Copyright Our Works?
www.spawn.org/marketing/copyright.htm
A succinct, readable summary of the benefits of registering a copyright.

Nolo Law
www.nolo.com
Nolo.com, "Law for All," is a great place to start your search for information on copyright issues. Just search for "copyright."

Novice Writer's Guide to Rights
www.writerswrite.com/journal/dec97/cew3.htm

Publishing Law and Other Articles of Interest
http://publaw.com/copy.html
Articles on a wide range of copyright, trademark, and rights issues.

United States Copyright Office
www.loc.gov/copyright/
Find out how to register your copyright, and download the necessary forms, from this site.

ELECTRONIC RIGHTS

Electronic Publishing and the Potential Loss of First Serial Rights
www.ivanhoffman.com/first.html

SFWA Statement on Electronic Rights
www.sfwa.org/contracts/ELEC.htm
The Science Fiction Writers of America position on electronic rights, including an open letter from a lawyer on rights issues involved in handheld e-readers.

RIGHTS IN WEB SITES AND E-MAIL

"C" Rights in "E" Mail
www.ivanhoffman.com/rights.html

Derivative Rights and Web Sites
www.ivanhoffman.com/derivative.html

Getting Permission to Publish: Ten Tips for Webmasters
www.nolo.com/encyclopedia/articles/ilaw/pub_permission.html
Do you want to use someone else's material on your site? Here's some tips on getting permission, and making sure that you don't infringe on another's copyright.

Proper Use of a Domain Name for Trademark Protection
www.arvic.com/library/domanuse.asp

Who Owns the Copyright in Your Web Site?
www.ivanhoffman.com/website.html

Whose Property Is It Anyway?
www.online-magazine.com/copyright.htm

CONTRACTS AND RIGHTS ISSUES

ASJA Contract Watch
www.asja.org/cw/cw.php
"Serves as Contract Information Central for freelance writers, keeping thousands informed about the latest terms and negotiations in the world of periodicals, print and electronic publication." You can check out a publication or its parent company in the database, and subscribe to a regular newsletter with information on publications that offer bad contracts and the results of contract negotiations (and lawsuits).

Journalist Electronic Rights Negotiation Strategies
www.nwu.org/journ/jstrat.htm

National Writers Union
www.nwu.org
Organization for writers, focusing on rights and related issues. Documents on various topics, including rights and copyrights, can be found at
www.nwu.org/docs/ dochome.htm.

Rights and Why They're Important, by Marg Gilks
www.writing-world.com/rights/rights.shtml

Selling International Rights, by Moira Allen
www.writing-world.com/international/ intrights.shtml
How to determine what rights you want to sell overseas, including geographic and language rights.

LAWSUIT INFORMATION

Supreme Court Opinions on *New York Times Co., Inc., et al. v. Tasini et al.*
http://laws.findlaw.com/us/000/ 00–201. html

"The *Tasini* Decision: Implications for the Future—An Interview with Charles E. Petit"
www.writing-world.com/rights/tasini.shtml

Random House v RosettaBooks
www.rosettabooks.com/pages/legal.html

<< CHAPTER 9 >>

PROTECTING YOUR WORK FROM PIRACY

A COUPLE OF YEARS AGO, the staff of the now-defunct writing newsletter *Inklings* made the distressing discovery that one of their articles had been substantially "copied" and sold to another online writing newsletter. The discovery was made by the even more distressed original author, who recognized her work even though the other "writer" had, to some extent, "rewritten" the article (basically by paraphrasing it line by line). The official statement issued by *Inklings* was that the second article bore a "substantial similarity" to the original. The editor of the second publication was mortified, and immediately offered to pay the original author what she would have received if she herself had submitted the piece.

Such an incident falls under the definition of "plagiarism" as offered by *Webster's Ninth New Collegiate Dictionary*: "to steal and pass off (the ideas or words of another) as one's own; [to] use (a created production) without crediting the source; to commit literary theft; [to] present as new and original an idea or product derived from an existing source." But is it copyright infringement?

Not necessarily. Copyright protects only the specific expression of your ideas—i.e., the exact form in which you wrote or recorded them. It does not protect those ideas themselves. Therefore, technically, if someone rewrites or paraphrases your material, even if literally "line by line," this may not qualify as an actual "copyright infringement." However, it is likely to qualify as an "unfair use" of your material, and an "infringement of rights."

This incident calls attention to the vulnerability of a writer's work, whether published online or in print. Ironically, however, a work's very accessibility online is also at times its best protection; as happened with *Inklings,* readers of one online publication are likely to read others as well, and therefore likely to catch a writer who attempts to "borrow" material from one to sell to another.

The Internet also offers an unprecedented ability to track down "original" sources of "borrowed" material. An intensive search using a few well-chosen keywords from the suspect article can often turn up the original source. (A check on another article by the "borrowing" author showed that it was substantially copied from another source as well.)

By the same means, you as a writer can take steps to safeguard your own material. Every so often, it's a wise idea to select a few key phrases or names from one or more of your articles and run a search online to see whether these phrases "turn up" somewhere they shouldn't. Proper names are an excellent search tool; if, for example, you've written about a specific person, company, or location, these details are not likely to be altered in a "stolen" article. Also, search now and then on your own name, to determine whether someone is using your material on their Web site without permission. (This is often done with the best intentions, and no intent to "steal"; people often mistakenly believe that they can post "good content" on their site without permission from the original author.) Google is a good search engine for this "safety check"; another alternative is to use a meta search site such as Dogpile (which searches several engines simultaneously).

In the long term, the individual who lost the most from this incident was the offending writer. This person lost at least two markets, as well as the value of a good reputation. If the individual fails to learn a lesson from these events, chances are that someone, someday, will carry things a step further and file a lawsuit—especially if the individual attempts to use such methods in higher-paying venues.

For here, indeed, is the ultimate irony: This individual was willing to copy another's work and risk the loss of reputation for the grand fee of—$15!

The article below, written by copyright lawyer Charles Petit, explains in detail what to do when you've discovered that your work has been infringed upon.

FINDING AND SINKING ELECTRONIC PIRATES

BY CHARLES PETIT[1]

FINDING PIRATED WORKS AND INFRINGEMENTS is the obvious first step. You should periodically search the Internet for your works, and should pay attention when someone else indicates your works may be found there.

Identifying the infringer comes next. This may not be as simple as it sounds, for both legal and practical reasons. For legal reasons, it is important to know who provides the access services used by the infringer. This often requires use of *Whois, ping, traceroute,* and *finger* tools, and deciphering message headers. A suggested toolkit for Windows users—keeping in mind the usual financial resources of writers, which is to say virtually none—includes:

- **Whois,** which helps identify who owns a given domain, and who provides services to it. While one can surf directly to one of the registrars' Whois servers, they do not cross-reference very well, and tend to be seriously overloaded. Helper utilities include ANALOGX WHOIS ULTRA (225 k), WORKSHELL WHOIS (1.1 MB), NETLAB (456 k), and several others. I have tested each of these three; they're reliable and easy to install and use.
- **Ping,** which functions to identify the actual machine on which transmissions originate. This can be helpful when the target is, for example, a university, which may have thousands of Web servers in its domain.
- **Traceroute,** which technically does not require an additional tool, as it is a low-level command built into Windows9x and later. However, the Windows command is pathetic, requiring use of the command-line interface, which closes the result window when the trace is complete. Traceroute is important in identifying both the machine and who provides services to smaller sites.
- **Finger,** which is more often useful on internal networks than on the Internet, because the finger function also provides a number of back doors into a machine and therefore *should* be either directly disabled or filtered out by a firewall. This is a tool of last resort, because it is useful only while the infringing individual is actually logged in.

Once you know who is actually infringing your work, you need to see who else may be responsible. This means a trip to the LIBRARY OF CONGRESS Web site to consult the Service Provider DMCA Agent Directory. (Note: You must have Acrobat Reader installed to use the directory.) This is important because it will confirm and expand the results of the Whois query performed earlier.

SINKING PIRATES

Once you find an infringement online (or in e-mail), you should take some action. This need not be an immediate filing of a lawsuit, except in special circumstances. You must balance your own desires for the piece with the probable risk and reward of taking actions. No self-help guide can make that decision for you. This guide lays out options for you to consider, but should *not* be taken as a formula or progression. In order of increasing seriousness:

- **Send a direct notice to the infringer.** Remain polite and professional, as in the sample letter below, no matter how provoked you may be. This step can be skipped in particularly egregious circumstances, such as outright plagiarism. However, if used, it will eventually become part of any court record, so don't say anything that will embarrass you or lead to counterclaims.
- **Send a DMCA notice.** This is an inexpensive option, and a major tool in combating electronic piracy. After reviewing the sample letter below, copyright holders should consider the following:
  - Only the copyright holder or an authorized agent of the copyright holder (such as a lawyer, family member, or literary agent) may send a DMCA notice.

- All facts must be accurate and attested to under penalty of perjury. Although "perjury" means "knowing," don't rely on an "ostrich defense" if something seems odd or uncertain—get legal advice. I wish more corporations and businesses would do so when confronted with a claim!
- Descriptions need not be exhaustively detailed, particularly as addresses (particularly Web site addresses and network news message identifiers) change frequently and unpredictably. The statute requires only that the letter "substantially provide" the information in question. If an unsophisticated individual could find the infringing material from the address information in the letter, it "substantially complies."[2]
- There are no "magic words" that must be quoted in the letter, nor must a work's copyright be registered before sending the letter—contrary to the claims of many parties, including major ISPs such as AOLTimeWarner (and its subsidiaries) and Verio.
- Do not rely solely upon an Internet form provided by an ISP that purports to comply with the DMCA's requirements. These forms may be convenient, but they do not provide you an adequate record of your own—and they are frequently inadequate in the first place.
- Print a copy of the DMCA agent designation from the Copyright Office's directory. If you could not find the service provider's data in the directory, make a signed and dated note of that failure, and (if possible) list all of the names you used attempting to find it. Service providers do not get the benefit of the DMCA's safe harbors if they do not comply with the public notice requirements.
- **Notify the service provider.** Again, this is an inexpensive option. Copyright infringement violates the terms of service of virtually every service provider. The sample letter below (free to copy and use) may be helpful in obtaining assistance from the service provider. Unfortunately, this doesn't always work, and it raises the stakes by involving a third party in the dispute. Reasons that it may not work include bureaucracy, willful refusal to act, explanations by the infringer that satisfy the provider that the infringer has the right to use your work, conflicts of interest, and just plain ignorance. *Accurate assertions of fact are critical; an inaccurate assertion of fact could expose you to a lawsuit or counterclaim for defamation.*
- **Get sound legal advice.** Although it is possible to take steps beyond these, you should not do so without legal advice (even if you intend to do the work yourself to cut costs).

LEGAL ADVICE

You need legal advice if:

- You are the creator of a work, but are unsure whether you hold the copyright.
- You are the holder of a copyright, but are unsure whether a use merely exceeds that which you granted to a publisher.

[2]See *ALS-Scan, Inc., v. RemarQ Communities, Inc.* (4th Cir. 2001); *RIAA v. Napster* (9th Cir. 2001).

- You have taken appropriate self-help steps without obtaining a satisfactory result.
- The infringer is, or appears to be, located in any of the following countries, which either are not signatories of the Berne Convention on Copyright or do not have adequate systems in place to resolve copyright disputes. This is not an exhaustive list, and you should keep in mind that several top-level domains are global (.com, .net, .org, .edu). This makes use of *Whois* particularly important in those domains.

Afghanistan (.af)	Moldova (.md)
Angola (.ao)	Montserrat (.ms)
Belarus (.be)	Myanmar (.mm)
Bosnia and Herzegovina (.ba)	Nepal (.np)
Brunei (.bn)	Pakistan (.pk)
Cambodia (.kh)	Saudi Arabia (.sa)
Cayman Islands (.ky)	Slovenia (.si)
Chad (.td)	Syria (.sy)
China (People's Republic of) (.cn)	Turkmenistan (.tm)
Cyprus (.cy)	Tuvalu (.tv)
Djibouti (.dj)	Uganda (.ug)
Ethiopia (.et)	United Arab Emirates (.ae)
Iran (.ir)	Uzbekistan (.uz)
Iraq (.iq)	Vanuatu (.vu)
Laos (.la)	Vietnam (.vn)
Latvia (.lv)	Yugoslavia (.yu)
Lithuania (.lt)	

The effectiveness of the systems in place in a number of other countries, such as Russia (.ru), remains highly doubtful; however, the systems at least do exist.

- There is more than one copyright holder (such as for a jointly authored article), and not all copyright holders either are aware of the infringement or have agreed with the particular action taken and result (or lack thereof).
- The infringer has not republished the entire work, and asserts that the infringement is "fair use." As a general principle, there is *no* fair use defense to republishing an entire work, even for scholarly or other commentary. There are exceptions, though, and the scope of the fair use privilege (17 U.S.C. § 107) is not for the fainthearted—or nonlawyer—to determine.
- A previously authorized distributor (generally publisher) has gone or is going through bankruptcy or another change of ownership other than voluntary dissolution. The Bankruptcy Code (Title 11) has many traps for intellectual property, and the various laws of corporate governance have even more.
- The rights you granted to a previously authorized distributor have been assigned to a third party, and you do not have the paperwork for the

assignment between the two parties. A letter from your previous publisher is helpful, but you really need the assignment itself. In the best of all possible worlds, a complete copy of such an assignment routinely would be forwarded directly to the author. This is not the best of all possible worlds.

Although there is a great deal that one can do without a lawyer's assistance to assert a copyright, there are many pitfalls once one moves past a simple, obvious infringement. There is no substitute for legal advice from an attorney whose practice includes copyright law.

Finding a lawyer is easy—we're in the Yellow Pages under "Attorneys." Finding the *right* lawyer can be much more difficult. First, although under the Model Rules of Professional Conduct lawyers cannot claim to be "specialists" (except in patent and bankruptcy law), we are—even more so than physicians. The difference is that there is no certification for legal specialties.

You should attempt to find a lawyer who is used to working on the "left side of the v." Even within intellectual property law, publishing law, and sport and entertainment law, attorneys tend to specialize. For example, I work almost entirely on the author's/creator's side. I can provide advice to a publisher (and have) on how to structure a contract; my advice, however, will be colored by my strong pro-author bias. Unfortunately, the majority of attorneys who do practice in one of these areas work on the distributor (or "middleman") side, which can warp the perspective of any advice. Attorneys who do not practice in the area can often be more dangerous than they realize, as there are many terms of art and industry customs that are, at the least, inconsistent with what one learns in law school (even in a copyright class).

That said, here are four places to begin searching for a lawyer (plus, of course, you may contact me). I have listed them in the order I suggest trying them.

- If you are a member of one of the major writers' organizations, the organization may have a staff attorney or outside counsel whom you can consult. He or she is almost always aware of any similar circumstances, which can prove very helpful.
- The VOLUNTEER LAWYERS FOR THE ARTS can often provide some basic advice. Keep in mind that the VLA is a group of volunteers, and not ordinarily litigation counsel for authors. However, the VLA is an excellent source of advice.
- One can attempt to use the AMERICAN BAR ASSOCIATION LAWYER REFERRAL SERVICES. However, for copyright and publishing law issues, this may be useless outside of a major metropolitan area. There is a nominal cost to use the system.
- Last, and definitely least, are the various online lawyer directories. The principal ones include MARTINDALE-HUBBELL and FINDLAW'S FIND A LAWYER. These indices, contrary to their public posturing, are not very inclusive, and are almost completely unverified. Martindale-Hubbell purports to rate lawyers; don't bother relying upon them, because a lawyer must pay a fee and request a rating. West's system is similar. Even aside from these problems, the accuracy of the system leaves a great deal to be desired.

SAMPLE LETTERS

MODEL LETTER TO COPYRIGHT INFRINGERS[3]

[date sent]

[return address]

Dear [Sir / Madam]:

On [date], I noticed that your [site/e-mail newsletter/electronic message/ electronic product] [exact name and URL, ISBN, or ISSN, if available],[A] dated [apparent date of infringement],[B] includes an [attributed/unattributed] copy of material that infringes on my exclusive right in the [story/article/ review] [writer's title]. This work originally appeared in [publication data].[C] According to my records, I have not authorized this use.

Please contact me immediately so we can work out either an appropriate agreement for this use or an agreement to terminate this use.

Sincerely,

Arthur Author

NOTES

A. Proofread all identification information carefully.
B. It is very important to ensure that dates are correct. Frequently, electronic sources do not have dates. If the material allows you to approximate the date, state so; otherwise delete the reference to the apparent date of infringement.
C. If the work has not yet appeared, but is scheduled to do so, give as much information as you have available. If the work was self-published by you (for example, on your own Web site), indicate that.

MODEL DMCA NOTICE TO COPYRIGHT INFRINGERS

[date sent]

[return address]

Demand Under the Digital Millennium Copyright Act

Dear [Sir/Madam]:

On [date], I noticed that your [site/email newsletter/electronic message/electronic product] [exact name and URL, ISBN, or ISSN, if available],[A] dated [apparent date of infringement],[B] includes an [attributed/unattributed] copy that infringes on my exclusive right in the [story/article/review] [writer's title]. According to my records, I have not authorized this use.

Pursuant to the Digital Millennium Copyright Act, this letter serves as actual notice of infringement in the event of legal proceedings. The information in this notification is accurate, and under penalty of perjury, I state that I am the owner of an exclusive right infringed by the specified material.[C]

Sincerely,

Beth Buchsbinder

NOTES

A. Proofread all identification information carefully.
B. It is very important to ensure that dates are correct. Frequently, electronic sources do not have dates. If the material allows you to approximate the date, state so; otherwise delete the reference to the apparent date of infringement.
C. As this paragraph makes clear, this is no longer open to negotiation, but is a demand for immediate action. Allow no more than ten business days for a response.

MODEL DMCA NOTICE TO SERVICE PROVIDERS

[date sent]

[return address]

Demand Under the Digital Millennium Copyright Act

[user or site name of infringer][A]

Dear [Sir/Madam]:

A [Web page hosted by your service/communication originating on your service], designated [full URL or message identification], retrieved [date and time],[B] infringes upon my exclusive right in [title]. I have attempted to resolve this directly with the account holder without satisfaction. Please remove the referenced material from your service and take other appropriate action against the account holder to prevent future infringement.

Pursuant to the Digital Millennium Copyright Act, this letter serves as actual notice of infringement in the event of legal proceedings. The information in this notification is accurate, and under penalty of perjury, I state that I am the owner of an exclusive right infringed by the specified material.[C]

Please contact me promptly to confirm the action you have taken.[D]

Sincerely,

Clarisse Curmudgeon

NOTES:

A. Although this is not completely necessary, it will be helpful when dealing with a repeat infringer—and you may not know whether this is the first infringement by this user.
B. Proofread all identification information carefully. It is very important to ensure that dates are correct. Frequently, electronic sources do not have dates. If the material allows you to approximate the date, state so; otherwise delete the reference to the apparent date of infringement.
C. As this paragraph makes clear, this is no longer open to negotiation, but is a demand for immediate action.
D. Allow no more than five business days for a response.

RESOURCES

TRACING SOFTWARE

AnalogX Whois Ultra
*www.analogx.com/contents/download/
network.htm*

NetLab
*ftp://ftp.ccit.edu.tw/Windows/Windows95/
WinSite/netutil/netlab95.zip*

Workshell Whois
www.workshell.co.uk

ATTORNEYS

**American Bar Association/Lawyer Referral
Services**
*www.abanet.org/legalservices/lris/direc-
tory.html*

FindLaw's Find a Lawyer
http://lawyers.findlaw.com

Martindale-Hubbell
*http://lawyers.martindale.com/xp/
Martindale/home.xml*

Volunteer Lawyers for the Arts
*http://arts.endow.gov/artforms/Manage/
VLA2.html*

COPYRIGHT AND FAIR USE ISSUES

Charles Petit's copyright information site
www.authorslawyer.com

Copyright and Fair Use
http://fairuse.stanford.edu

Links to articles and other resources on
issues of copyright, multimedia rights,
and fair use.

Copyright Clearance and Fair Use
*www.lib.rochester.edu/copyright/
default.htm*
Links to articles and resources on fair use
and how to obtain permission to reprint
copyrighted material.

Copyright Infringement
*www.computerbits.com/archive/1999/
0400/copyright.html*
Excellent article discussing what constitutes infringement, and how to avoid it.

Is Your Work on the Web?
www.sarahwernick.com/web.htm#article
This article by Sarah Wernick will help you
find out whether your work is being used
online (or your magazine articles sold by
databases) without your permission.

**Giving Credit and Requesting Permission:
Guidelines for Using Material Other than
Your Own**
www.oreilly.com/oreilly/author/permission
A book chapter covering issues of copying, quoting, and obtaining permission
for use of other authors' materials.

(For more information on rights and
copyright, see Resources, chapter 8.)

CHAPTER 10

PERILS, PITFALLS, AND SCAMS ON THE WEB

WHILE THE WEB ABOUNDS WITH opportunities and resources for writers, it has its share of pitfalls and traps for the unwary as well. Sadly, many shady individuals and organizations have found the Web an excellent place to hunt for amateur, inexperienced, and "desperate to be published" writers. Some of these pitfalls will do little more than waste your time, but others can waste a significant chunk of your money as well. Some should be approached with a "buyer beware" mentality—and others should be shunned like the plague.

Two items that fall into the "buyer beware" category are "freelance job sites" and "author showcase/syndication" sites. Neither of these categories are actually scams, or in any way illegal. However, there is considerable doubt among professional authors as to whether these sites really deliver what they promise. The writer who wishes to sign up in hopes of finding work or selling more material should do so with a full understanding of the risks involved.

AUTHOR SHOWCASES AND SYNDICATION SERVICES

BY DEBBIE RIDPATH OHI[1]

IT SOUNDS LIKE AN AUTHOR'S dream come true. Just hand over your written pieces to one of these services, and let them sell your writing for you! No need for time-consuming market research or networking, which gives you more time to do actual writing. But does it really work this way? I surveyed authors, editors, and those who run author and syndication services to find out.

The goal of author showcases and syndication services is to help writers sell their work. The difference between the two types of services is somewhat blurry in terms of how the two terms are used by the services themselves, however. For the purposes of this article, I will refer to both as "showcase services" for authors, online services which offer authors the space to post their writing or who offer to actively market their articles and columns to content buyers.

In theory, editors and other content buyers will visit the site, looking for material to purchase. Some of these showcase sites offer their services for free, but most charge a monthly fee or take a percentage of the transaction's profit. AUTHORLINK, for example, evaluates submitted manuscripts for potential listing in the showcase. A listing contains a short synopsis, excerpt, and author résumé, and involves a fee. If a listing interests an editor or agent, they can request the full manuscript.

SOME STATISTICS

Authorlink was one of the few who posted their statistics online, and is also one of the oldest, having been online since early 1996. They have about 800–1,000 writers listed. According to founder Doris Booth, Authorlink has signed more than 400 writers with agents in the past three years, and has helped sell seventy-six titles. "This is more than some of the large New York agencies sell annually," says Booth. "And we don't take agency commissions unless we're in a sub-agenting role."

FEATUREWELL.COM has more than seven hundred writers registered, including established names like Andrei Codrescu, Jimmy Breslin, and Robert Reich. They only work with experienced journalists. Featurewell.com's CEO David Wallis says that their service is fairly successful for writers "as long as writers' expectations are realistic. No one gets rich from reprints. We sell about $2,000–$3,000 of stories per week. Sixty percent generally goes to the writer. I consider syndication 'literary lotto.'" The site claims to have more than eight hundred clients who browse material on the Featurewell.com. "Some browse, some buy on occasion, some buy all the time."

Many of the showcase services I surveyed, however, were unable to provide data on their success rates, mainly because they had no way of accurately tracking the number of visits by content buyers and the number of resulting contacts made or manuscripts sold. In many cases the setup was very casual, so that anyone could post or view material without having to register. THE WRITE BIZ does not track how many of its showcased pieces are actually sold, for example, but site owner Alex Salisbury says that he receives an average of four to six inquiries a month about how to contact a particular author.

CONCERNS ABOUT SHOWCASE SITES

Writers have a number of questions about such sites, including:

What If Someone Steals My Material?

Barbara Florio Graham is an author and teacher as well as a long-time member of the Periodical Writers' Association of Canada (*www.pwac.ca*), and says she's cautious about using online manuscript showcases. "I'm wary of this method of selling your writing," says Graham. "It's just too easy for someone to 'lift' your work from a Web site, remove your byline, and either adapt it or use it intact to enhance their own Web site (or to sell outright, even though they know this is plagiarism)."

Some showcase services only post excerpts on their sites, granting full access only to registered members. CORRESPONDENT.COM posts a very brief synopsis of articles, for example, but requires membership to access the full text. Authorlink publishes only a synopsis and a short excerpt from its book-length manuscripts. "If an editor or agent makes a request then the author himself/herself sends it directly to the requesting party," says Doris Booth.

If I Post Material to a Web Site, Can I Still Sell "First Rights"?

John Hewitt, editor of WRITER'S RESOURCE CENTER, believes that online publication negates first rights. "Publishing on the Internet is just like publishing anywhere else, there can be only one first." He points out that you can still offer first print rights to print publications. "How the individual publication feels about that is up to them. Writers should remember, however, that if you have written a story once and keep your research, a rewrite can turn a reprint into a first publication again and quickly solve your problem."

Sheri McConnell, founder of the NATIONAL ASSOCIATION OF WOMEN WRITERS, doesn't believe that most editors consider posting material online the same thing as being published. "For instance, if someone posts their information on our Member Portfolio page, I do not consider it published by the NAWW. Now, if I publish it in *NAWW Weekly*, then it is considered published."

When considering using an author showcase, be sure to read over the terms of service or contract carefully before signing up. Humor writer Carole Moore turned down a contract from a medium-sized syndicate service after reading their contract, which indicated that the company would have all rights to her material while she was under contract. It also specified that they would have complete control over all promotional activities, including whether or not it was done. "Which meant that if they chose not to promote any aspect of my work, it would just sit there and decay and I couldn't do anything about it," said Moore. "I decided not to sign on."

Do Editors Use Author Showcases?

Do editors actually browse online showcases for material? Many of the magazine editors I surveyed said they did not use manuscript showcase services. Doug Bennett, publisher of *Masthead* magazine, didn't even know this type of service existed. "We assign articles to freelance writers directly, or they pitch us story ideas directly." Many editors said they have enough trouble keeping up with the amount of unsolicited material that they already receive.

Authorlink, however, gets an average of 68,000 unique visitors a month and Doris Booth says that this number includes editors, agents, writers, and readers. "We know that major publishers visit us often, because their URLs frequently show up in our reports, and they tell us they visit the site when we talk to them in person." Michele Pezzuti, an editor at McGraw-Hill, confirmed that she ended up buying author Dee Hubbard's *Slim to None* manuscript after first reading an excerpt on Authorlink. She says that the writing was strong and the message so unique that she decided to show the manuscript to others at McGraw-Hill. "Everyone was very supportive, excited, and we are all geared up for its release in 2003." Paul Dobransky says that he's had his Authorlink pieces requested by editors at HarperCollins, Penguin, McGraw-Hill, and HarperSanFrancisco.

Other authors said they liked online showcases because the services helped with name recognition, even if there were no direct sales. Josh Aterovis hasn't sold any of the half-dozen columns he had posted on GAYLINKCONTENT.COM, but says he doesn't mind because there were no upfront fees. "Several of the columns I have posted are on there for free for the community to use as long as they credit the author (me). A few are on there for sale. I haven't sold any, but I did get a job writing a monthly column for Gaywork.com, a division of Monster.com. I've also found that my free columns are being used on sites around the Internet. I feel anything that builds name recognition is a good thing." Tracey Rosenblath says that posting material on FOR THE LOVE OF WRITING resulted in sales. Rosenblath is a technical writer, but wanted feedback for her fiction writing. She attributes the sale of several short stories, poems, essays, and a monthly feature assignment to her postings to fortheloveofwriting.com. Several editors mentioned that they had first seen her work on the community critiquing site.

Though Amy Chavez hasn't made many direct sales through Correspondent.com, she has sold several pieces because of editors who have seen her work on the site. "My experience has been that it hasn't helped me sell lots of reprints of my work, which is what I had hoped for when I signed up for the service," says Chavez. "However, the editors have contacted me to do articles. This is, of course, the better end to be on as it guarantees an editor's interest in an article idea, and you don't have to waste time querying your own ideas to magazines or newspapers who may not be interested in your idea anyway." Chavez has made most sales through a working relationship she has developed with an editor at Correspondent.com. Chavez says that her Correspondent.com contact works hard to pitch writers' stories through one-on-one contact with editors.

How Easy Is It to Get Syndicated?

Some online showcases offer syndication services, meaning that they will distribute your articles or columns to newspapers and magazines.

Getting syndicated is difficult despite these encouraging statistics, according to Craig Branson of the American Society of Newspaper Editors (*www.asne.org*). "It's a good idea to have a current base of operations in place—a local newspaper or magazine, for example—that is running your stuff already—perhaps for free—to build up clips and a reputation. But it's very, very hard to get picked up by syndicates and even harder to self-syndicate." Featurewell.com's CEO David Wallis warns writers not to expect to get rich through syndication, and adds: "Also, everybody wants to be a columnist. The competition is stiff, so you better have a compelling idea and strong samples to have a shot."

"Writers seem to feel that they have to be syndicated to feel as though they've reached the big time," Carole Moore says. "For the vast majority, that's simply not going to happen. Not in a day and time when really good writers are being cut loose from newspapers."

Many of the online services that market themselves as author showcases are not effective in helping writers sell their work, because content buyers do not use them. The services that do work are effective mainly because they are active in building and maintaining relationships with editors and agents. "We believe that most mere online showcases don't work very well," says Doris Booth of Authorlink. "Our success is built on personal relationships with the publishing community, and frequent face-to-face contact, facilitated by our online activities—not the other way around." Featurewell.com screens its material by using only experienced journalists, as does Correspondent.com, and Correspondent.com actively markets some of its writers' pieces through individual relationships with editors.

Some writers found that even though the online showcases they used did not result in many (or even any) direct sales, they found the exposure was worth it, or that they got other assignments because of editors who had seen their work online. Amy Chavez says that some of these services can also provide a degree of added protection to writers regarding kill fees or getting paid for their work. "I just signed a contract to do a monthly column for a Belgian print magazine, which was a result of Correspondent.com. The entire negotiation of the contract has gone through the editor at Correspondent.com. This means that if the Belgian magazine for some reason decides not to pay me, they risk their reputation with Correspondent.com as well. I've never had problems being paid by a magazine, but I know many writers who have."

Again, however, much depends on the quality and reputation of the service. Before you sign on with a showcase service, make sure you do your research. Carole Moore advises authors to have someone who knows the business read the contract or terms before they sign up. Some questions to answer while researching a service:

- What costs are involved?
- What rights are you giving away? Do rights revert back to the author once a contract expires? What happens if an author decides to withdraw his or her material?
- What promotion, if any, does the service do to market your work?
- How does the site attract editors and other content buyers?
- Does the site have customer recommendations and statistics available for public viewing? Do they have a way of tracking their success?

Even if you do get an editor or agent interested in your work as a result of a showcase service, be sure to do research to confirm that the interest is legitimate. Ginger Hanson said that when a company contacted Authorlink to request her complete manuscript, she decided to look up information about them before submitting the full work. She searched various publishing and writers' market directories for information about the company as well as information about the books they claimed to have published by other authors. She was unable to find anything. As a result, she decided that the company was probably a vanity press that did not support its published authors, and decided not to submit her manuscript to them.

"Showcasing your work at Authorlink still means a writer has to know the publisher before they send a submission," notes Hanson. "Usually, a writer researches the publishing companies and then chooses one that matches their manuscript. Services such as Authorlink turn that concept around. The publisher contacts you, but a match between material and publisher is still important. A reputable publisher is a must." Ginger Hanson has since sold a two-book deal to Kensington Publishing Corporation because of Authorlink exposure.

After having tried a few services, Carole Moore has opted to promote her writing services through her own Web site rather than use a showcase or syndication service. "All the effort put into these sites might pay off for some people. But I think it's much more effective to establish your own online presence. Put up your own site and let people find your work," says Moore. "I compare it to Wal-Mart. If you post your work on one of these sites, then, yes, you might have hundreds of people looking at your stuff—but most of them will be other writers checking you out. And you're sitting on a shelf, next to dozens who do the same thing. Instead, put up your own site and become a little boutique. The kind of place where discriminating shoppers go and spend the afternoon."

Sheri McConnell believes that online author showcase services can work. "However, I don't think a writer should use them as their only marketing tool. A writer should create a complete marketing plan to have a successful writing business." Writers should also be aware that poorly written material will not sell, whether or not it's being featured in an online showcase. Properly researched, an online showcase service can help increase your exposure and sales, but a writer should use it to supplement rather than replace his or her own efforts. "Three things are key in freelancing: writing well, pitching well, and collecting the money," says Craig Branson. "If you do any of these poorly, you probably should be doing something else."

ONLINE MARKETPLACES: MONEYMAKERS OR MADHOUSES?

BY LORALEI WALKER[2]

WITH THE EVER-INCREASING AMOUNT of work being outsourced by large and small corporations, it's no wonder that the number of online marketplaces is also on the rise. While many of these sites offer free memberships to freelancers, the new trend is toward charging a monthly or a yearly fee. Is it worth the time, the effort, and the money? The answer to that is best left to the individual, but here's some information that may help you make that decision:

HOW ONLINE MARKETPLACES WORK

While there are many online marketplaces, there is only one giant. ELANCE has managed to corner the market on all of the best jobs out there. Others include GURU, BULLHORN, and SMARTERWORK, just to name a few.

Each site works slightly differently. For all sites, you create a profile, listing your skills, expertise, recent experience, etc. Smarterwork requires that you become qualified as an "expert" in any category that you wish to look for work. You may either take a short test and qualify with at least 75 percent correct answers, or you may submit a letter outlining your qualifications. For Guru.com, you can also submit professional references, and choose whether or not to display various sections of your profile. With eLance, all categories you fill in will be displayed on your profile. eLance also gives you the option to create a portfolio of your work that can be viewed by prospective clients. Other marketplaces do not offer the opportunity to create a portfolio, but they all allow you to direct a person to a URL where your work may be seen. If you are a new writer, or one whose work has previously only appeared in print, you might want to create a simple Web site where your work may be viewed. If you have any published work, list when and where each piece was published. If not, then just fill your site with a few great examples of what you can do. (See chapter 13 for tips on setting up an effective author Web site.)

Once your profile is in order, it is time to search the site for projects you are interested in. While each site works differently, the concept is the same. Buyers post jobs, and service providers search the database for projects, using categories or keywords. Then comes the pitch. This is where service providers (that's you) state their qualifications and try to convince the buyers exactly why they are the best person for the job. Some use experience, others use education and work background, and, unfortunately, some use a bid price that is far below standard.

The problem with offering work for little or no pay in order to gain experience is that it may come back to haunt you. On eLance, monies earned within the last six months are visible when you place your bid. If you wish to bid closer to standard pricing on a project, a buyer need only view your feedback history to see what you have accepted previously for similar projects, and ask you to work for the same price again.

With Guru, you choose whether or not to display your contact information to prospective buyers when you make your pitch, allowing the buyer to contact you directly. On eLance, direct contact between buyers and providers is not permitted; they do, however, offer a private message board that may be initiated by a buyer in order to discuss projects, pay, etc., with service providers. Another option for buyers is to view profiles according to category. Depending on which marketplace a buyer is using, they may either contact you directly or invite you to place a bid on a project. eLance also offers a section of featured providers, with a rotation of providers set by a schedule based on earnings, feedback, etc. In order to be featured with any regularity, however, you must be working and being paid through their system consistently.

COUNTING THE COST

At the time of this writing, eLance's monthly fee is $75 per month for a basic service provider (with a discounted annual fee of $360). For a "select" service provider status, which gives one "exclusive access to select projects," monthly fees are $250 per category (e.g., "Web site design," "writing and translation," etc.), with discounted annual fees of $1,200. eLance also charges a 5 percent transaction fee on all projects originating through the site. However, at the time of this writing, five thousand service providers were listed in the writing and translation category—but only seventy projects.[3] On average, a person would have to bid on thirty to forty job listings to be awarded one project.

Although Guru remains cost-free for the freelancer, Bullhorn and Smarterwork both charge a 10 percent fee on any monies earned by the service provider. Smarterwork charges an additional 4 percent "administration" fee, as well as a membership fee of 500 Euros. Bullhorn charges $39.95 for access to the "Project Exchange" section, where jobs are posted. While these and other marketplaces have much more realistic fee and membership guidelines, the difference in the number of jobs listed is striking. The search at Guru for writing jobs turned up six opportunities;[4] Smarterwork came in close second at having four, and Bullhorn coming in third, offering an astounding zero job postings in its copy writing section.[5]

IS IT WORTH IT?

While a person could sign on for many of the marketplaces hoping to increase their chances of finding work, the sad truth is that doing so might just be a waste of time. When reviewing the different online marketplaces, I found that the majority of job postings were listed on a number of different sites, with some listed on as many as five marketplace sites. Essentially, what this means is that you could spend hours searching and posting for jobs on a number of sites, only to have the project awarded through a site where you haven't placed a bid.

Another disheartening fact is that with so many providers out there, competition is fierce, and buyers know it. Buyers look for the best deal—and unless they have received poor quality work in exchange for a lower-than-standard rate, they usually look for the best price as opposed to the most qualified person. I have also seen cases where a buyer will send a message to a number of service providers, stating that they have been offered work for bargain-basement prices, and asking whether the service provider be willing to offer an even lower price. This is done to create a "bidding frenzy" amongst providers, and is often very effective. There are

[3]This article was originally written in 2001. When I checked Bullhorn in August 2002, the "Writing and Translation" section offered eighty-six listings, of which eighteen were "select" (meaning one could not bid on them without having a "select" membership in that category.
[4]In August 2002, Guru.com offered twenty-one listings under "writing" and three under "editing."
[5]In August 2002, Bullhorn offered no listings under either Creative Writing or Technical Writing jobs; I did not bother checking further.

also many new writers willing to work for substandard rates, and sometimes even for free, just to build a portfolio, making it nearly impossible to compete for projects.

Online marketplaces may work for some, but for most writers, there's still no substitute for building your own client base, researching markets, and sending out queries and submissions the old-fashioned way!

THE SERVICES DESCRIBED IN THE previous two sections are by no means illegal. Their benefit to the writer, however, is dubious—and a writer should be cautious about handing over money to such an organization without being absolutely certain of receiving a benefit in return. Such sites often claim to be alternatives to the "standard" way of doing business—but often, that "standard" way is still the *best* way (and sometimes the only way).

Other "opportunities" for writers, however, are outright scams. Unscrupulous agents, subsidy publishers who don't deliver, and book doctors who offer to make a manuscript "saleable" are just a few of the perils writers face. Unfortunately, these types of predators actively hunt for amateur, inexperienced, and "desperate-to-be-published" writers on the Internet, stalking their prey in newsgroups, discussion lists, and chat rooms. Here are some of the more typical scams facing writers online:

UNSCRUPULOUS AGENTS

AS THE WEB HAS BECOME crowded with would-be authors, wannabe authors, and authors who will do just about anything to "get published," it has also become crowded with sharks who recognize those authors as ideal prey. Among those who cruise the discussion boards and writing lists for potential "clients" are unscrupulous agents, who make their money by convincing authors to pay in advance for services that they may never receive.

Granted, not every agent who charges a fee is necessarily running a scam (although I have yet to meet a professional author who has anything good to say about fee-charging agents). The problem is, a fee-charging agent is making money off the wrong person: You. A reputable agent makes a decision about representing a client based on whether he or she believes that the client's work can be sold successfully to a publisher. If the agent feels that the work can't be sold, or that he or she is simply not the right agent (or with the right connections) to sell that work, the agent will say no. In short, a reputable agent won't take on your work unless fairly *sure* that he or she can make money by selling it.

A fee-charging agent doesn't have to worry about that, because he or she is already making money from *you*, whether the *work* sells or not. While many no doubt do make an attempt to market the work of their clients (or they wouldn't still be in business at all), the incentive to select *only* work that can be marketed is gone. The agent earns a fee whether you get published or not—and since that removes any incentive to be selective about clients, it means that there is absolutely no guarantee that by signing with a fee-charging agent, you will have any better chance of getting published.

Here's a letter from a writer who has had a range of unpleasant, but all too typical, experiences with fee-charging editors:

> First of all, I signed a six month contract with————.[6] She charged me $175 up front, but explained her reasoning and I felt, if she fully represented me, the charge was justified. The editor I am working with now thinks I made a big mistake. I'll chalk up the $175 to hard earned experience, but my obligation to this agency is for another six months, and that concerns me the most. If she is going to sit on my work, then I'd like to be free to pursue the other two agents who have expressed interest in the novel.
>
> The experiences I have had so far are full of red flags. I have had a total of five agents respond favorably to my query letters. My query e-mail was responded to within hours of being received [by one agency] and I was told to submit my manuscript according to the guidelines posted on their Web site. To my chagrin, they wanted $150 along with the submission; however, there was a "no fee" option and that is the one I chose. About two weeks later a secretary called me and said that the agent wanted to talk with me. She asked me to call back the next day at an appointed time, which I did and we talked for an hour, on my dime. She told me the novel was some of the best writing to come across her desk in a long time, but that she didn't like the structure or the protagonist. She had her own ideas and wanted to "consult" with me for a fee of $9,500, after which I would have a suitable manuscript to submit to other agents. She would not guarantee representation! I was floored, to say the least. I told her I would take a few of her editing suggestions and make the corrections myself. Three days later my manuscript was returned to me with a terse letter telling me that if I resubmitted the novel it would cost me $95.
>
> Then I heard from a Canadian agent, who also wanted $175, as well as from the agent I actually signed with.
>
> Then two days ago I got a phone call from another agent. She said she would represent me, but the manuscript needs work and if I got it edited, she would take it on. She had an editing service in mind, which charges $6.50 per 250 words at a cost of $3,450. She even went so far as to give me their Web site, however, the Web site said they charged $6 per page at a cost of $3,180. I just received the sample edit back. I agree with 90 percent of the changes; however the agent wrote the cover letter to the fax! I thought this editing service was not associated with her, I guess I was wrong.
>
> Not wanting to be pushed into anything, I finally did some research on my own and found that these agents are all poorly rated by

---

[6]Names of agents and agencies have been removed. However, all the agents who were referenced in this letter appear in the various warning sites listed in the Resources section.

Agentresearch.com. If the agent I've signed with is really working for me, as an agent should, would a publisher be willing to edit a manuscript or should I proceed with hiring someone?

This unfortunate author apparently got hit by every scam in the book; fortunately, she only signed one agreement and lost no more than $175. However, as this letter shows, the potential for loss is significant!

That doesn't mean that editors and book doctors are fraudulent. There are many excellent, reputable editors and book doctors—and unfortunately the cost of a high-quality manuscript edit *is* high. And, sadly, very few publishers are willing to provide the type of editing service for a manuscript that they once did, which means that if your manuscript isn't just about perfect "as is," it may have less chance of getting published. The scam, however, is when agents and editors work together to bilk a writer of money with promises of acceptance and publication—as with the cases below.

AGENTS AND BOOK DOCTORS: WOODSIDE AND EDIT INK

IN FEBRUARY 1999, THE WOODSIDE Literary Agency of Queens, New York, was ordered to stop its Internet publishing scheme, provide restitution to consumers, pay penalties and costs to the state, and post a $100,000 bond to protect consumers in future business dealings. Here's an excerpt from the official press release of the Office of the New York State Attorney General:

> The Attorney General's office had received complaints from dozens of consumers, many of whom said they lost as much as $400 in fees to Woodside. The company lured would-be authors with glowing evaluations of writing samples, and then imposed steep charges for further review and processing of manuscripts. Consumers who paid an initial reading fee of as much as $150 were informed that their work was "publishable." They were then asked to pay an additional $250 contract fee. To lend credence to the scam, Woodside told authors that only five percent of submissions were accepted by the agency. In reality, the company offered contracts to anyone who paid the initial reading fee.
>
> The Attorney General's Office investigated Woodside after receiving complaints from writers who grew tired of the company's repeated solicitations through literary-related news groups and bulletin boards. In an effort to test Woodside's literary standards, a group of writers actually submitted a bogus writing sample that was filled with nonsensical prose, and grammatical and spelling errors. Woodside later requested the author's entire manuscript—and a fee.[7]

[7]Press release from the Office of the New York State Attorney General, *www.oag.state.ny.us/press/1999/feb/feb17a_99.html*, posted February 17, 1999.

Woodside was also accused of harassing writers who attempted to warn others of the scam by posting warnings on newsgroups or by e-mail. In some cases, writers were threatened with legal action when they tried to spread the word about Woodside. According to Attorney General Eliot Spitzer, "This is another example of how scam artists are using the Internet to cheat consumers out of their hard-earned dollars. Internet users and all consumers must be on guard against unscrupulous businesses."

Another such unscrupulous firm, and perhaps the most widely publicized, is Edit Ink, run by four residents of Buffalo, New York, and one California man. The participants ran a "fictitious literary agent and publishing house business" that defrauded more than 3,600 writers nationwide. According to the Office of the New York State Attorney General:

> This phony literary service generated approximately $4.75 million in revenues. Consumers were duped into believing that their manuscripts showed "great promise and excellent commercial possibilities" but required professional editing. The participants then made referrals to Edit Ink, a Cheektowaga firm which charged hopeful writers up to $2,000 per manuscript. What was not disclosed to the consumers, however, was the fact that these fake literary agents were receiving a 15 percent kickback from Edit Ink for every referral. After resubmitting their edited writings to the literary agent or publishing house, the victims were informed that their manuscript had been rejected.[8]

The operators of Edit Ink were fined $2 million in civil penalties, with additional fines for damages to the victims. According to Spitzer, "These victims placed their hopes and dreams in fraudulent literary agents and publishing companies only to be deceived into paying for an overpriced editing service, lied to about the qualifications of the editors, misled about the potential for acceptance by a publishing company, and ultimately rejected by fictitious literary agents or publishing houses. It is equally important that we fight to get substantial refunds for these consumers."

Despite the conviction against Edit Ink, this particular scheme lives on—or tries to. In October 2001, the subsidy print-on-demand publishing firm Xlibris sent a letter to more than 20,000 agents and editors, encouraging them to refer unpublished writers to Xlibris, who would then encourage those writers to pay for print-on-demand services (typically costing $1,000 or more). Agents and editors would receive a referral fee of $500 for every author who actually signed up. "The idea is simple," said the letter. "You send Xlibris your slush pile—the authors you've rejected. These are authors whom you've deemed aren't yet ready for mass market. Xlibris introduces them to print-on-demand self-publishing as a viable alternative." Authors and author advocates pointed out the similarity between the Xlibris letter and letters sent by Edit Ink—and Xlibris quickly rescinded the offer.

[8]Press release from the Office of the New York State Attorney General, *www.oag.state.ny.us/press/1999/feb/ feb22b_99.html*, posted February 22, 1999.

SUBSIDY PUBLISHING SCAMS

AUTHORS WHO WOULD "DO ANYTHING to get published" are especially vulnerable to the promises of subsidy publishers. While most professional authors regard subsidy publishers as anathema, most are not actually "scams"—they are simply companies that take your money and deliver a "published" book that is virtually impossible to sell. Such a book is not considered "published" by any professional standards; it won't receive reviews, it won't get into bookstores, it won't qualify as a "publication" credit applicable to membership in a professional organization (such as Romance Writers of America or Science Fiction Writers of America). It's simply a book-shaped hunk of pages that makes authors feel good. But it's not, technically, a *scam*.

Unfortunately, a handful of subsidy publishers go a step farther, and take authors' money without delivering even that "hunk of pages." One such publisher is Northwest Publishing of Utah, founded in 1992 by James van Treese. Van Treese worked through a network of literary agents, who received kickbacks for referring their clients to Northwest. The company claimed to be selective in the manuscripts it chose for publication, but in reality, any author willing to pay the price could be published.

The scam lay in the fact that the books were never actually published. While a handful would be printed to send to the author, the author was told that the rest were "warehoused," when in fact they were never printed at all. According to charges brought against Van Treese, much of the authors' money was actually gambled away in Las Vegas. In 1997, Van Treese and his son were charged with twenty-two second-degree counts of communications fraud, securities fraud, tax evasion, and racketeering.

In 1997, Charles and Dorothy Deering launched a subsidy publishing company called Sovereign Publications, following the same model. The Deerings also operated a fraudulent literary agency, which served to direct clients to the publishing house. Again, authors generally never saw the books that they had paid thousands of dollars to print.

The most recent entry in the subsidy scam sweepstakes is Press-TIGE Publishing, run by Martha Ivery, aka Kelly O'Donnell. As Kelly O'Donnell, Ivery ran several fee-charging literary agencies, as well as a vanity publishing house. Ivery was noted for soliciting clients through newsgroups, chat rooms, and discussion groups. She also obtained mailing lists of writers through conferences and other sources. According to lawyer Charles Petit, "Many complaints and extensive documentation demonstrate that Press-TIGE doesn't print the books that authors pay for, had no ability to do so, and probably never intended to do so." Authors with claims against Ivery (e.g., books paid for but not produced) were encouraged to file with the court. During the hearing, Ivery admitted to operating yet another vanity publishing house, New Millennium, in Leeds or Catskill, New York. According to Petit, "Ivery admitted under oath that she unilaterally transferred some unfulfilled publishing contracts from Press-TIGE to New Millennium."[9]

[9]Charles Petit, "Press-TIGE Publishing Files for Bankruptcy," 27 July 2002, *www.authorslawyer.com/l-publishers.shtml.*

There are circumstances in which subsidy publishing (particularly electronic or print-on-demand subsidy publishing) can be a viable way to get one's book into print. It is not, however, considered a professional or commercial form of publication under any circumstances, and is generally considered a means of taking advantage of amateur or desperate authors. However, a reputable subsidy publisher will at least deliver the promised book! At time of writing, this case has not been resolved, but you can follow the latest twists and updates (and find out what to do if *you've* been involved with this publisher) at WRITER BEWARE.

WRITING CONTESTS AND POETRY.COM

THE INTERNET HAS MADE IT possible for organizations around the world to advertise writing competitions—and to attract entries from around the world. The majority of these contests are legitimate, sponsored by reputable organizations (or even individuals), and fulfill their promises (whether those promises are of cash prizes, publication, or other awards). However, there are always those who recognize that "desperate-to-be-published" writers often see a contest as a shortcut to fame and publication—and are thus easily parted from their cash.

Many writers fear that *any* competition that charges an entry fee must be a scam. This is by no means true. In fact, the vast majority of competitions charge fees—both to fund the awards themselves and, often, to help support the organization sponsoring the competition. Writing contests are one way that many literary magazines stay in business, for example. And one of the most well-known "questionable" competitions charges no fee at all, as we'll see below.

It's not always easy to determine whether a competition is legitimate, a scam, or simply a not-so-well organized effort by an amateur organization. Here are some things to watch out for when considering a competition:

- **How does the size of the award compare to the size of the entry fee?** If a competition is charging $5 for entries and offering only $25 in prize money, this isn't much of a prize. Your profit would be no more than $20 *if* you win.
- **Does the prize depend on the number of entries?** Many individuals run contests to promote their service or business. While they may promise huge prizes (often $5,000 or more), you'll discover in the fine print that these prizes depend on the number of entries. The actual "purse" will depend on the total amount of revenue generated from entry fees, minus whatever amount the contest sponsor chooses to keep!
- **Does the entry fee seem unreasonably large?** Most fees range from $2 to $10 (or a comparable amount in non-U.S. currency). Screenwriting competitions tend to charge more (usually between $25 and $50). However, even a reputable organization may charge an unusually large fee; I know of one well-known writing association that charges $45. Competitions involving novel-length manuscripts (or portions thereof) also tend to charge larger fees.

- **Is the organization legitimate?** That can be hard to judge as well, as anyone can slap up a Web site and sponsor a competition. However, you can usually determine, by poking around the site, whether the sponsor seems to be a recognized organization, such as a literary publication, writers' group, or something similar. If the competition is annual and has been running for several years, that's usually a good sign as well.
- **Can you get more information?** Does the competition offer clear contact information, including an e-mail, for inquiries?
- **What type of publication is offered, if any?** Many competitions offer publication in the organization's magazine or e-zine, or in an anthology. Try to determine whether this is a reputable publication, one that would be a good credit on your résumé—or a fly-by-night "zine" that is simply looking for content.
- **What rights are demanded?** Most competitions do not ask for any rights to non-winning entries, and only limited rights to winning entries. Beware of competitions that demand the rights to your material whether you win or not, as well as those that ask for all rights to winning entries.

It's also a good idea, if you have doubts about a contest, to do a search on the name of the competition either through a search engine (such as GOOGLE) or through GOOGLE GROUPS, where you can research whether the competition has been discussed in newsgroups. Newsgroups are usually the best place to pick up discussions of unethical competitions.

These warnings are all very well, but *none* of them really apply to one of the best-known "almost-scam" contests on the Web: Poetry.com (also known as the International Library of Poetry). This "competition" charges no entry fees, demands no rights, offers "publication," and has been in business for years. It's not accurate to declare that Poetry.com is an actual "scam," as this implies that it is doing something illegal, which so far has not been demonstrated (although it *was* profiled on ABC's *20/20*). What Poetry.com does is prey upon the amateur poet's desire to be "published."

Simply put, Poetry.com offers a "contest" that no one can lose. Suspicious poets have tried, submitting verses on everything from flatulence to absolute nonsense syllables, still to receive a glowing letter of praise indicating that the poem has won the "first round" and is eligible to be a finalist for the actual cash awards. In the meantime, the poem will be included in a "special anthology" that the poet is invited to buy.

This anthology is where Poetry.com makes its money. The anthology appeals to the poet who yearns to see his or her work in print—for only $49.99. (Nor does one have to be *too* amateur or desperate to be tempted; I've fallen for this one myself.) Less savvy poets fondly suppose that this is a "publishing credential"—but other poetry publications are well aware that publication in one of the ILP's anthologies is meaningless. Additional warnings about the ILP can be found in the "Warnings" section of WRITERSWEEKLY.

HOW CAN YOU SPOT A SCAM?

HOW CAN YOU SPOT A less-than-legitimate offer? The quick answer is: "If it's too good to be true." Here's how to recognize a potential rip-off:

- **A person or organization contacts *you*, without having seen your work**. For example, if an "agent" contacts you out of the blue and offers to look at (or represent) your work, sight unseen, *for a fee*, this is not likely to be a legitimate offer. Reputable agents don't go hunting clients, and they certainly don't offer to represent someone whose work they haven't even seen. Nor do reputable agents charge fees to writers. An agent earns a commission by selling your work to a publisher; if the agent doesn't feel that he or she can effectively market your work, that agent won't accept you as a client. An agent who is earning money in advance from the *writer*, however, has little incentive to try to sell that work to a *publisher*.
- **A person or organization suggests that you are "almost ready to be published," but that your work needs a bit of polish**—and then recommends someone who, for a fee, can provide that polishing. This type of scam is usually accompanied by promises that make it sound as if the person *will* accept or represent you after you've paid for the editing. Beware of any individual who tells you that you can "get published" by paying certain fees for various services in advance.
- **A person or organization promises that by paying for their service, you can bypass the established method of doing business with agents, editors, and publishers.** This type of offer always sounds good to writers, who are (understandably) frustrated by the time-consuming and often disappointing method of submitting queries, synopses, proposals, and manuscripts. However, while writers may be searching for an alternative to this approach, agents and editors are *not*—they still expect writers to follow "standard procedure."

The bottom line is simple. If it sounds too good to be true—if it promises to fulfill your dreams for just a small fee by bypassing standard publishing practices—then it probably *is* too good to be true. Unfortunately, when it comes to getting published, there does not seem to be any real alternative to "doing it the hard way"—i.e., improving one's skills and learning the business.

RESOURCES

AUTHOR SHOWCASE & SYNDICATION SITES

Authorlink
www.authorlink.com

Correspondent.com
www.correspondent.com

Featurewell.com
www.featurewell.com

ForTheLoveOfWriting.com
www.fortheloveofwriting.com

Gaylinkcontent.com
www.gaylinkcontent.com

Write Biz, The
www.thewritebiz.com

FREELANCE MARKETPLACES

Bullhorn Exchange
http://talent.bullhorn.com/Bullhorn
Exchange

eLance
www.elance.com

Guru
www.guru.com

Smarterwork
www.smarterwork.com

SCAMS AND WARNINGS

13 Warning Signs of a Bad Poetry Contest
www.winningwriters.com/warningsigns.htm
What to watch out for before sending that
poem—or that check.

**Avoiding Writing Scams: Advice from Those
Who Know, by J.A. Hitchcock**
www.writing-world.com/rights/
scams.shtml

Before You Write that Check
www.writer.org/scamkit.htm
A good article on scams against writers.

**Dave Barry on the International Library of
Poetry**
http://windpub.org/literary.scams/
D-Barry.htm
Dave Barry's hilarious column about
submitting a poem to this group when it
was still "The National Library of Poetry."

**How to Protect Yourself from Questionable
Agents, by Marg Gilks**
www.writing-world.com/publish/agent/
agents.shtml

Poetry Awards/Frequently Asked Questions
www.poets.org/awards/faq.cfm
Tips on determining whether a contest is
a scam.

Poetry Contest Scams
http://windpub.org/literary.scams/ilp.htm

Preditors and Editors/Agent Listings
http://anotherealm.com/prededitors/
pubagent.htm
This site is a good place to look for
warnings against agents who are "not
recommended."

Vanity Poetry Contests
www.poets.ca/pshstore/sidebar/vanity.html

Web Resources that Help You Identify Scams
www.winningwriters.com/
scambustingsites.htm

Writer Alerts!
www.nwu.org/alerts/alrthome.htm
Warnings about nonpaying or problem
publishers from the National Writers
Union.

Writer Beware
www.sfwa.org/beware

Victoria Strauss's excellent compilation of tips, warnings, and updates about a wide variety of hazards to writers.

WritersWeekly Warnings Reports
www.writersweekly.com/warnings/ warnings.html
This is a great place to check on websites and publishers that (a) have a reputation for slow or nonpayment, or (b) are going out of business or are rumored to be having troubles.

You Too Can Sniff Out Scams!
www.yudkin.com/scams.htm
An excellent article by Marcia Yudkin that covers six telltale signs of a scam—the key being that if (a) it sounds too good to be true or (b) they want your money upfront, watch out!

<< CHAPTER 11 >>

PROMOTING YOUR BOOK ON THE WEB

I F YOU'RE THE AUTHOR of a book, the Internet provides a marketplace that you can't afford to ignore. Dozens of promotional opportunities are available online—and unlike old-fashioned marketing methods that involve printing hundreds of flyers and paying for hundreds of stamps, many of these opportunities are absolutely free. At most, they are available for the cost of a connection and Web site space.

TEN WAYS TO PROMOTE YOUR BOOK ON THE WEB

THE FIRST STEP IN BOOK promotion is often to develop an effective "author site." Chapter 12 discusses a variety of ways in which you can use such a site to promote your books. Once you've built that site, however, don't stop. You can use it as the focal point for a variety of promotional efforts, including the following:

WRITE ARTICLES FOR OTHER SITES

An excellent way to attract readers and build name recognition is to offer content to other sites. Whether you write fiction or nonfiction, you can develop informational articles that will be valuable to visitors and act as a lure to bring those visitors back to your own page. Consider the following possibilities:

- **Offer nonfiction articles or FAQs on the topic of your nonfiction book.** Look for both specific and general sites. For example, if you've written a book on breast cancer, look not only for sites that address that specific issue, but sites on health in general, women's health, nutrition, stress, and other topics that could relate to your own. Offer an article or FAQ that focuses on the interests of visitors to that specific site.

- **Offer nonfiction features on topics related to the background of your novel or other fiction.** For example, if you've written an Arthurian novel, look for sites that cover history, folklore, British travel, and related topics. If you've written a Victorian romance, consider covering various aspects of the period for sites likely to be visited by enthusiasts of Victoriana. For example, you might include sites covering costuming, collectibles, and other topics not clearly related to reading or writing.
- **Offer tips for writers that relate to your writing expertise or genre.** Consider offering a brief article or FAQ to one or more of the many writing sites online. You could discuss writing techniques that relate specifically to your work (e.g., "How to Research Victorian Customs") or general writing issues ("How to Find a Publisher").
- **Use your imagination.** What other topics could you address that might interest potential readers of your book? As you surf the Web, keep your eyes open for sites that such readers are likely to visit, and ask yourself what you could provide for that site that would inspire a reader to click the link to your own page. One way to find potential sites is to do a search for sites that already include a link to your page. On GOOGLE, for example, just enter "link:www.your address" as the search parameter. Another way to find sites that might appreciate your input is to search on your own name, or the title of your book.
- **Provide a bio.** Many sites can't pay for content, but they will generally offer you space for a bio and provide a direct link back to your page. Consider including your e-mail address for questions and feedback as well.

WRITE FOR NEWSLETTERS

No matter what subject you write about, there's likely to be a newsletter (or e-zine) that covers it, or at least something closely related. Search for newsletters and e-zines in one of the many directories online (see chapter 5 for a list of such directories). Most are free, so you can read a sample copy to determine the focus of the publication at no cost. Many newsletters post the most recent issue and/or archives of back issues on a Web site; others ask you to subscribe to receive the most recent issue. Once you've familiarized yourself with the style and content of the publication, contact the editor with an article idea. While many newsletters can't pay for material, they will list your URL, and some will provide a free classified ad for your book in exchange for your article.

SUBMIT YOUR BOOK FOR REVIEW

Many sites and newsletters review books. Look for book review opportunities in newsletters, e-zines, and sites that cover topics related to your book. Look also for book review sites that cover specific genres. Some of these are related to genre organizations; others are independent. Search for sites that focus entirely on book (or media) reviews. ABOUT.COM and SUITE101 offer pages specifically dedicated to literature, books, authors, and genres, as well as subject-specific pages that might also be willing to review your book. Develop a list of potential online reviewers and ask your publisher to include them when sending out review copies (most publishers are less likely to do this research on their own).

ADD YOUR URL TO "AUTHOR" LISTS AND LINKS

A number of sites list links to author pages on the Web, including pages hosted by authors and pages about authors. Look for author lists on genre-specific sites, general writing sites, and sites devoted to reading or literature. Join author Webrings, both general and specific. If you write nonfiction, look for Webrings that focus on the topic of your book. (Most author lists focus on fiction.) Visit YAHOO! and look under the "genre" directories for author listings; then submit your own URL for inclusion.

JOIN DISCUSSION GROUPS

Use GOOGLE GROUPS to find newsgroups and e-mail discussion lists that relate to your writing. Be creative. Don't stop at lists that focus on writing or literature. Look for lists that discuss subjects you've addressed in your writing, whether fiction or nonfiction. For example, if you've written a novel about an abusive relationship, consider looking for lists that discuss abuse issues, psychology, or related topics. Don't "advertise" your book to the list, but instead, become a participant and offer helpful advice in response to questions. Include your book title and URL in a discreet signature block to let participants know who you are and where to look for more information.

PROVIDE INFORMATION ABOUT YOUR BOOK
TO ONLINE BOOKSTORES

AMAZON.COM provides a number of opportunities for authors to promote and even "hand-sell" their books (see below). Other online bookstores also offer promotional opportunities. Some feature author interviews, and most provide a "review" section where you can include information about your book. Check a book-search site such as BOOKFINDER.COM to find out what online bookstores carry your book. Then visit each of those stores to find out what you can do to promote your title. Ask friends and customers to provide reviews. If you choose to place your own book description in a "review" section, be sure to note that you are the author; don't try to fool readers into thinking that you're a "happy customer." Keep your description short and free of hype.

PARTICIPATE IN ORGANIZATIONS RELATED TO YOUR WRITING

Search for sites that relate either to the type of writing you do (e.g., a genre organization) or to the subject of your writing. Find out how you can become active in the organization. If the organization sponsors conferences or seminars, you may be able to promote your books through these gatherings. Many organizations (such as the NATIONAL ASSOCIATION OF WOMEN WRITERS) also provide free Web space for members, where you can list your title and excerpts from your book or other information.

MAKE YOURSELF AVAILABLE FOR INTERVIEWS

Many sites are willing to interview authors. Look for interview opportunities with online bookstores, genre organizations, writing or topical newsletters and e-zines, and "guide" sites such as About.com and Suite101.

PROMOTE YOUR BOOK THROUGH "BOOKSTORE" PAGES

Search for personal and professional sites that offer a "bookstore" page (usually in conjunction with an associates or referral program sponsored by an online bookstore). Contact the host of the site to suggest that your book be added to the page. If you have self-published your book, you can set up your own affiliate program through CLICKBANK, offering other sites a percentage of sales made through their site. If you click on the "Register Products" button, you are taken to information on how to become a vendor. This includes information on how to set up your own affiliate program. Another way to find sites that might host your book is to search on a related or competing title.

PROMOTE YOUR ONLINE EFFORTS OFFLINE

For many readers, the Web is the first place they'll look for more information about a book or author. However, you may *meet* those readers offline—and when you do, you'll want to be able to direct them to your Web site. Be sure that you've added your URL and e-mail address to your business cards and professional stationery. Consider developing postcards that display your book cover on the front, and a brief blurb and your URL on the back. Custom-made bookmarks are another tool that many writers use to promote their books. Some writers even include their promotional cards, flyers, or bookmarks in anything they mail out—including their regular bills!

Whatever method of promotion you use, be sure to include your URL. Keep track of sites that list your URL, so that if it ever changes, you can contact them to update it. If possible, provide a link from your own site to the site that is promoting you. Link to articles you've written, interviews that you've given, and transcripts of author chats. If you're going to give a chat, announce it on your own site in advance.

TIPS FROM AN E-PUBLISHED AUTHOR

BY SHERY MA BELLE ARRIETA[1]

FOR ALL MY E-BOOKS, MY #1 tool is writing royalty-free/free reprint articles. Short articles (300–500 words) related to my e-books are able to help me spread the word about my e-books. Even though many balk at the idea of writing for free, my free articles have generated me the $3,000 + just for my last e-book on creating profitable e-mail workshops. In promoting my first three e-books, I used my writing/writer-related newsletters.

---

[1]Copyright © 2002 by Shery Ma Belle Arrieta. All rights reserved. Reprinted with permission from a personal e-mail from Shery Ma Belle Arrieta, author of four e-books, including *How to Create and Profit from Your Own E-mail Workshops in 3 Days or Less*. Information on Arrieta's books can be found at *http://ewritersplace.com*.

When I released my e-book on e-mail workshops in December 2001, I spent $75 on e-zine advertising (solo ads and regular e-zine ads). From that, I profited approximately $550. The rest of my sales for this particular e-book came from my affiliates, who promoted my e-book for me for free. For every sale they made, I gave them 50 percent of the e-book's selling price.

I also partnered with e-zine publishers and allowed them to customize one of my e-mail workshops for their subscribers. Their customized copies carry their affiliate links as they "sponsor" the free e-mail course.

On top of this, I update the e-book every four months, making my e-book more attractive and providing that value-added dimension to buyers (because they will never have to pay again to receive all future updates and revisions).

To date, I have about seventy-nine affiliates promoting this e-book for me, and the only place now where I promote the e-book is on my e-zine that deals with the topic of e-mail workshops and e-mail courses.

As for distributing my e-books ... First, all of my e-books are in PDF. For the first three e-books, I e-mail copies to buyers. For the last e-book, there is a protected download page.

First, while it is important for us writers to write what we know and write about what we want or are interested in, we shouldn't forget our audience. Thus, if you're interested in self-publishing an e-book, especially a nonfiction e-book, it's very important to determine your niche, and to determine if there is an interest in the topic you're planning to write about. It also pays to observe the latest trends—what types of informational products are selling, how are the top sellers doing it, what are the most cost-effective ways of marketing it online, etc.

Second, it's also very crucial to have a marketing plan from the beginning—even before you write your e-book. No matter how good your e-book is, it's going to be a flop if you don't know how to market it. So it can be very helpful to form a good relationship with e-zine publishers and site owners and people who are your e-book's target audience, even when you're only contemplating writing your e-book.

Third, have a strategy for promoting your e-book. Sure, you're a writer, but once you're done writing your e-book, you become a marketer/promoter. Think of ways you can market your e-book without breaking your bank account. In my case, I am marketing my e-book solely on the Internet, so I write free articles, do joint ventures with e-zine publishers, set up an affiliate program with an attractive commission, track my promotional campaigns and compare which ads are pulling the highest response, publish an e-zine related to the topic, and constantly promote my URLs.

Fourth, marketing and promoting your e-book is not a one-shot deal. It requires daily promotion. Brand yourself. In the free reprint circle, I am known as the expert on e-mail workshops and e-mail courses, and now that sequential autoresponders and e-mail courses are becoming more and more popular, my name is quickly being recognized as that of an expert on the subject, and this is just because I wrote the first and only e-book dealing with the creation of e-mail workshops and e-courses. So name recognition should be one of your goals.

And lastly, have fun doing it—from writing to promoting to giving support to your customers, because once you establish a good and reliable reputation with them, they will be more likely to become repeat customers.

PROMOTING YOUR BOOK ON AMAZON.COM

ONLINE BOOKSTORES ARE ONE OF the greatest boons to authors and small publishers. By linking your title directly from your Web site to its electronic bookstore page, you greatly increase the chance of catching those impulse buyers who want your book *now*. If you're distributing your own books, selling them through an online bookstore bypasses the problem of accepting credit cards on your Web site.

The trouble with online bookstores, however, is that buyers cannot browse before they buy. They can't hold your book in their hands, examine the cover and "blurbs" (including reviews), and flip through its contents. To buy a book online, one must take the risk of buying sight unseen.

Recognizing this problem, Amazon.com is taking steps to help authors and publishers (including small presses) promote their books more effectively. The site offers programs that enable self-publishers, small presses, and authors who distribute their own books to compete on virtually equal terms with the major presses—"leveling the playing field," as merchandising manager Dan Camacho puts it.

To get a sense of the possibilities, it's a good idea to read both the author and the publisher guides from Amazon.com, no matter which category you fall into. As an author, you can contribute significantly to the way your title is displayed—and you can encourage your publisher to take additional steps to enhance sales.

Here are some of the options recommended by Amazon.com:

MAKE SURE YOUR TITLE IS ACTUALLY LISTED IN THE AMAZON.COM CATALOG

Most books that have an ISBN and are available from a North American publisher, wholesaler, or distributor are added to the Amazon.com database automatically. In addition, most publishers take care of submitting necessary information (including your book cover, table of contents, etc.) to Amazon.com. However, if you're a self-publisher, or if your book was published by a small/independent press, you may need to add the information yourself. See Amazon.com's CATALOG GUIDE for details.

ENCOURAGE "IMPULSE PURCHASES" BY LINKING YOUR TITLE TO AMAZON.COM

Your "detail page" on Amazon.com lists basic information about your book, including the title, author, publisher, price, discount (if any), and how long it takes to ship. To find your "detail page," search for your title or ISBN. If you join Amazon.com's ASSOCIATE PROGRAM, you'll be able to earn a percentage for every sale of your book that is made through your Web site—and you'll also receive a report every quarter that shows how many books are sold.

SEND ADDITIONAL MATERIAL FOR YOUR DETAIL PAGE
TO AMAZON.COM

If you self-published your book, you can submit information about it directly to the Amazon.com catalog, including:

- Your cover, as a GIF or JPEG file
- A description of your book, up to 1,000 words
- An excerpt of your book, up to 1,000 words
- A table of contents (omitting page numbers, formatting, etc.)
- Reviews of your book or, more accurately, quotes of published reviews of up to 150 words each, including the name and date of the publication in which the review appeared
- Back cover copy, up to 1,000 words
- Inside cover flap copy, up to 1,000 words
- Your author bio, up to 1,000 words
- Author comments, up to 1,000 words (if you haven't already completed this information online)

Check Amazon.com's Catalog Guide (see Resources) carefully for the precise format in which to submit your information.

ASK YOUR PUBLISHER TO PARTICIPATE IN THE
LOOK INSIDE THE BOOK PROGRAM

Amazon.com now posts scanned pages from a number of titles, making it possible for readers to literally browse through a book. Generally, these pages will include the table of contents and the index, along with a sample chapter or pages chosen at random. Publishers (including self-publishers) can submit titles for inclusion in the LOOK INSIDE THE BOOK program. If your publisher hasn't participated, contact Amazon.com directly and ask whether, as the author, you can submit material.

JOIN THE ADVANTAGE PROGRAM FOR SELF-PUBLISHERS

If you are a self-publisher, you can join the ADVANTAGE program. Through this program, Amazon.com will stock a small quantity of your titles, so that books can be shipped directly from their warehouse. The advantage of the program is that you can market books directly through Amazon.com and offer immediate shipping (otherwise, Amazon will have to order books from you, which means that posted delivery time will be from four to six weeks). The disadvantage is the fee; Amazon.com receives 45 percent of all sales. The program includes:

- Inclusion in the appropriate "Browse Subjects" category
- Cover scanning
- Immediate shipping
- Online order tracking
- Monthly payments
- Marketing assistance

At the time of this writing, no other online bookstore has offered authors the same opportunities for self-promotion as Amazon.com. This may change in the future, as other bookstores recognize the role authors can play in promoting (and increasing the sales of) their books. In the meantime, it's still a good idea to get your book listed by as many online bookstores as possible, simply to make it available to as wide an audience as possible.

"CHATTING UP" YOUR BOOK

BY MARYJANICE DAVIDSON[2]

AUTHORS SEARCHING FOR WAYS TO promote their work often worry about cost. But one of the easiest and cheapest ways to get the word out is no more difficult or expensive than your teenager's computer habit. Online chats let you push your work, connect with your audience, and even establish business contacts for future work. However, many writers don't do them, perhaps due to stage fright or lack of awareness. If you're not using this valuable promotional tool, you should be. Following are tips for getting a chat started, running the chat smoothly, and following up to your best advantage.

First, figure out the purpose of your chat. Are you promoting a new release? Trying to stir interest in your backlist? Looking for feedback on a new style of writing (or new genre) you've undertaken? Without a clear reason for being there, you may find your chat drifting. As with a business appointment (which, after all, it is), you want to have goals in mind.

Once you know what you're going to chat about, the next step is to find a site which will help promote your idea. A good beginning is to go to a search engine, type "writer chats" and check out the opportunities that pop up. You can also narrow it by genre, e.g. "science fiction writer chats."

Once you've found a Web site, send the chat coordinator an e-mail offering a chat, and explain why you'll draw traffic. For my chat, "Escaping the Slush Pile," I pitched not only my relevant nonfiction release, but the fact that I have a full-time, nonwriting day job, write for several publishers in several genres, have sold eleven manuscripts in less than three years, and am raising two children. The chat coordinator was intrigued to receive an e-mail from someone who apparently never slept and wrote just about anything, and proposed a chat date.

Perhaps you're a neurologist who writes medical thrillers. Or you're a private investigator who writes mysteries, and can give chat participants a chance to find out how a real gumshoe thinks. Or you're an ex-con who writes true crime. All of these will make great chat topics.

Once you have a chat date, don't panic. Unfortunately, I did. As the date and time approached, I was tempted more than once to call it off. I, blabbermouth supreme, was overwhelmed by the burning question: What was I going to *say* to all those people?

The way to get around this problem is to have friends e-mail you questions for practice. Or think up questions you fear the most (in my case, it's the dreaded, "What is your book about?" I can never sum up 250 pages in three sentences), and formulate answers for them. With a little self-directed practice, you'll be a lot less nervous.

A week or two before the chat, promote it. Mention it on your e-mail lists and tell friends and family. Put it on your Web site, with a link to the chat site. Do it once or twice before the chat, so people can put it on their calendar, and again on the day of the chat.

Now. The big day is finally here. The coordinator has introduced you, and hundreds of (well, dozens of ... okay, maybe ten) people are waiting breathlessly for your words of wisdom. Here are the rules.

- **Obey chat etiquette.** In most chats, the host will introduce you and moderate. It's bad form to answer a question before the host calls on the person asking. Picture yourself as a guest in a classroom, and the teacher calls on kids as they raise their hands. The moderator is looking out for you, so if you're feeling overwhelmed, say so. Most chat rooms enable you to "talk" privately with the chat host. In one chat, I had a person asking question after question without waiting for others to be called on. The host privately contacted her and told her to back off, which she did.
- **Prepare, prepare, prepare.** Have your opening paragraph ready to go before the chat starts. At show time, you can just paste it into the chat. This way everyone in the room isn't silently waiting while you frantically type your hello. Mine went like this: "Hi, everyone! Thanks for joining us this evening. I hope I can answer your questions about avoiding the slush pile. I've got a book available on this topic; you can get more information at my Web site: *www.usinternet.com/users/alongi*. And now ... bring on the questions!"
- **Know your topic.** Hand in hand with preparation is knowing your topic. There's nothing worse than being asked a question you can't answer. In my slush pile chat, imagine if I hadn't been able to describe what separates a good query letter from a bad ... I would have sounded like an idiot, not to mention unprofessional.
- **Have five or six key points** you want to get across about yourself, your book, or your issue ... again, *before* you start. For one of my chats, I wanted chat participants to know my book was available, to know this wasn't my first release (read: I had a good publishing track record), what sorts of topics my book covered, and how to write an effective query letter.
- **Potty time.** Go to the bathroom before your chat starts; you sure won't be able to in the middle of the chat. And watch the water intake, particularly if you're scheduled to chat for more than an hour. I speak from bitter experience on this one.
- **Mention your Web site.** Mention your URL more than once. Ideally, the people you chatted with will want to know more about your work. You want them to have a place to go post-chat.
- **Be nice.** Answer your audience's questions personally (*"Well, DogLover, I think the hardest part of writing is sitting down and doing it."*). In addition to common courtesy, this will help people know what question you're addressing.

- **Long answers are better.** Here's a typical question. *GoodWriter: MJ, is it okay to send an electronic query or should you just snail mail?* Don't simply reply, *"It depends on where you're submitting."* There may have been several more questions asked while you formulate your reply, making it difficult for your audience to know what question you're answering. Try, *"GoodWriter, an electronic query can be used instead of snail mail, but you've really got to know your market. Make sure they accept e-queries before submitting."*
- **Jack be nimble.** It helps to be a fast typist. For me, the questions often come hard and fast. As I type one answer, three more people ask questions. Although it sounds a bit scary, these chats are my favorites; the time races by and it's loads of fun. If you have trouble keeping up, don't be afraid to type something like, "Bear with me, folks, I'm typing as fast as I can!" People will understand.
- **Numbers don't matter.** Speaking of people, don't fret about the number of participants … there's just no way to judge a successful chat based on who comes. My coordinator told me he'd seen anywhere from five to twenty people show up for a chat, and it had nothing to do with the author's name or topic (in our culture, it probably has more to do with TV reruns than anything else). If there are only two or three people in the chat room, you'll have plenty of time to be thorough and answer their questions.
- **Offer free stuff!** If you can, offer giveaways (usually copies of your latest release). It increases interest and attendance. Alternatively, offer free chapters. During my chat I suggested anyone who wanted a free sample chapter from *Escaping the Slush Pile* should e-mail me. The result was a self-promoter's dream.
- **Follow up.** After the chat, the coordinator will often post a transcript at his Web site. This is wonderful for you, because it's more free promotion; link to it! For months afterward, I received private e-mails from people who either participated in the chat or saw the transcript and had questions about my upcoming release. Also, send a thank-you to the chat coordinator afterward for their help, and don't forget to e-mail them a few months later to ask if they'd like to do another chat.

To keep your name and product fresh in people's minds, try to do at least one chat a month. It won't take much of your time (or, better, your money), and the benefits can be huge. In my case, chats cost me a few minutes of promotion the week of the chat, and an hour out of my life the day it takes place. Which, given that I normally would have spent that hour gorging on coffee ice cream and watching *Simpsons* reruns, is time well spent indeed.

ON THE INTERNET, AS ANYWHERE else, the key to a successful promotion is persistence. Think of the Web not as a giant shopping mall, but as the world's biggest library. Your contribution to the flow of information will be the best possible advertisement for your writing—and with luck, you should see the difference on the bottom line of your next royalty statement.

RESORCES

GENERAL BOOK PROMOTION RESOURCES

Authors on the Highway
http://publishersweekly.reviewsnews.com/index.asp?layout = authorsMain
A place to list your upcoming book signings, speaking engagements, and other "on the road" promotional activities.

Book Marketing Update
www.bookmarket.com/index.html
Although the primary focus of this site is to promote a newsletter and other products, it offers a variety of free reports and other materials of use to self-published authors or authors seeking to promote their own books.

Book Promotion Resources
www.writing-world.com/promotion/index.shtml
This section on Writing-World.com includes articles on book signings, speaking engagements, interviews, and other book promotion techniques, as well as a series of articles on book promotion by MaryJanice Davidson.

E-mail Newsletters: A Growing Market for Freelancers
www.contentious.com/articles/1–10/editorial1–10.html
An article on how to write for e-mail newsletters.

E-mail Signatures
www.apromotionguide.com/sig.html
Tips on using your e-mail signature for promotion.

EventCaster
www.netread.com/calendar
Offering a talk or a book signing?
You may be able to announce your event to local news media free through this site.

Literary Times
www.tlt.com/news/itiner.htm
Provides a place for romance authors to post events, such as chats and book signings.

Midwest Book Review/Publisher Resources
www.midwestbookreview.com/bookbiz/pub_res.htm
Among a vast array of links, this site includes a good selection of book review sources.

Press Kit
www.writing-world.com/press/current.shtml
Debbie Ridpath Ohi's column on book promotion.

Your Free Book Promotion Countdown Checklist
www.geocities.com/~lorna_tedder/virgins.html
Extensive list of things to do to promote your book before and after publication.

AUTHOR AND WRITER CHAT SOURCES

Gotta Write Network
http://hometown.aol.com/gwnlitmag/index.html

iVillage Readers and Writers Channel
www.ivillage.com
Skip past the introductory ad to reach the site.

TalkCity
www.talkcity.com
A site dedicated to talk and discussion, including author chats and general

reading chats (e.g., "SF&Lit Chat, a discussion of the best and brightest in SF&F literature"). Transcripts of previous chats also available.

WordsWorth
www.wordsworth.com/www/present/interviews
A bookstore that hosts author interviews and author promotional pages.

Writer's BBS
www.writers-bbs.com/chat.html
Offers chat rooms, discussion forums, and an e-zine entitled, *Fish Eggs for the Soul.*

Writer Space
www.writerspace.com
An author community focusing on romance and mystery.

ORGANIZATIONS THAT HOST WEB SITES

Horror Writers Association
www.horror.org

Mystery Writers of America
www.mysterywriters.org

Romance Writers of America
www.rwanational.com

Science Fiction Writers of America
www.sfwa.org

SFF Net
www.sff.net
Hosts author pages in a variety of genres, plus links to other author pages.

PAGES LISTING AUTHOR SITES

Authors
http://contemporarylit.about.com

Children's Book Council Authors and Illustrators Page
www.cbcbooks.org/html/links.html

One Woman's Writing Retreat
www.prairieden.com

Romance Writers of America/Author Websites
www.rwanational.org/author_websites.stm

SFF Net/People Pages
www.sff.net/people.asp

Useful Links for Romance Writers and Readers/Authors
www.jaclynreding.com/links
Use the pull-down menu at the top to be directed to author links or other parts of the site.

WritersNet
www.writers.net

Yahoo! Directory/Genres
http://d1.dir.dcx.yahoo.com/arts/humanities/literature/genres
Check under your preferred genre for the "Authors" category, and submit your listing.

AMAZON.COM PROGRAMS FOR WRITERS

Amazon.com
www.amazon.com

- Advantage program—for small presses, self-publishers, and authors who distribute their own titles:
www.amazon.com/exec/obidos/subst/partners/direct/direct-application.html
- Associates program—offering a commission for selling books (including your own) from your Web site:
www.amazon.com/exec/obidos/subst/partners/associates/associates.html

- Catalog Guide—describing how to include supporting material (such as chapter excerpts, reviews, etc.) on your book's "detail" page: *www.amazon.com/exec/obidos/ subst/ partners/publishers/ catalog-guide.html*
- Look Inside the Book program: *www.amazon.com/exec/obidos/subst/ partners/publishers/look-inside.html*

BOOK-SEARCH SITES

AddAll Book Searching and Price Comparison
www.addall.com

Searches thirty-four bookstores for titles and price comparisons.

BookFinder.com
www.bookfinder.com
This site will search bookseller databases online (including electronic bookstores and databases provided by "real-world" bookstores) to locate your title and provide a comparison of prices and shipping information.

<< CHAPTER 12 >>

DO YOU NEED A WEB SITE?

OR THE FIRST TIME IN history, writers have access to something they've craved since the first cuneiform was chiseled: Access to worldwide publicity at virtually no cost. The Internet offers writers an opportunity to promote their books, reach out to their fans, establish their expertise, and enhance their professional standing with editors. Establishing a Web site can cost as little as $10 a month—or less, if you choose a free Web hosting site.

More and more writers—from best-selling authors like DIANA GABALDON to relative unknowns who have just launched their first title—are recognizing the importance of setting up a professional author site. Such a site can serve a variety of purposes, and produce a range of benefits, as Debbie Ridpath Ohi discusses in this excerpt from her "Press Kit" column on Writing-World.com.

THE IMPORTANCE OF AN AUTHOR WEB SITE

BY DEBBIE RIDPATH OHI[1]

JEANINE BERRY HAS MORE THAN one publisher, so she finds her Web site essential. "How else are you going to get information about all your books together in one place?" She uses her site to display her book covers, posts excerpts and reviews, and posts a monthly newsletter "and other features to keep readers coming back."

Children's author Nancy McArthur says her Web site is "like an easily updated color brochure that can be called up any time, anywhere, and be printed out as needed." She provides a FAQ, author bio, suggestions and class activities for teachers and librarians. "I get e-mails out of the blue from children, parents, teachers, and librarians who probably wouldn't communicate with me otherwise. I also got a very lucrative writing assignment from an educational publishing company that found me through my Web site."

Cindy Vallar is the author of a Scottish historical novel and has added related resource information to her site. She says that people checking out her site for reference information will often come back and buy her books, as well as recommending her site to others. Vallar was recently asked to do workshops for other writers because of the information on her site.

Sophia Dembling says the mail link on her site encourages readers to send her feedback, which she enjoys. She also likes the international exposure that having a Web site can bring. "Though the book is in bookstores in Texas only, I've had hits from France, Australia, Austria, China, and other countries."

Joyce and Jim Lavene publish romance and mystery titles under various pseudonyms. They have one site for each genre, and also do an opt-in promotional mailing by e-mail with approximately a hundred subscribers.

Julie H. Ferguson says that her site has helped her writing and speaking career. "I really try hard to do all my communications electronically. I also sell my books, e-booklets, and fully narrated CD-ROMs of my workshops on my Web site. This side of the business— and let's face it, writers have to sell their work to make a living—is key. I believe that I will eventually make more money through my Web site than through public appearances and writing articles, etc."

Former *Inscriptions* editor Jade Walker's Web site has changed over time. When she was a full-time freelancer, Walker's site included her résumé and best clips. Web-savvy editors will often check out freelancers through Google before they hire, Walker says, and adds that the fact that you can maintain a Web site "tells potential clients about your ability to write, edit, do graphics, and creatively design a page in HTML. In today's market, just being a writer isn't always enough to pay the bills. You need to be multitalented."

Now that Walker has a full-time job in the media, the purpose of the site has changed to emphasize her editorial skills and book projects. "My Weblog keeps readers informed about my everyday writing adventures and interests. The 'books' page promotes my publishing achievements. And in time, my weekly column will either be syndicated or published as a collection in book format. Until then, each column brings in new readers, and helps reinforce my need to write on deadline."

Burr Hazen's windsurfing instruction book was originally supposed to be published in print form with sixteen chapters. Now he's selling each of the chapters as individual e-books instead. In the first six weeks, and well before he started actively promoting the site, Hazen had already sold 250 books.

Carole Moore says that through her site she has already received a wide variety of job offers and inquiries. "My work has been carried by CompuServe and reprinted in many different countries," says Moore, "Any writer who wants to be a contender who doesn't have a Web site, needs to regain consciousness. Going online was a great move for me. I just wish I'd done it sooner!"

BEFORE YOU RUSH OUT TO set up a home page, however, stop and take a deep breath. The Internet is flooded with sloppy, unimpressive, cutesy, trivial, or heavy-handed "writer" pages. As a professional, you want something that says more than "Hi, my name is Bob, click here to read my *stories*, click here to see a picture of my *dog!*" Before you launch, take some time to determine what your readers (or potential readers) might wish to see on your site—what would be likely to bring them there, and bring them back.

The key word in building an author Web site is "content." Most readers are *not* interested in a site that is primarily one big, electronic, slow-loading adver-tisement. It's important to avoid giving the impression that the only thing you want from visitors is their money. While your motivation for building a Web site is certainly going to be based on what you can *get* from that site, the mechanism for developing a successful Web site is based on what you are willing to *give*. Put another way, while you may be wondering what benefits a Web site will bring to you, your readers want to know what benefits you have to offer *them* for visiting.

FIVE TYPES OF AUTHOR SITES

FOLLOWING ARE SUGGESTIONS FOR THE type of *content* you might wish to include on your site, depending on its purpose. (Chapter 13 discusses how to design and promote your site.) Note, however, that before you post any previously published materials on your site (such as book excerpts, short stories, or articles), you must be sure that you own the rights to do so. As mentioned in chapter 8, if you've sold all rights, all electronic rights, or exclusive electronic rights to your work, you may no longer have the right to post it on your site. Some publishers will make exceptions for personal Web sites, so if you're not sure, ask!

THE CLIP SITE
One of the questions often asked by writers who are sending out queries electron-ically is "how do I handle clips?" Editors do not want you to send clips as attach-ments, but many still wish for an opportunity to review your previously published work. The answer, in many cases, is to develop a "clip" site—a Web site where you can post samples of your best work for editors to view. Such a site should include:

- **An introductory home page** that provides an overview of your credentials and a list of the clips available on the site. If possible, organize your clips by topic area. If you have written on a variety of topics, you might wish to provide a top-level table of contents on this page that lists the topics on the site (e.g., pets, gardening, travel). Each of those categories would then lead to a more detailed menu of the clips posted on that particular topic. Your home page should also include your contact information. (For security and privacy reasons, most writers now prefer to post only an e-mail address rather than an actual mailing address.)

- **Selected clips of your best work.** Note that I said "selected"—you don't need to post everything you've written since your first essay was published in the high school paper. Editors don't have time to wade through a mass of material; give them the highlights. Be sure that you own the rights to the material you are posting; if you've sold exclusive (or all) electronic rights to a piece, you may not be able to post it on your own site. (Many electronic publications, however, will make an exception for personal Web sites.) When posting clips, it's best to format them as independent HTML files, rather than simply scanning magazine articles and posting them as image files. Image files are cumbersome and slow to download, and a magazine clipping may contain copyrighted elements that don't belong to you (e.g., artwork, etc.). If you prefer to scan your clips, convert them into text files (and be sure to proofread them for errors).
- **Copyright information.** To further protect your work, make sure that you include a copyright notice on every clip. In your copyright notice, list the title of the material, the copyright date, your name, the name of the publication in which it appeared, and the date of publication. (This information will also be useful to anyone using your material for research.) Your copyright notice might look something like this:

"Ten Ways to Get the Most from the Internet"
© 1997 by Ima Good Author.[2]
Originally published in *Write Write Write*, October 1997
All rights reserved. For reprint information, contact *IGAuthor@myisp.com*.

A clip site of this type also works well for writers of short fiction and poetry. While editors of fiction or poetry publications are less likely to visit your site to read your previously published works, such a site can be a good way to attract readers and fans.

THE EXPERT/INFORMATION SITE

Some writers focus upon a particular area of interest, expertise, or passion. For others, writing is a secondary interest, in support of or in the context of a special interest, hobby, career, area of study, etc. If you fall into one of these categories, your goal may be not so much to convince editors that you are a brilliant *writer*, but that you are an expert on the subject that you write about. Or, you may be interested primarily in promoting a better understanding of your field or subject. In this case, you may wish to develop a Web site that functions more to *educate* visitors than to showcase your writing (although it can easily do both). Such a site would be likely to include:

[2]Use the HTML code "©" for the copyright symbol (©).

- **A home page that describes or introduces the subject area itself.** Title this page in such a way that anyone interested in the subject will be easily able to find it. Choose keywords that would be likely to be chosen by someone searching on your subject, and make sure that those words appear near the top of your page (where they will be given more weight by search engines). Make sure that someone visiting your home page will be able to determine, at a glance, what subject is being covered by the site, what materials and resources you are offering, and how to access those materials.
- **Comprehensive information.** The best way to establish your expertise on a subject is to provide expert information. This could include articles you've published on the topic (which will also serve double-duty as a "clip" site), or perhaps a FAQ about the topic, or even material that you write specifically for the site itself (rather than for publication elsewhere). You might want to post a regular column, such as a news update column that keeps visitors in touch with developments in your field, or a Q&A column in which you answer questions posed by your readers. Your goal is to ensure that someone coming to your site will come away with worthwhile, useful information (and perhaps a desire to come back and learn more). Don't tease the visitor by promising information you don't deliver, or by suggesting that the reader can find out the answers to questions you pose on the site by buying your books; this kind of "bait and switch" site simply turns off potential readers.
- **Links.** Surf the Web for other high-quality sites on the same subject, or on related subjects. Remember that visitors rely on you to be selective, so don't add a link to a site you haven't personally screened. Contact the hosts or Webmasters of the sites you're linking to and invite them to offer reciprocal links to your own site. Check your lists of links regularly, removing dead links and updating those that have changed.
- **A bookstore.** Consider offering a "bookstore" of titles related to your subject (including your own!). This will give readers the benefit of your expert recommendations, and show editors that you are keeping up with new titles in the field. Plus, by linking your book recommendations to an online bookstore such as Amazon.com or Barnes & Noble through an affiliate program, you'll earn a percentage each time a visitor buys a book through your site. Often, your affiliate fees will more than support the cost of hosting your site itself.
- **Your credentials.** Keep your bio short and professional. Focus on anything that supports your standing as an expert: education, credentials, job history, personal experience, etc. Let visitors (and editors) know that they can trust you as a source. (Your credentials could appear on your home page, or on a separate page within the site.)

THE NOVELIST'S SITE

Novelists are finding the Web an excellent place to highlight past, present, and future books of all types and genres. Thanks to the Web, novelists no longer seem remote and unreachable figures; many encourage fan feedback by offering an e-mail address and responding to readers' comments and questions. Such a site often includes the following elements:

- **A home page** that clearly lists your name (e.g., "Welcome to the Joan Q. Novelist Web Site"). Keep in mind that most fans will search for your work by author name, not by title, so your name should be prominently listed toward the top of your home page. Make sure the reader can immediately determine what you are offering on your site—e.g., chapter excerpts, other fiction, background and research information, etc. Your site should be more than an online order form for your books. This page might also include the titles of your novels, and possibly cover images (though you should be cautious about posting too many images on your front page, as this can cause it to be slow to load).
- **An author bio.** Fans will want to know more about you, so satisfy their curiosity with a brief, professional biographical sketch (and a photo, if you wish). This is a good place to discuss how you began writing, why you write the types of books you do, your expertise relating to those books, your future writing plans—and, of course, how many cats you have. Many writers also post copies of interviews that they have provided for the media or other Web sites.
- **A bibliography.** Many authors provide a list of all their writings, including short stories, awards, and any other credits.
- **Descriptions of your books.** This is your chance to give readers a better summary (and teaser) than they will find on the backs of your books. Try to include images of your book covers as well. (A quick way to obtain cover images is to search for your books on Amazon.com; you can download either the thumbnail-size image on your book's "detail" page, or click on that image for a larger version.) If you are providing lengthy descriptions of more than one novel, create a separate page for each. These pages might also include selections from positive reviews of your book.
- **Excerpts.** Selections from current or forthcoming novels are often a major attraction on novelists' sites—and an excellent sales tool as well. Such excerpts give readers something to take away, but also leave them hungry for more. Choose an excerpt that a reader can understand without having read the rest of the book—but ends with a cliff-hanger that will make the reader *want* to read the rest of the book. (You may need your publisher's permission to post such an excerpt.)
- **Background information.** Is your novel set in a particular historical period, locale, or cultural milieu that readers might want to learn more about? Your Web site is an excellent place to answer questions, post background history or details, explain unfamiliar terms and concepts, and provide links to other sources of information on the Web.
- **Writing tips.** Many of your fans undoubtedly dream of writing the types of books you write. Give them a hand by offering some advice on writing in your field or genre. Such a section will also improve your chances of receiving links from other writers and organizations in your field, because other writers and organizations will regard it as a useful site for writers as well as readers.

- **A news page.** Let readers know when your latest book is coming out, what awards you've won, when you'll be appearing on television or radio talk shows, when and where you're giving talks or book signings, and anything else of a newsworthy nature. Some authors also provide links to fan sites, book reviews, and online interviews.
- **Links.** No site is complete without a few links. Choose those that relate to the general purpose and content of your site—other sources of background information or other sites for writers in your genre. You might also seek reciprocal links with other authors in your field.
- **Other works.** Some authors use their Web sites to archive previously published stories. This works well if the stories are relevant to the novel you're trying to promote. Be careful, however, about posting material that is likely to shatter the image your fans have of you as an author; this could have a negative effect on the works you're currently trying to promote.
- **Ordering information.** Make sure that visitors can find out where and how to get your books. One easy way to prompt sales is to link your book titles to an online bookstore, such as Amazon.com.

THE NONFICTION-BOOK AUTHOR'S SITE

The key difference between a fiction and a nonfiction author site is that while fiction readers tend to be author-focused, nonfiction readers tend to be subject-focused. A Web site designed to promote a nonfiction book, therefore, should usually focus on the subject of the book, and include:

- **An introductory home page** that will attract visitors searching for information on your subject area. Your name may be less important than keywords that describe the subject. To be indexed properly in search engines, those subject keywords should be close to the top of the page.
- **Information of value to readers.** The best way to promote a nonfiction book is to offer useful *free* information. Turn your site into a resource on the topic of your book. Offer FAQs, articles, and other forms of information that will help the reader immediately. Avoid, at all costs, the appearance that the information is just a plug for your book or that you're manufacturing some sort of hype or crisis that your book will solve. Make sure that visitors can benefit from your site itself, whether they buy the book or not; this will also encourage referrals.
- **Links.** A good way to make your site a genuine resource is to include a list of links to other sites covering similar topics. This will help convince visitors that you are genuinely interested in sharing information, rather than simply trying to peddle a product.
- **Your credentials.** Before accepting your advice or information, readers will want to know why they should trust you. Readers won't want personal details here, but information about your education, experience, background, and anything else that will demonstrate your qualifications will be helpful.

- **A summary of your book.** On a nonfiction site, it helps to keep book promos low-key. Offer a summary of the book, along with a cover image, on a separate page that also includes ordering information (such as a link to an online bookstore).

THE WRITING SITE

Initially, one of the most common features of any author site was a selection of writing tips. Now, sites for writers have proliferated beyond count. There's still room on the Web, however, for high-quality writing advice.

The best approach to a writing-tips site today is to move beyond general "how to write" (or "how to format your manuscript") topics and focus on your area of specialty. What can you offer writers that isn't easily found elsewhere? Focus your site on writing for a specific genre, category, or field.

For example, if you're a mystery writer, share tips on how to become a mystery writer—or how to become a better mystery writer. Don't just talk about writing techniques, but tell your readers where to find helpful research information, such as sites that cover forensics or police procedures. Offer links to publishers of mystery books or short fiction. Seek reciprocal links with other mystery sites. Offer a "contest" page that lists writing contests for amateur mystery authors. Offer links to mystery e-zines. Offer a bookstore of how-to books for mystery writers.

A writing site will need much the same type of content as an expert site, including:

- **An informative home page** that describes the types of writing tips that will be offered. If your name is well known in the field, make sure it is prominently displayed on the page. If readers are more likely to locate your page through an information search than an author search, however, move your name and biographical information to a lower position on the page and keep the topical information toward the top.
- **An array of top-quality information.** Again, consider posting previously published articles, FAQs, a column, and anything else that will help writers (and would-be writers) improve their skill. An important consideration to keep in mind is the quality of your own writing: Be sure that your information not only discusses good writing, but models it as well! Nothing will detract from a writing page as quickly as flawed grammar, spelling and punctuation errors, or errors in content.
- **Links.** If you're offering a general writing site, you can go crazy with links. If you're specializing in some field, however, limit your links to the area that your site addresses. For the mystery writing example, one might include links to mystery writers' organizations, sites of other mystery writers, sites that address the how-tos of mystery writing, and sites that provide useful research or reference information for mystery writers. A good selection of links helps establish you as a resource site and will encourage related sites (such as other mystery authors and organizations) to link back to you.
- **A bookstore.** Rare is the writing site that doesn't offer a selection of the best writing books on the topic. If you've published (and are promoting) your own

writing book, consider listing it both on your bookstore page and also on a separate page of its own, where you can offer an expanded summary and a cover image.

- **Writing samples.** If you're a novelist, you may wish to incorporate a "tips for writers" section into a site designed primarily to promote your novels. If you write short fiction, consider posting samples of some of your previously published works. These can serve several purposes: to attract readers, to serve as clips for future editors, and to stand as examples of the techniques you discuss in your "tips" section. Again, be sure that you own the relevant rights to the material you post.
- **Your credentials.** If you're a fiction writer, describe your writing background and feel free to add some personal information. Consider including a bibliography page of published works, along with cover images of your books. If you're discussing nonfiction writing, keep your bio professional, listing credentials and credits but leaving out such personal details as how you started writing. (However, it's perfectly okay to mention that you have a spouse and twenty cats!)

Needless to say, these aren't the only reasons writers launch Web sites—and in many cases, these reasons may overlap. You're certainly free to mix and match the items listed above, as well as to add items of your own. Be cautious, however, about attempting to develop a Web site that serves too many purposes at once (e.g., to promote your novel, showcase nonfiction clips, help writers, and establish your expertise in a completely unrelated area). Many writers have several separate career tracks. If you're one of them, consider creating a separate, stand-alone Web site (with its own home page) that supports each of your career goals.

FIVE THINGS EVERY WRITER'S WEB SITE NEEDS

NO MATTER WHAT THE PURPOSE of your site is, you want it to function smoothly and present an attractive "face" to your visitors and customers. To accomplish this, certain elements are essential, including:

A USEFUL TABLE OF CONTENTS

Whether you think of it as a table of contents, a menu, or a site index, your site needs one (or several). A typical approach is to offer a general, first-level TOC on your home page that provides an overview of the contents—e.g., Articles, Bibliography, Resources, etc. A second-level TOC can then be developed for each section—for example, under "Articles," you should list all the articles posted on your site. However, beware of building in too many layers of menus (e.g., Articles >> Articles for Writers >> Fiction Articles >> Short Fiction >> Finally, The Actual Article List). Remember that each layer of menus adds an extra barrier between your visitors and your content—and another opportunity for that visitor to grow impatient and move on to a more accessible site.

In addition to your main TOC, be sure to include a version of the top-level TOC on each page of your site. This enables visitors to navigate within your site without having to return to the home page.

ANNOTATED LINKS

Every site needs links—and one of the best ways to please visitors is to annotate those links with a brief description. Let visitors know, in a line or two, what to expect when they visit the recommended site. In addition, it's a good idea to include not only the title of the site, but the actual URL. Then, if visitors print out your material to read later, they can determine what the URL is without having to go back to your site. (I learned this when I distributed copies of my own articles at a conference—and realized that a list of underlined site links with no actual URLs wasn't terribly helpful!)

Check your links regularly to make sure they still active. If you're daunted by the thought of doing this manually, don't despair: There's an easier way. Simply submit your URL to a link-checking site (see the Resources section of chapter 13), and you'll receive a list of inactive or inaccurate links within minutes. You can also purchase inexpensive software to check your site's links.

A COPYRIGHT NOTICE

Actually, you may need not just one, but several copyright notices on your site. The first should be a blanket copyright notice that covers your entire site. This should be posted prominently on your home page and might read something like this:

Flights of Fantasy—Copyright © 2003 by Joan Q. Novelist
All rights reserved on all material on all pages in this Web site, plus the
copyright on compilations and design, graphics, and logos. For information
on reprinting material from this site, please contact JQNovelist@myISP.com

Keep in mind, however, that many visitors may arrive at your site indirectly, either through a link or a search engine that takes them to one of the subordinate pages on your site rather than the home page. If you post articles, columns, or clips on your site, therefore, you may also wish to include a separate copyright notice with each article. (See The Clip Site, on pages 161–62, for an example of a single-page copyright notice.)

A HIT COUNTER

The best way to find out whether your site is serving its purpose is to track the number of visitors it receives. To do this, you'll need a counter not only on your home page, but on each separate "content" page. This will enable you to determine which aspects of your site are attracting attention and which are being ignored. For example, if your home page registers two hundred visitors in a single month and your article on "The Importance of Flossing" registers only two, you know that only 1 percent of your visitors are interested in this article—a good clue that you might want to swap it for something more enticing.

Your hit counter should provide some indication of the longevity of your site. For example, you might want to incorporate it into a phrase such as, "You are visitor number [XXXXX] since January 1, 2003." This is also a good place to include a "last updated" date, to let visitors know how fresh your material is. On the other hand, if you don't update your pages, leave this information off, or visitors will get the impression that your material might be old news, no matter how timeless it is.

An alternative to the hit counter is to sign up with an ISP that offers a Web tracking service. Many ISPs include this type of service (which is generally provided by a separate company, such as WEBTRENDS) as part of their "business" Web-hosting packages. Rates for this type of package vary widely; but can be as low as $15 per month. A Web tracking service can be useful if you have a large number of pages and don't want to have to create (and check) a counter for each individual page. You'll be able to determine how many people visit your site each day (or even each hour), where they visit from, and what search engines and keywords are being used to locate information on your site. You'll also be able to track errors in your site (e.g., pages not found due to a faulty internal link). However, such services generally track only the most popular pages of your site; they won't give you the statistics on every page.

CONTACT INFORMATION

Unless you prefer to toil in seclusion, include an e-mail address so that your visitors (and fans) can contact you. On your bookstore or links pages, you may want to invite visitors to suggest additional references or links. (It's wise to have a policy about the types of links you will accept—for example, no commercial links—so that you can explain, if necessary, why you are choosing not to add a particular link.) Another way to solicit feedback from your visitors is to incorporate a guest-book into your site.

THREE THINGS YOUR WEB SITE CAN DO WITHOUT

IN DEVELOPING A WEB SITE, as in writing itself, it's as important to know what to leave out as what to leave in. Certain elements can significantly detract from the professionalism of your site, including:

UNPUBLISHED WRITINGS

Many would-be writers view the Internet as the ideal place to self-publish material that they have been unable to market. Unfortunately, the only result has been to convince savvy surfers that self-published stories, poems, or novels on a Web site are an indication not of professionalism but of desperation. Even if your unpublished materials are of the highest quality, posting them online is likely to tarnish your professional image. (Note that this does not apply to materials written specifically for the site itself.) Also, as I mentioned in previous chapters, posting your unpublished materials online raises a question of whether you have used up "first rights" to those materials. Many publishers will regard such materials that have appeared online, even on a personal Web site, as "reprints," which means that by posting your unpublished work online, you could be reducing (or losing) your chances of selling that work later.

TOO MUCH PERSONAL INFORMATION

If your goal in developing a Web site is to advance your writing career, be sure to keep it as professional as possible—which means making sure that it won't be confused with a holiday newsletter to friends and family. This is not the place for news about your grandchildren or photos of the family pets. That doesn't mean that you can't develop a personal site, but you'd be wise to keep it separate from your writing site. At most, add a discreet link that points readers to "Joan Q. Novelist's home page."

LINKS TO EVERYTHING

Resist the temptation of offering links to every site on the Web that interests you, no matter what its subject. No matter whether you are a veteran rock-climber, an armchair archaeologist, or a connoisseur of filksinging groups, leave those personal-interest links off your professional page, unless they somehow relate to its focus.

THE GREATEST DANGER OF ALL

THE GREATEST DANGER OF A writer's Web site is not what you put on or leave off. It is the speed with which such a site can consume your writing time.

The temptation to tinker with a Web site is hard to resist. There's always the urge to redesign your pages, add new elements, rewrite your menus, add better graphics, or simply to surf for new links or new ways to promote your site. Moreover, it's easy to justify such tinkering as "working to promote my novel" or "gathering important information."

Before you quite know what has happened, however, you'll have spent the entire day tinkering—without adding a single word to that article or story you're trying to complete by deadline. (Trust me. I know.) Designing and maintaining a site can be an excellent way to promote your writing and advance your career, but it should not be allowed to *replace* writing. High-tech procrastination is still procrastination. If necessary, ration yourself to only so many hours of site development per week or month. Otherwise, you may end up with the perfect writer's Web site—and nothing for it to promote!

RESOURCES

ARTICLES ON WEB SITE DEVELOPMENT

Building a Writer's Website
www.sff.net/people/victoriastrauss/
victoria%20strauss%20whywebsite.html
Ideas and design tips from fantasy author
Victoria Strauss.

**Concise, Scannable, and Objective: How to
Write for the Web**
www.useit.com/papers/webwriting/writ-
ing.html
The results of a study by John Morkes and
Jakob Nielsen on how users "read" online,
with tips on writing for an online audience.

Jakob Nielsen's Alertbox
www.useit.com/alertbox
Numerous articles on Web site design,
content, readability, and related issues.

Usable Web
http://usableweb.com/index.html
"A collection of 1317 links and
accompanying information about human
factors, user interface issues, and usable
design specific to the World Wide Web."

(For HTML and Web site development
resources, see chapter 13.)

AUTHOR WEB SITES LISTED IN THIS CHAPTER

Stephanie Barron (Francine Matthews)
www.francinemathews.com

Jeanine Berry
http://clik.to/Jeanineberry

Sophia Dembling
www.YankeeChick.com

Julie H. Ferguson
www.beaconlit.com

Diana Gabaldon
www.dianagabaldon.com

Burr Hazen
www.windsurfingbible.com

Joyce and Jim Lavene
www.joyceandjimlavene.com

Nancy McArthur
http://junior.apk.net/~mcarthur

Carole Moore
www.thehumorwriter.com

Cindy Vallar
www.cindyvallar.com

CHAPTER 13

DESIGNING AND PROMOTING YOUR SITE

WHILE CONTENT IS ALL-IMPORTANT IN attracting visitors to your Web site, design can make the difference between keeping those visitors and driving them away. A poorly designed site, with pages that are difficult to download or navigate or that offer no clues as to their content, is likely to be dismissed as not worth the effort.

Building a Web site doesn't have to be intimidating or expensive. While some writers hire designers to develop and maintain their sites, the truth is that if you can handle basic word-processing tasks (let alone desktop publishing), you can easily construct a Web site. The issue is not so much how your Web site looks, but how easily the user can access the information you consider important.

I'll share a little secret with you: The only people who are really impressed by glitzy site designs are other designers. The rest of us may think a Java-based fire-breathing dragon is cute, but it's not what we came for. And for some of your visitors, too much design can actually get in the way.

Think of assembling your Web site as similar to assembling a book. No matter what your content may be, certain elements need to go in certain places. You'll need a table of contents that will enable a reader to quickly locate your material. You'll need chapters, or a similar division of content. You might also want an index, a copyright notice, an author bio. You may wish to include illustrations, but those should be chosen to enhance your content and not simply to dress up the page. Finally, your site must be accessible. If the Internet is analogous to a vast electronic library, you want its patrons to be able to locate your book on its shelves.

MAKING YOUR SITE "USER-FRIENDLY"

WHILE THERE IS NO SINGLE right way to construct a Web site, certain consid-erations are likely to win the hearts of your visitors and encourage them to recom-mend your page to others. For example, while today's array of multimedia bells and whistles can be tempting, it's vital to remember that not everyone has the fastest modem, the most sophisticated processor, or the latest browser. If your site takes so long to download that a visitor could brew a pot of coffee while waiting, or if your rotating globe or fire-breathing dragon causes the user's browser to crash (tak-ing the system with it), visitors will move on. More importantly, they won't recom-mend your site to others or link to your page.

Whether your goal is self-promotion or a desire to educate and inform others, it simply doesn't make sense to erect technological barriers between your material and your audience. The following elements all have the potential to create such barriers and should be considered carefully:

MAKE YOUR SITE EASY TO VIEW

Ideally, a page should fit within the width of a typical computer screen or browser. (Keep in mind that some users may access your site through a laptop with a small screen.) If a page is too wide for the screen, users must scroll horizontally as well as vertically to view your material.

An easy guideline is to think of your page as just that: a page of paper. If your material won't fit within the width of a normal sheet of paper, it won't fit certain browser windows either. While many elements of your site may be flexible and adapt to different window widths, make sure "fixed" items (such as tables and large images) can be contained within that page size. If your site design is based on tables, keep in mind that specifying column widths can prevent your page from adapting to the user's screen or printer.

If you use frames, this will further limit the amount of space available for viewing your page. An oversized left-hand menu frame can cause your viewing frame to shrink dramatically. Some pages that look fine on a full screen don't work nearly so well when shrunk to a three-inch window.

MAKE YOUR SITE EASY TO PRINT

The same guidelines apply to printing: If your material won't fit on a sheet of paper, it will have to be reduced or printed horizontally. Reductions may make parts of your page hard to read, and horizontal printing is just plain annoying. (Again, basing your site design on tables with specified column widths can affect the user's ability to print out pages.)

Always test your site's printability. Check your images: Do they print properly or create black boxes on the page? Tables with a colored background may also print as black boxes with some browsers, which means the user won't be able to read the content. Light fonts on light backgrounds may print as "shadow fonts" that are hard to read. Background images and "wallpaper" may also interfere with the text overlay, and while white text on a black background usually prints properly over a background color, it may not print correctly over an image. Also, make sure your images are sized to fit the spaces you've established for them. If the actual image file you're using is larger than the space, it will often overprint your text.

MAKE YOUR SITE EASY TO NAVIGATE

When a visitor hits your front page, he or she should be able to determine immediately what your site has to offer and how to find it. Your front page should indicate what the site is about—e.g., your works as an author, or a particular subject area, or a specific book. It should include a meaningful table of contents that indicates what can be found elsewhere on the site—articles, book chapters, links, your bio.

If your site includes several different sections—e.g., a set of sample chapters, a series of articles, etc.—then you may need to have some second-level tables of contents. For example, your front page might have a link to "articles," leading to a second table of contents that lists the articles available on your site. (See the previous chapter for details.) Beware of using too many tables of contents, however—visitors are likely to leave if they can't find content by the third or fourth click.

Make sure that visitors can return to your home page, or reach other major parts of your site, from anywhere within the site. While you don't have to have a complete table of contents on every page, you should have a list of the basic sections, such as the home page, your bio, the bookstore, your links, etc. Many designers run this basic navigation table along the top or bottom of each page, or in the left margin.

Keep your front page short, so that the reader doesn't have to scroll endlessly to find out what's available. It's all right for internal pages (such as book chapters or articles) to be long, but the first page should put it all in front of the visitor as quickly as possible.

If possible, keep individual chapters, articles, columns, etc., to a single page each. Readers don't like having to click from one page to another just to finish a chapter or article. Some commercial and magazine sites use the annoying ploy of putting a paragraph or two per page, requiring one to keep clicking to finish an article. The purpose of this is simply to increase the site's overall hit rates; it doesn't please visitors. Try, however, to keep the text portions of your pages to 40 k or under; if you have a *very* long text, it's okay to split it into two sections. Also, try to keep graphics to a minimum on long articles or chapters, or the pages may be slow to load.

Finally, be sure to *check* your internal links. Nothing is more frustrating to a visitor than clicking on an interesting-sounding article or excerpt—and going nowhere. If you move your pages, be sure to change your links.

USE COLORS AND FONTS THAT ARE EASY TO READ

Though it may seem boring, dark type on a pale background still creates the most readable page. Be cautious about mixing colored fonts and backgrounds. What looks good on one browser may not work well on another, and what appeals to one user may seem absolutely ghastly to another.

Pale fonts on pale backgrounds are notoriously hard to read. Patterned backgrounds can also interfere with readability. The smaller the font, the more difficult it will be to read—and italics reduce legibility even further.

Some people find white (or light) fonts on black extremely hard on the eyes, while red or glaring yellow text on black can be positively painful. Colors that possess a comparable "grayscale" (i.e., they would appear as the same shade of gray on a black-and-white monitor or printer) cause a "jitter" effect as the eyes struggle to distinguish between them.

Be conservative with font sizes as well. While a huge headline may be appropriate for the top of a page, it will be distracting anywhere else. Italics can be difficult to read; consider using boldface or caps for titles or emphasis. Tiny font sizes should be avoided—remember that they will become even smaller if the page must be reduced for printing.

CHOOSE GRAPHICS WISELY (AND SPARINGLY)

Used effectively, graphics enhance a site's content; used ineffectively, they can detract from a site's usefulness and appeal.

The primary problem is the size of many graphic files. Image files often require large amounts of memory, and consequently require lengthy download times. For this reason, some users surf with images off, choosing to download graphics only after determining whether the site's content is of interest.

Even smaller graphics, such as lines and bullets, can slow loading time, especially if a page includes a number of graphic elements. Image-heavy pages affect a user's ability to move easily between different sections of your site, especially if the user must repeatedly return to a graphic-laden (and slow-loading) menu or list of links to select new options.

While it would be absurd to suggest that one avoid images entirely, one can take steps to make graphics easier for all users:

- Use only those images that contribute to a site's content. Avoid graphics that are little more than bells and whistles that add no functionality to a site.
- Keep graphic files as small as possible. When using a program such as Photoshop, for example, save JPEG files at a lower resolution (72 dpi, preferably) to reduce file size.
- Include an "Alt" ("alternate text") tag with every image icon so that users can determine the content or purpose of a graphic before downloading it. This tag enables you to give your image a title or caption that will be displayed when the image itself has not been loaded. It is particularly useful if you incorporate navigation functions into images—for example, your "contact me" image could have an "alt" tag of "contact." A line of HTML such as <IMG SRC = "Contact.gif" ALT = "Contact"> will ensure that the word "contact" will be associated with the image icon when the image itself is not displayed.
- Keep graphics to a minimum on pages that a user is likely to have to reload frequently, such as a menu or list of links.
- Specify height and width sizes for images. This enables text to download first, so that a visitor can begin to explore your page without waiting for all the graphics to load.

- Make sure that your graphic files themselves are sized to fit the space in which you want them to appear. For example, if you want an image to fit in a space that is 150 pixels square, make sure that the image itself is 150 pixels square. While a larger image file will be reduced by most browsers to fit the specified parameters on screen, an oversized image may *not* be reduced when printing—which will cause your images to overprint the rest of your page.
- When embedding menu or navigation instructions in graphics, provide an alternate, text-only set of instructions somewhere else on the page (e.g., at the bottom).

USEFUL EXTRAS

In addition to the basic elements of a site (i.e., your content), you may wish to add some "extras" that will either help your visitors—or help you determine what is working and what isn't. Here are some free or inexpensive options that can dress up a site:

- **Your own domain.** I've included this as an "extra" because many writers still prefer to use free ISPs (such as Geocities/Yahoo or Homestead), or an author site such as SFF.net. However, more and more authors are registering their own domains. The cost ranges from $15 to $35, depending on the registry you use and the number of years you sign up for (the minimum is one). You can register as a .com, .org, .net, .biz, .info, or .name (among other options). The downside of having your own domain name is that you will have to pay for an ISP to host it, which will generally run at least $9.95 per month. (You can also register a "virtual" domain that points to another address.) The positive side, of course, is that having your own domain name makes it much easier for visitors to find you; they can search for "www.yourname.com" rather than "www.someISP.com/directory/yourdirectory/yourindex.html." (See Resources, chapter 2, for several sites that provide lists of domain registries.)
- **A search function.** If you have a huge amount of information on your site, consider making it searchable. PICOSEARCH provides a free search function that enables visitors to enter a keyword and obtain a list of pages within your site that contain that word. Results are ranked by closeness of match—for example, a page will be placed higher on the list if the search term appears in the page's title, or appears frequently within the text of the page.
- **A guestbook.** This enables visitors to give you feedback on your site, and leave their contact information—a useful feature if you'd like to collect visitor e-mails for future promotional efforts. (If you do so, make sure that visitors know that you will be using their e-mails for this purpose.) A guestbook can be set up with a simple CGI script.
- **A hit counter.** As I mentioned in the previous chapter, setting up a hit counter enables you to track your visitors—and announces the popularity of your site to those who visit. Some ISPs provide a hit counter for their clients; others require you to use one that is offered through a separate service (generally at no charge). Some hit counter programs will enable you to put a counter on every page of your site; others work only for the site as a whole.

- **Web-tracking software.** Often, you can obtain a Web-tracking service (such as WEBTRENDS) from your ISP, usually by signing up for a "business" account rather than a personal account. The costs of such accounts vary widely, so research ISPs for a good rate. (Don't assume that you need to find a local ISP; often, the best price and service may come from a host in a different state.) A Web-tracking service gives you statistics on the number of visitors to your site, where they come from, what pages are most and least popular, any errors encountered on your site, and more. You can also sign up for such services separately (see Resources).
- **A bookstore affiliate.** Many writers earn a bit of extra income from their site by setting up an affiliate program through an online bookstore such as Amazon.com or Barnes & Noble. An affiliate program enables you to earn a percentage (from 5 to 15 percent) on books sold through your site. All you need to do is set up some sort of bookstore page (or display book covers/titles on any page of your site) and add a link to the online bookstore. You'll receive a percentage of sales made to any visitor who either clicks through and buys the book you've displayed—or who clicks through from your site and then buys some other book or product. Other types of affiliate programs (e.g., to magazines such as *Writer's Digest*) are also available.

ELEMENTS TO USE WITH CAUTION

One of the attractions of the Internet is the many ways that one can create a high-tech "look." However, elements that lead to a flashier-looking site can also lead to problems for some users. Exercise caution when considering the following design elements:

IMAGE MAPS

These have become increasingly common, and are attractive—but they can still cause problems. Some image maps involve large graphic files that are slow to load, delaying the user's ability to navigate the site. Some users prefer to surf with images turned off to save download time, and won't welcome an entry page that offers no navigation clues beyond an icon or flock of icons. I've also found that image maps are often fraught with errors, leaving one unable to access the promised section or page. If you do use an image map, consider including a text-based menu elsewhere on the page (e.g., at the very bottom) as an alternate form of navigation.

FRAMES

These once caused problems for older browsers, but most newer browsers handle them well. However, they can still be frustrating to the user. One of the most frustrating problems I encounter with frames is a framed site that is too wide for the screen, and too wide to print. Frames also make it difficult for a user to bookmark a specific page within your site, or return to that page through the browser's "history" command. They can also bypass a browser's "forward" and "back" buttons, making navigation more difficult. When a page is printed, the user must be careful to select the correct "framed" window, or he is likely to end up with a printout of the frame menu and no content (with a frame, one can print the frame itself or the framed content, but not both). Finally, frames can be annoying if you link to a number of other sites, which must then be displayed within your frame. This may make the linked site more difficult to view and navigate, as well as to bookmark.

There is also a legal question as to whether it is a violation of copyright to link to another site and thereby cause it to be viewed within the context of your own frame (which, by the way, also precludes the display of the URL of the linked site). Several court cases have already arisen over this issue, but no firm conclusion has yet been reached. Fortunately, it seems that frames are becoming less popular as other design elements (such as left-margin image maps) take their place. If you do wish to use frames, consider offering a "no-frames" option as well.

AUDIO AND VIDEO

Recently, I visited a site that greeted me with the warning that I needed a Real Audio plug-in to fully appreciate its content. A second warning told me that I should also download a MIDI program. A third warning then popped onto my screen—but before I could read it, my browser crashed. Needless to say, I haven't gone back.

There's nothing wrong with adding audio or video elements to your site—but make sure that they don't interfere with a browser's operability. Even newer browsers may not have all the plug-ins needed to handle such functions. Audio and video extras should be just that: optional extras that users can choose to explore or ignore.

After constructing your site, it's a good idea to test it—not only with your own browser, but with others, including older programs. If you don't have access to other browsers, use a program such as BCENTRAL FREE WEB TOOLS to determine your site's accessibility from different platforms and programs.

BELLS AND WHISTLES

It's tempting to dress up your site with a host of multimedia features, such as animation, video clips, audio files, Flash, or Shockwave. While such features can add visual pizzazz, however, they often don't enhance your content—and they can prove a problem for some users. Don't assume that everyone who visits your site has the latest version of Explorer or Netscape, or that they've downloaded all the right plug-ins to handle your "extras." Many of your visitors may be at the low end of the technological literacy scale. (I've actually had visitors ask me what a "browser" is.) While anyone can technically download the "latest" software, many of your visitors may be using older systems and equipment (either by choice or from economic necessity). Even for the most up-to-date users, multimedia elements can slow the speed at which visitors can access the more important material on your site—and combinations of multimedia effects can cause even the most streamlined browser to crash. The bottom line is, if a special effect doesn't add to the underlying purpose of your site, leave it out—no matter how snazzy it may be!

MAKING YOUR SITE "SEARCH-ENGINE FRIENDLY"

SEARCH ENGINES ARE TO THE Internet what card files are (or once were) to libraries. If those search engines can't find you, many potential visitors won't be able to find you either. The problem is, no two search engines work exactly the same way. A good overview of how different engines retrieve, index, and rank sites can be found at SEARCH ENGINE WATCH ("How Search Engines Work"). It's also important to know how they *don't* work: Certain design elements can actually prevent you from receiving a high ranking or from being indexed at all. The following tips will help you ensure that your site can be located, retrieved, and indexed effectively:

DON'T HIDE YOUR MENU IN AN IMAGE MAP
Many search engines can't read image maps, and therefore can't index keywords from your menu. Thus, if your home page consists of nothing but an image map, it might not be indexed at all—and if it is, it may not be associated with relevant keywords.

Image maps also prevent many engines from "crawling" from your home page to your secondary pages. Most engines use your links to explore the rest of your site—but if those links are hidden in an image map, those secondary pages may not be retrieved or indexed. Since those pages often contain important content that may boost your site's ranking in a listing of search results, it's vital to make them accessible to search engines.

If you want to use an image map, be sure you also provide a text menu on the same page. This will not only ensure that search engines can index and explore your site, but will also help visitors whose browsers don't handle graphic files well—or who simply prefer not to download large graphic files just to determine what's on your site.

THINK TWICE ABOUT FRAMES
Frames can also create problems for search engines. Like image maps, they may hinder an engine's ability to link to your secondary pages from within a framed menu. In fact, many search engines don't "see" frames at all. A frame is composed of several separate files, including a master file that tells browsers how to assemble those files into the frame displayed on the screen. A search engine may locate only that master instruction file—which often doesn't have the information that needs to be indexed. And since the instruction file doesn't include your internal links, the search engine won't be able to explore the rest of your pages.

One way to bypass this problem is to incorporate indexing information under a "noframes" tag on the master page. More information on this option, along within links to frames resources and tutorials, can be found on the SEARCH ENGINE WATCH site ("Search Engines and Frames").

USE META TAGS
Some search engines use meta tags and others don't. Since you won't be penalized for incorporating meta tags, this simply offers you another chance to improve your index ranking.

A meta tag is a line of HTML code placed within the <HEAD> section of your document. Two meta tag are used in indexing: the "description" tag and the "keywords" tag.

The "descriptions" tag consists of up to 250 characters that describe your site. For those engines that use tags, this is the description that will appear in your listing. Make sure your description is tailored toward the audience you are trying to attract. Determine how your site can benefit that audience, and list those benefits or resources in the tag.

The "keywords" tag lists the keywords under which your site should be indexed. For example, if you write romance novels, you might include such keywords as "romance," "romance writing," "romance fiction," and perhaps your name and the title of your novel. Spend some time brainstorming all the possible keywords someone might use to locate a page about you and your writing, and include those in the tag.

Here's an example of the placement of meta tags:

```
<HEAD>
<TITLE>Tips for Writers</TITLE>
<META  name = "description"  content = "Articles  on
writing skills, finding a publisher, copyright issues,
and  electronic  rights;  resources  for  fantasy/SF
authors; contests; critique groups; research and writ-
ing links.">
<META name = "keywords" content = "writing, writers,
writing tips, freelancing, freelance writing, pub-
lishing, fantasy, science fiction, writing contests,
writing resources">
</HEAD>
```

Never use meta tags to "spam" a search engine. "Spamming" means repeating the same keyword dozens of times in hopes of obtaining a higher ranking. Most search engines are programmed not only to ignore spam, but to reject pages that include it. Other spam techniques include placing keywords in a "comment" tag that is read by search engines, but not by browsers, or in "hidden" text (text that is the same color as the background and can't be seen by the viewer). Again, these tricks may result in the rejection of your page.

CHOOSE AN EFFECTIVE TITLE

Actually, each of your pages will need two titles: the hidden title that serves as the official label for your Web site (but isn't viewed onscreen) and the title you choose for the page itself. These titles don't have to be identical. Your hidden title is included within the <HEAD> section of your document. This is the title that will be listed in a search engine, at the top of a user's browser window, and in a user's navigation menus and bookmark files. If you don't choose a title, search engines and browsers will use the first readable characters of your page, which may not be descriptive or informative.

If you want to include the same master title on each page of your site, use sub-titles to distinguish one page from another. This will help users locate and return to specific pages while navigating your site. For example, you might title your home page:

```
<TITLE>ANNIE AUTHOR'S BOOK PAGE</TITLE>
```

but label your bookstore page:

```
<TITLE>ANNIE AUTHOR'S BOOK PAGE: Books for Writers
</TITLE>
```

In addition to your hidden title, you'll also want to give appropriate titles to your pages themselves, just as you'd title an article or story. Since these titles are also likely to show up in your search engine listing (because they're near the top of your page), think carefully about the impression they'll make. A title like "Links for Romance Writers," for example, is more likely to attract serious writers (and romance readers) than "My Favorite Links to Really Cool Stuff."

PLACE DESCRIPTIVE CONTENT TOWARD THE TOP OF YOUR PAGE

Search engines that don't use meta tags will index the first 100–250 characters of your text as your site description. It's important, therefore, to make sure the first readable text on your page is also descriptive of its content. That text should be something other than image tags, menu items, or similarly noninformative material.

The easiest option is to simply provide a brief description of the page's content as a sort of abstract beneath the title. You could even repeat your meta description tag, since it won't be visible to browsers. If your first item is a menu, make sure its contents are descriptive: "Articles on Writing" instead of simply "Articles," and "[My Book Title] Excerpt" instead of simply "Book Excerpt."

Keep in mind as well that many search engines index every word on your page, up to 1 MB of text. Such engines often determine keywords not by meta tags, but by the number of times a word appears on a page. To improve your chances of being included under the right keywords, therefore, make sure your entry page uses those keywords frequently (and appropriately!). Move content that doesn't relate to your central topic to another section of your site.

If you're determined to have a graphics-only entry page, place descriptive information in a comment tag or hidden text, so that it can be indexed by a search engine without appearing on the user's screen. Or, consider submitting a different page for indexing purposes that is more reflective of your content.

TEST YOUR SITE

After you've done everything possible to ensure that your site is indexed properly, test it. Several sites on the Web will examine your site, free of charge, and report on its effectiveness in several areas (such as search-engine readiness, accessibility, design, HTML accuracy, and link problems). One is META MEDIC, which analyzes the suitability of your meta tags and provides a simulated example of how your site will be listed in a typical search engine index. Microsoft's BCENTRAL site also provides a variety of free tools to help you check the operation of your site. These reports will give you additional hints on how to improve and upgrade your site.

PROMOTING YOUR SITE

ONCE YOU BUILD IT, WILL they come? Constructing an accessible, navigable, attractive site is only half the battle; the other half is promotion. Fortunately, there are several steps you can take to promote your site that cost nothing more than time:

- **Register your site with all major search engines,** including Google and AltaVista. Don't rely on a program that promises to submit your site to all the major engines. Instead, visit each site yourself and follow the instructions under the "add URL" option.
- **Use free site registration programs to submit your URL to additional search engines and directories.** While most registration sites want you to purchase a registration package, many (such as SUBMITAWAY! and AUTO SUBMIT) still offer a limited range of free submission services. While it's not clear how effective these registration services are, they can't hurt.
- **Register your site with major directories.** While Yahoo! is the best-known directory on the Web, you can find many others through sites like the LIBRARIANS' INDEX TO THE INTERNET, which offers hundreds of categories to choose from. You can also submit your URL to various categories within smaller directories, such as My Virtual Encyclopedia. (A number of directories are listed in the Resources section of chapter 3.)
- **If your site includes writing tips, invite the major writing resource sites to add your URL.** If appropriate, offer a reciprocal link in your own resource section. But don't stop at the majors. Actively solicit links from any writing site you come across, including those hosted by individual writers like yourself.
- **Submit your site information for inclusion in author lists,** such as the miscellaneous author list maintained by SFF.net.
- **If your site includes nonfiction topics, search for sites that cover similar topics.** Ask for reciprocal links whenever appropriate, but don't hesitate to suggest a link to your site even when you can't offer one in return. For example, many pet owners link to my pet loss site[1] because of their interest in the topic, even though I don't offer links to personal pages in return.
- **Watch for potential link sites whenever you surf the Internet.** When you add a site to your page, contact the site host and inform them of the link, and invite them to link to you in return.
- **Look for newsletters or e-zines that cover topics relevant to your site, and submit your URL for review.** Again, if appropriate, offer a reciprocal link; however, many newsletters provide news of new or "just discovered" Web sites without requiring reciprocity.
- **Join newsgroups and discussion lists relevant to your site.** Don't advertise your site on such lists; however, if someone raises a question that your site answers, it's usually acceptable to provide the URL. If not, send the URL information by private e-mail.

[1]The Pet Loss Support Page, www.pet-loss.net.

- **Exchange links with authors of books similar to your own,** either of the same genre or on related topics.
- **Ask your publisher to post a link to your Web site.** Your publisher may also be able to post an expanded author bio or an excerpt from your book.
- **List your site name (or book title) and URL in your e-mail signature block.** This is considered a discreet, acceptable way to advertise your site to newsgroups and discussion lists—as well as to anyone else with whom you correspond.
- **Include your URL and e-mail address on your business card and letterhead.** (You may also want to include it on more personal correspondence, such as your holiday newsletter!)

Finally, be sure to check your promotional efforts regularly. To find out whether your site is indexed in the major search engines, for example, run a periodic keyword check to determine whether (and where) your listing appears. If it doesn't appear, resubmit it. If it doesn't appear within the top one hundred listings (or even the top ten), use a program such as META MEDIC to help you determine whether you can improve its ranking. Also, visit the sites that *do* receive high rankings and see if you can determine ways to improve your own site's rating. View the source code for high-rated sites, for example, to determine what meta tags they use.

You can find out how many people have added links to your site by conducting a URL search. On Google, for example, simply enter "*link:www.yourdomain.com*" in the search box to find out who links to your site.

Keep in mind that search engines can't keep up with changes to your Web site. When you remove a page, it may remain in a search engine's index for months—but potential visitors won't be able to find it, or you. You can solve that problem by replacing any page you delete with a "redirect" message (using the same URL) that offers a link back to your main menu:

> Hello! You have reached a page that has been moved or deleted from this site. Click here to return to *Annie Author's Tips for Romance Writers*; click here to reach the *main menu*.

Web sites don't become popular overnight. Most become popular through word of mouth—but it's your job to get that word started. Be patient, be diligent, create the best site you can—and one morning you'll check your hit counter and be astonished by the results.

SIXTY TICKS FOR A GOOD WEB SITE

BY RICHARD WALLER[2]

Impression on first entry

[ ] The URL/domain name is appropriate and meaningful
[ ] The surfer sees something meaningful within 8 seconds
[ ] The site name and product/purpose come up instantly
[ ] The first page is less than 20 k, and images are kept small
[ ] Text is visible while graphics are loaded (WIDTH = , HEIGHT =)
[ ] Graphics are named (using ALT =) with full text content

The Home Page is exciting, interesting, attention-grabbing

[ ] There is useful information on the Home Page
[ ] The home page looks good, and has a clean, uncluttered look
[ ] The important information is on the first display seen

The Home Page contains the key facts

[ ] Name of organization (preferably in H1 heading)
[ ] Shows business, products, where based
[ ] Shows the sort of information available in the site
[ ] Shows how to contact the company [or individual]
[ ] A mail to: reply form
[ ] What to do about faults, comments, suggestions
[ ] Title is meaningful
[ ] Meta statements are accurate
[ ] Site description mirrors the title and meta description

Links are clear and meaningful

[ ] It is clear which are internal and which are external links
[ ] Not more than seven options on any menu
[ ] Image-links are appropriate
[ ] Image-links are supported by text-links and ALT tags
[ ] External links are shown with the full URL

The whole site has a structure

[ ] It is clear what the structure of the site is
[ ] Useful content is not more than three clicks from the home page
[ ] There is a List of Contents or a Site Map with links to every page
[ ] Each Web page has links back to the Contents or Site Map
[ ] There are appropriate links to other useful pages

All the pages obey the same rules
[ ] Each Web page has a proper title
[ ] The title shows why users should look at this page
[ ] Titles are consistent with the words used in links to this page
[ ] Meta statements are provided where appropriate
[ ] Text is shown in centered tables (say 500 pixels wide)

Long Web pages have their own structure
[ ] Long Web pages are used when it is useful to print as a whole
[ ] Avoid long centered tables; use several short ones
[ ] Users are warned if access time is likely to be long
[ ] Each displayed part of the Web page has a heading or color
[ ] There is a list of contents for the page
[ ] At useful intervals there is an escape link back to the contents

All Web pages have a reference
[ ] Author and name of organization on each page
[ ] Accreditation or acknowledgement of the source of data is shown
[ ] Web page URL is shown for reference if page is printed
[ ] Date created or last updated on each Web page
[ ] Pages that may be printed have company and/or contact information

Useful external links are provided
[ ] Links are provided to relevant sources of information
[ ] Links to associated organizations are provided
[ ] Information readily available elsewhere is not repeated
[ ] There is a description of who each link is to, and why

The Web site achieves its purpose
[ ] It is clear what the purpose of this Web site is
[ ] The apparent purpose has been achieved
[ ] There are appropriate images and color
[ ] It has a professional, planned, workmanlike, friendly image
[ ] There is appropriate scope for user interaction, Java, JavaScript
[ ] The reply forms are easy to use and relevant to the need
[ ] There is some humor or light relief
[ ] I am tempted to return in the future

The whole Web site has been tested on several browsers
[ ] Netscape
[ ] Internet Explorer
[ ] Mozilla

Score: 40–50 is excellent. 20–40 is only average. Less than 20, and you have a problem.

WEB SITE DEVELOPMENT AND HTML TOOLS

Bare Bones Guide to HTML, The
http://werbach.com/barebones
A listing of every known HTML tag, plus tutorials and links to other Web design resources.

bCentral Free Web Tools
www.bcentral.com/products/free.asp
A variety of free tools for Web site development, testing and promotion, including a meta tags tester, link tester, counter, spell checker, and search engine submitter. (Scroll to bottom of page.)

Beginner's Guide to HTML, A
http://archive.ncsa.uiuc.edu/General/ Internet/WWW/HTMLPrimer.html
An excellent primer on HTML, with easy instructions and examples of how formatting will appear on the page. Includes instructions on tables and graphics, plus links to other resources.

Color Specifier
http://users.rcn.com/giant.interport/ COLOR/1ColorSpecifier.html
An easy-to-use chart of colors for use in backgrounds or fonts, showing the color, the name of the color, and the HTML code.

HTML Goodies
www.htmlgoodies.com
Tutorials, primers, images, software, and a host of other resources on HTML, Java, and Web site development.

Matt's Script Archive
www.scriptarchive.com
Free CGI scripts that can be used to create forms, feedback messages, forums, visitor counters, site search

tools, and more. Also offers links to other free script and shareware pages.

PicoSearch
www.picosearch.com
Enables you to build a free search function into your Web site.

Search Engine Tutorial
http://northernwebs.com/set
Tips on how to improve your site's search engine ranking, including how to use meta tags effectively.

Search Engine Watch/Search Engine Submission Tips
http://searchenginewatch.internet.com/ webmasters
Includes "Checking Your URL," "How Search Engines Work," "How to Use Meta Tags," "Search Engines and Frames," "Search Engines Features Chart."

Web Style Guide
http://info.med.yale.edu/caim/manual/ contents.html
A useful tutorial on designing Web sites, with illustrated examples.

Web Wonk: Tips for Writers and Designers
www.dsiegel.com/tips/index.html
A variety of tips and resources to improve one's Web site.

PROMOTION AND SEARCH ENGINE REGISTRATION

@Submit!
http://uswebsites.com/submit
Free search engine submission site.

Auto Submit
www.autosubmit.com/promote.html
Free search engine submission site.

Bobby
http://bobby.watchfire.com/bobby/html/en/index.jsp
A free service that analyzes your Web page and provides an analysis of its accessibility and compatibility with various browsers.

Go Net-Wide
www.gonetwide.com/gopublic.html
An extensive list of URL submission sites and other promotional links (some free, some fee-based).

HTML Goodies/Ad Banners
www.htmlgoodies.com/primers/bannerprimers.html
An excellent series on how to promote your site or newsletter through development and strategic placement of ad banners. (Also explains how to track responses to your banners.)

JimWorld
www.jimworld.com
Formerly known as *VirtualPromote,* this site offers a number of promotion techniques, tools, and tutorials. Though aimed at commercial sites, many tips also apply to writing sites (especially if you're promoting a book or product).

Librarians' Index to the Internet
http://lii.org

Meta Medic
www.northernwebs.com/set/setsimjr.html
Check your meta tags for validity, length, and repetition. The program generates a simulated "search engine listing" to demonstrate how your site is likely to appear in a search.

Midwest Book Review/Publisher Resources
www.midwestbookreview.com/bookbiz/pub_res.htm
Among other excellent resources for publishers, this page includes a set of links for submitting your URL directly to major search engines.

Promotion World
www.promotionworld.com
Tutorials, articles, tools, interviews, reviews, and ideas for website design and promotion.

Site Owner Link Tester
www.siteowner.com/badlinks.cfm?LID=229
An excellent, free service that analyzes and rates your site's meta tags, HTML, spelling, links, and browser accessibility. This is a quick and easy way to verify whether your links are accurate. The program provides a detailed report on each area.

SubmitAway!
www.submit-away.com/auto-submit.htm
A site that submits your URL to a variety of search engines for free.

Top 10 Ways to Irritate Your Visitors
www.virtualpromote.com/top10.html
If you don't believe me, check this list of things not to do when designing your Web site!

(See Resources, chapter 2, for sites that list ISPs and domain registries.)

WEB TRACKING SOFTWARE

1.2.3.Count.com Traffic Analysis
www.123count.com

TulipStats Web Stats
www.tulipstats.com

Webtracker
www.fxweb.com/tracker

WebTrends
www.netiq.com/webtrends/default.asp

Search on "web tracking service" for more options.

<< CHAPTER 14 >>

PUBLISHING AN E-ZINE OR E-MAIL NEWSLETTER

N THE PRINT WORLD, THE cost of launching one's own magazine, or even a newsletter, has always been prohibitive. Online, however, the cost of production and distribution can be almost nonexistent—meaning that nearly anyone can start a magazine or newsletter of one's own. And because an electronic publication can be read by anyone anywhere in the world at no extra cost to you, this is a great way to build yourself an international audience and reputation.

An electronic publication can be a way to add to the content of your Web site, attract new visitors, build a mailing list, and contribute to your promotional efforts. It can also be a way to educate and inform, or simply to entertain. Many top-name authors offer brief newsletters to inform fans of new releases, book signings, and other events; nonfiction authors often launch newsletters to help establish their credentials and provide more information on their subject.

Because an electronic publication is so easy and inexpensive to develop, the Web is flooded with e-zines and e-mail newsletters of every description. Before you decide to launch one of your own, therefore, it's a good idea to check around and make sure that no one else is already hosting something similar. One way to do this is to check an e-zine directory (see Resources); another is to search for keywords on TOPICA or YAHOO! GROUPS.

TEN QUESTIONS TO ASK BEFORE LAUNCHING A ZINE

WHILE PUBLISHING AN E-MAIL NEWSLETTER or e-zine *is* relatively easy and inexpensive, there are a number of things to consider before making the decision to launch one. Otherwise, you may find yourself grappling with a monster that devours more of your time and energy than you ever imagined, leaving you with little or no time for the writing that your zine was supposed to be about in the first place. Take the time to answer the following questions before you launch:

WHAT IS THE GOAL OF YOUR PUBLICATION?

What do you want to achieve by launching your "zine"? Do you want to attract more visitors to your Web site? Do you want a vehicle through which to inform fans and readers of your forthcoming works? Do you want a publication that will attract more readers to your published books (fiction or nonfiction)? Is your primary goal to educate readers about a subject that is important to you? Do you wish to entertain? Or are you simply trying to fulfill a dream of having a publication of your own? (If so, what type of publication would satisfy that desire?)

WHAT WILL YOUR PUBLICATION BE ABOUT?

Most successful zines have a well-defined focus that attracts a specific audience. If you're publishing a fiction zine, does it focus upon a specific genre or subgenre (e.g., science fiction, or time-travel science fiction)? If you're publishing a non-fiction zine, is the subject broad enough to sustain the publication week after week, month after month? Or are you likely to run out of ideas and material after a few issues?

WHO IS YOUR AUDIENCE?

Define the types of readers who would be interested in your publication. Where will you find them? How will you attract them? Have you found newsgroups or discussion lists where such readers gather, and where you could announce your publication? Are there other zines on similar topics with which you might swap links or ads? (If there are already a number of other publications on the topic, you may also wish to ask what you can offer that will attract readers to *your* zine.)

HOW OFTEN WILL THE PUBLICATION BE PRODUCED?

E-zines are often updated monthly, while newsletters are more likely to come out weekly or biweekly. Generally, the less frequent the newsletter, the longer it will be. Keep in mind that once you set a schedule, readers will expect you to keep it. Subscribers won't tolerate too many missed deadlines; if you promise to deliver your newsletter every Monday, be sure that you can follow through on that promise.

WHERE WILL YOU GET MATERIAL?

This is perhaps the most important question of all. You may have a wonderful idea for a newsletter, but do you intend to do all the writing and research for every issue? If so, you've set yourself a significant and time-consuming task. (Be careful, too, that your newsletter doesn't turn into an "all-you, all-the-time, *me*-zine.") If you don't want to do all the writing yourself, that means you'll need to find material from other sources. Here, the adage "you get what you pay for" is very true. While you will undoubtedly be able to find free material, it's often free for the very simple reason that no one is willing to buy it. You may find that you need to do a great deal of editing to make that "free" material presentable. If you choose to pay for contributions, you'll end up with better content—but also with higher costs.

HOW MUCH TIME ARE YOU WILLING TO SPEND ON YOUR ZINE?

A regular publication takes more time than you might imagine, even if you're not doing all the writing yourself. Your schedule will include planning time, design and format, administration, correspondence (with your readers, writers, sponsors, and sources), promotion, research, surfing, trouble-shooting, and the ever-present "miscellaneous tasks." Be sure that you can balance these demands with your regular writing.

HOW MUCH MONEY ARE YOU WILLING TO SPEND ON YOUR ZINE?

There is a direct trade-off between the investment of time and the investment of money. The more money you are willing to spend, the more time you will be able to "buy back." For example, you'll save a great deal of writing time if you're willing (and able) to buy articles from other writers. Similarly, you may want to pay someone else to handle the design of your Web zine. However, unless your newsletter is a completely altruistic labor of love (and you're independently wealthy), the question of putting money *into* it often turns into a question of how to get money *out* of it (which will be discussed below).

HOW WILL YOU PROMOTE YOUR PUBLICATION?

Once you've defined your readership, you'll need to take active steps to let them know about your publication and entice them to visit and/or subscribe. While there are many ways to do this (some of which will be described below), it can be a time-consuming process.

WILL YOU OFFER THE PUBLICATION FOR FREE OR CHARGE FOR SUBSCRIPTIONS?

The vast majority of e-zines and e-mail newsletters are available at no cost. Those that do charge generally provide high-end or "marketable" information. For example, several newsletters that offer extensive information on writing markets (such as WRITE MARKETS REPORT and FREELANCING4MONEY) charge for subscriptions, because they are marketed to professionals who use the information in their business. Other, more general writing newsletters have attempted to charge for subscriptions, however, and received little response. Because so much information *is* available for free on the Web, you have to offer something *very* special (and worth paying for) to attract paid subscribers.

SHOULD YOU OFFER AN E-ZINE OR E-MAIL NEWSLETTER?

The final decision you will need to make is on the format of your publication. Each has its advantages and disadvantages, including format considerations that will influence your choice of content and design. The sections below explore each format.

BUILDING AN E-ZINE

THE ONLY SIGNIFICANT DIFFERENCE BETWEEN an e-zine and an ordinary Web site is that an e-zine is regularly updated, offering a new issue at specific intervals. Older issues are often archived on the same site.

An e-zine offers tremendous flexibility in terms of design and presentation options. You could, for example, design your magazine to look much like a print publication, with columns, sidebars, and graphics. You can also go beyond print by incorporating multimedia elements such as animation, audio, and video clips. For example, if you feature an interview with a famous author, you could include an audio clip of the interview, so that readers could hear the author's words in her own voice. Finally, you can add links to material outside your e-zine for more information.

E-zines also enable you to present material in a nonlinear fashion, through hyperlinks that let the reader choose which elements to read, in which order. Don't fall into the design trap of artificially breaking articles into separate pages, however. This practice arose from the desire to track visitors to find out whether they actually read the entire article, but only adds frustration to the reading process. Clicking on a "continue" button and waiting for a new page to download is nothing like flipping a magazine page! If an article is naturally linear, put it on a single "page," unless it is exceptionally long (more than 50 k) and would take excessive time to download.

Be cautious about adding too many bells and whistles to your publication just to attract readers with a snazzy design. Remember that many people still use older equipment that doesn't respond well (or quickly) to a host of Java applets, giant images, complicated wallpaper, and animated features. Assess your audience profile: Is this a high-tech group, or a set of folks who just want easy access to solid information? Also, test your site to find out just how long it *does* take to download—if you could brew a cup of coffee while waiting for your site to load through a high-speed cable connection, imagine the irritation it's causing to people with a 56 k (or slower) modem.

Some e-zines open with a cover image that operates like the front cover of a magazine. While this can be attractive, be aware that it also adds an extra level of "noninformation" that a visitor must get past before finding your content. Make sure visitors can bypass this introductory image if they choose. Another thing that is likely to alienate visitors is to open your e-zine with an audio or video file that must be downloaded—especially if the user must obtain a special plug-in just to view it. If you do want to provide such an intro, be sure that users have the option to bypass it.

Other e-zines open directly to a table of contents. This will serve as your primary navigation tool, so make sure it is clear and easy to access. Beware of frames that don't allow the reader to return easily to the contents section. Cute titles are fine, but be sure your subtitles give readers an idea of what your publication is about. This page should also point the reader to instructions on how to subscribe (if necessary), how to contact you, and how to find back issues. It should also include (or point to) your copyright notice. You may wish to add a contents bar to each page or article, so that readers can navigate within your site without returning to the table of contents.

Each issue of your e-zine should be clearly dated. Once an issue has expired, you'll need to archive it and provide a contents entry for back issues. If you archive older materials, you'll need to discuss archival rights as part of any contract with your writers and artists. (See the sample contract at the end of this chapter, and the Archival Rights section in chapter 8.)

CREATING AN E-MAIL NEWSLETTER

AN E-MAIL NEWSLETTER IS GENERALLY easier to produce than a Web-based e-zine, as you don't have to deal with HTML, design issues, graphics, etc. All you need to do is prepare your material in a word-processing program and cut-and-paste it into an e-mail message. You can even prepare it directly in your e-mail program.

An e-mail newsletter can offer a wide variety of content. Many writing newsletters, for example, offer news items, information on markets, a selection of useful links, an article or two, and perhaps a regular or rotating column. Take a look at what other newsletters are offering, then decide what you can offer that is different or "better" than your competition.

Newsletter editors generally offer two different types of newsletters: Those that are completely self-contained, and those that offer links to a Web site for the actual content. A self-contained newsletter is just that: All the information is in the e-mail itself. It might also refer readers to additional information on your Web site, but that information would not be treated as "part" of the newsletter content. Conversely, a "Web-link" newsletter offers only portions of the featured articles or other content (such as the first paragraph or a summary), and directs the reader to a Web site for the rest.

Which is best? Different readers have different preferences. My own preference is for a self-contained newsletter, as I tend to want to read everything at once, and may not bother to click through to different articles. Other readers enjoy going to a Web site for more details. *WritersWeekly* uses the Web-link format, and since that publication has more than 67,000 readers at the time of this writing, it must be doing something right. One advantage of this format is that it keeps the text of your actual e-mail short. (You can use counters or Web-tracking software to determine how many people actually click through to the different features.)

Among the many decisions you'll need to make when preparing an e-mail newsletter is whether to archive back issues on your Web site. Such an archive gives readers an opportunity to catch up on features they missed, and gives potential subscribers a chance to review your publication before making a decision to sign up. If you do archive newsletters, archive them "in their entirety." This protects the collective copyright of each issue. Create a back-issue index that lists the primary features, columns, etc., in each issue. (An easy way to archive an e-mail newsletter is to use the "<pre></pre>" tags for "preformatted" text; that way, you don't have to HTML-format each issue for the Web.)

FORMATTING YOUR NEWSLETTER

Though an e-mail newsletter seems easy to design, it does pose some formatting challenges. Since text runs in one long column from beginning to end, you'll need to find a way to separate different sections, for example. Most of all, you'll want to ensure that your newsletter is easy to read by anyone, no matter what e-mail program they are using. Here are some tips on accomplishing that goal:

- **Avoid frills.** Resist the temptation to dress up your newsletter with fancy fonts or colored "inks." A newsletter with four or five different font styles and sizes, let alone colors, tends to look amateurish at best, and is likely to be distracting and hard to read. Keep in mind that many readers may not have the same fancy fonts that you have, so you can't be sure how "frills" will look at the other end.
- **Keep your font size readable.** Too many e-mails appear to have been written in microprint. Make sure that you are using at least a "normal" font size (10 to 12 points); never use "small."
- **Don't use HTML.** While some e-mail programs offer the option of automatically HTML-formatting outgoing messages, not all programs *accept* HTML-formatted e-mail. Thus, some readers are bound to receive a newsletter that is crammed full of HTML code—and virtually impossible to read. Stick to plain text.
- **Watch out for special characters.** The vast majority of newsletters I receive are chock full of "hieroglyphs" that are the result of using special characters such as smart quotes and em dashes. See Turning off the Gibberish in chapter 6 for tips on how to avoid smart-quote clutter.
- **Don't include graphics.** Though some e-mail programs will allow you to embed graphics and illustrations in the text of an e-mail, avoid the temptation. Many ISPs will "strip out" those graphics from an incoming message, and append them as attachments, which make many readers very nervous. In addition, graphics will add unnecessary file space to your newsletter.
- **Use simple dividers.** If you wish to place some sort of dividing line between sections and articles, use simple characters for this, such as a line of dashes, equal-signs, asterisks, etc.
- **Consider limiting line lengths.** Some newsletters limit line lengths to sixty-five characters or less. This can give a newsletter a more formal, formatted look (and avoid problems with certain types of e-mail programs). It is also useful if you're selling classified advertising, as you can specify the number of lines and characters per line that you're willing to accept.
- **Provide a heading.** At the top of your newsletter, include the title of the newsletter itself, the date, the issue number, and (perhaps) the URL of the associated Web site. You may also wish to include the number of subscribers here. Here's an example of the heading for my *Writing World* newsletter:

```
**********************************************************
          W R I T I N G W O R L D

   A World of Writing Information - For Writers
                Around the World

          http://www.writing-world.com

   Issue 2:14     10,034 subscribers     July 11, 2002
**********************************************************
SUBSCRIBE/UNSUBSCRIBE   INSTRUCTIONS   AT   END   OF
NEWSLETTER

**********************************************************
```

- **Include a masthead.** Whether you place your masthead at the top or bottom of the newsletter, it should include contact information (e.g., your name and e-mail), copyright information (the collective copyright for the newsletter itself), and information on how to subscribe and unsubscribe. Here's an example of the masthead from *Writing World:*

```
Copyright (c) 2003 Moira Allen
Individual articles copyrighted by their authors.
**********************************************************

Editor/Publisher: MOIRA ALLEN
(moirakallen@writing-world.com)
Managing Editor: PEGGY TIBBETTS (peggyt@xxxx.net)

Writing World is hosted by Listbox.com -
http://v2listbox.com

**********************************************************

Subscribers are welcome to recirculate Writing
World to friends, discussion lists, etc., as
long as the ENTIRE text of the newsletter is
included and appropriate credit is given.
Writing World may not be circulated for profit
purposes.

**********************************************************

Do not reply to this message to subscribe or
unsubscribe! To subscribe to Writing World, send
a  blank  e-mail  to  subscribe-writing-world
@listbox.com. To unsubscribe, send a blank e-mail
to unsubscribe-writing-world@listbox.com.
```

- **Include a table of contents.** Beneath your heading, including a table of contents that lets readers know what they'll find in the issue.
- **Keep it (relatively) short.** Some readers have ISPs that limit the length of incoming messages, and may truncate an e-mail that exceeds that length. In general, an e-mail newsletter shouldn't be longer than 50 k (and some ISPs won't even accept that). If you need to produce a longer newsletter, consider sending it in two parts. (However, this doesn't always work either. When I split *Writing World* into two sections, I found that many of my AOL subscribers never received the second half, for reasons we were never able to resolve.)

HANDLING SUBSCRIPTIONS

Most newsletter editors prefer to handle subscriptions through a list-management service. Services like Yahoo! Groups and Topica are free; others charge a fee based on the number of subscribers. A list-management service enables readers to subscribe or unsubscribe, or change their e-mail address, without having to contact you directly. (In spite of this, many readers will still contact you to subscribe or unsubscribe.) Most services will also automatically unsubscribe bounced addresses. The service will also provide you with a CGI script to place on your Web site to create a "sign up" box. Sending out your newsletter is easy: You simply e-mail it to the list service, which sends it out to your subscriber list.

The disadvantage of a free service is that it will place advertising in your newsletter, and you have no control over the ads that are placed. A second disadvantage is the quality of customer service; I've heard many complaints about the free services, but I've always received good support from the paid service that I use. The disadvantage of paid services, of course, is that you actually have to pay for them—and fees vary widely. The service I use (LISTBOX) charges $5 for lists of five hundred or less, and $10 for lists of a thousand subscribers.

Display your subscription information and "sign-up" box prominently on your Web site. Make sure it is clear to readers how to sign up, what they are getting, and that the material is free (assuming that it is). Also, include a clear link to your back issue archive, if you have one, so that potential subscribers can preview the publication before making a decision. It's also a good idea to include a privacy clause that assures readers that you won't use your mailing list for any purpose other than delivering the newsletter (including for your own personal promotional use), and that you won't sell it or give it to any other individual or organization.

Never subscribe people to your mailing list without permission. This is equivalent to "spamming" and is not appreciated. If you think that someone would appreciate receiving the newsletter, e-mail them personally and let them know about it, and ask if they would like to receive a sample issue—but don't simply put them on the list. (Most list-management services require a subscriber to confirm a subscription if it is submitted from another e-mail address.)

PROMOTING YOUR ZINE

Regardless of the type of publication you develop, your primary challenge is attracting readers or subscribers. If you sell advertising, your rates will be based on your circulation, so tracking subscriptions or site visitors is important.

Most of the recommendations on promoting your Web site (chapter 13) also apply to promoting your publication. Here are some other techniques:

- List your publication in a database of e-zines (see Resources, chapter 5, for a list of e-zine directories)
- Submit your publication to reviewers
- Exchange reciprocal links with related Web sites
- Swap ads (display or classified) with other newsletters on similar or related topics
- Send out a brief "press release" announcing your e-zine to other relevant zines or newsletters
- Offer a "site of the week" (or month) award to relevant Web sites, and providing each site with an award image that links back to your site
- Offer a free gift (such as a special report or e-book) to new subscribers
- Offer a more significant free gift to the "xth" subscriber (e.g., the hundredth subscriber, the thousandth subscriber, etc.)
- Include the URL of your publication (or its subscription e-mail address) in your e-mail signature block

The best promotion of all is "word of mouth." If you have a high-quality publication, readers will pass it along to their friends, their newsgroups, their discussion groups. Ultimately your readers will become your best, and most dedicated, advertisers.

WORKING WITH FREELANCERS

UNLESS YOU CHOOSE TO DO all the writing for your online publication yourself (which can be very time-consuming and not necessarily cost-effective), chances are that you're going to want to acquire material from other sources—specifically, other writers. Here, again, it's wise to heed the old adage, "You get what you pay for."

Sources of "free" Web and newsletter content abound. However, it is often generic material that isn't tailored to your publication or your audience. In addition, it is often free for a reason: No one would be willing to pay for it. While professional writers *do* occasionally work for free, those whose work is of a marketable quality expect to be paid market rates. If you're unwilling or unable to pay for material, that tends to limit your pool of contributors to those who *can't* sell their material, those who have *never* sold anything before, and those who are willing to do anything for a byline. Some of these writers may be competent, but many leave much to be desired.

Fortunately (or unfortunately, depending on your perspective), the online market tends to offer fairly low rates to freelancers. If you'd like to pay for work, you don't need to offer the moon; you'll find many high-quality writers who are willing to work for a few cents a word. You can also gather excellent material by offering a flat rate for reprints—particularly work that has not appeared online or in a similar e-zine. Many writers have sold material to smaller regional publications, and welcome the chance to earn another $20 or so from an online reprint.

You may also be able to obtain content by offering advertising space or other considerations. Some writers *are* willing to provide their material at no charge for promotional considerations. One question to ask, however, is how "exclusive" the material is. If a writer has sent the same article to twenty different newsletters, running it in yours isn't going to be much of a coup.

Regardless of whether you pay your contributors, you should still protect their rights, and yours, with a proper contract. This contract should spell out what payment (if any) is provided and what rights the author is licensing to your site. Many e-zines blithely state, "Oh, we don't take any rights, because we're not buying the material." Every writer should be aware, however, that simply having one's material published constitutes a *use* of rights—usually first rights, such as first electronic rights. This is true whether a contract has been issued or not, and regardless of whether the author is paid.

If you use the material of other writers on your site or in your newsletter, you will typically be using either first electronic rights or second electronic rights (i.e., reprint rights). Or, you may choose to use one-time electronic rights, which leaves the author free to sell the material elsewhere at the same time. If the material is used on a Web site, you may also need to specify a duration for those rights—e.g., "exclusive first worldwide electronic rights for a period of 30 (thirty) days." If you plan to archive back issues of your newsletter or material that has been posted on your site, you'll also need to specify a grant of archival rights.[1]

A contract protects you and your contributors. It also demonstrates to your writers that you are a professional, and that you respect the rights of your writers. The easiest method is to create an e-mail contract that includes the name and address of the contributor, the title of the article, the terms of payment (if any), and the rights you are requesting. Put a space at the bottom for your signature and for the signature of the contributor, and ask the contributor to print out a copy, sign it, and return it to you by mail or fax. When you receive the signed contract, countersign it and return a copy to the contributor. (You'll find a sample contract at the end of this chapter.)

MAKING MONEY FROM YOUR E-ZINE

MANY E-ZINES BEGIN AS LABORS of love—but when that "labor" becomes too intensive, or if you've chosen to pay for content, you may begin to search for ways to make your e-zine profitable. Such efforts tend to meet with varying success,

---

[1]Archiving back issues of a newsletter involves a somewhat tricky copyright issue. Technically, your newsletter issues are covered by your "collective copyright"—that is, a copyright that applies to each issue of the newsletter *as a whole*, exactly as it is published. This copyright belongs to you as the publisher, and covers the issue itself—but does not transfer ownership of individual articles by other contributors within that issue. Thus, you should be entitled to archive back issues of your newsletter *in their entirety* without obtaining special permission from contributors, but you are *not* entitled to archive individual articles separately without permission.

depending on the type of publication and the editor's "business savvy" and ability to exploit potential sources of revenue.

There are four basic ways to turn an e-zine into a source of income:

- Sell advertising
- Sell subscriptions
- Sell a product
- Solicit contributions

Many e-zines use a combination of these approaches.

SELLING ADVERTISING

Many editors of electronic publications support those publications by selling advertising space—including display advertising on Web sites and classified advertising in newsletters. The most successful ads are those that match the content and interests of the audience. For example, if your publication is about writing, your advertising should relate in some way to writing as well. If your publication is about pets, your advertising should relate to pet products and services. Your readers are not going to be interested in ads that don't relate to the content of your zine, and your advertisers will want assurances that your zine reaches an audience that is likely to be interested in their products.

The amount you can charge for ads depends primarily on your circulation (as measured either by distinct visitors to your Web site or subscribers to your newsletter). It also depends on what the market will bear. You may find that your subject area doesn't lend itself to "big ticket" advertisers—large companies with lots of money to spend. If the majority of your potential advertisers are likely to be smaller companies or individuals with limited advertising budgets, you'll need to price your ads accordingly.

While many complex rate calculations exist regarding "CPM" (cost per thousand), the easiest way to determine what to charge is to visit similar publications and check out their ad rates, as well as their circulation figures. Also, determine how many advertisers a publication actually has. If one publication charges high rates but has very few ads, while another charges lower rates and has many ads, that's a good indication of what that particular market will bear.

When setting your ad rates, keep in mind that you'll need to offer discounts for long-term advertising—e.g., three months, six months, one year, etc. Also, consider whether you wish to impose a "minimum" listing, especially for newsletter ads, so that you don't have to keep changing your ad list every week or month.

It's also wise to insist on being paid *before* you actually run any advertising. While most advertisers are honest, you *will* get stiffed from time to time. The exception is when you are dealing with a company that is well-known, reputable, and can only cut checks through an accounting department (which generally takes several weeks). I also recommend developing a contract to use with advertisers; you'll find a sample contract at the end of this chapter.

ONLINE DISPLAY ADVERTISING

If you have a Web zine, or a site associated with your newsletter, you can offer "display advertising." There are several basic types of display ads:

- **Banner ads** are rectangular and extend horizontally across your site. A common width is 500–600 pixels. Generally, such ads are not very deep (50–100 pixels).[2]
- **Button ads** are square, and range in size from fairly small (e.g., 50x50) to around 150–200 pixels square.
- **Rotating banner ads** are the same size as regular banner ads, but enable you to combine several ads in a single location. Each ad is displayed for a period of time, followed by the next. You can determine how many ads to include in the rotation and how long each one will be displayed.
- **Pop-up ads** open a separate window on the user's browser. These, however, are generally considered an abomination by most users, who close them as quickly as possible; software is also available to block pop-ups.

Including advertising on your site can be a complex design issue. While advertisers prefer their ads to be as close to the top of the page as possible, you don't want the ads to distract the reader from the content of the site. Typical locations include the top of the page, the left or right column, or the very bottom. If you think you'll want to sell advertising space, it's a good idea to incorporate this into your site design from the beginning.

Keep in mind that every ad on the site is a separate graphics file, and will add to the download time of each page. If you have a great many ads, this can make a page very slow to load—and very frustrating for visitors. Another factor to consider is whether you wish to accept animated ads. While a little animation can be a good thing, a little also goes a long way. It can be distracting if every ad on your page is blinking, flashing, whirling, or doing other strange things.

Another decision to make is whether ads will appear throughout your site, or only on the main index/entry page. If you decide to place ads only on the "front" page, be sure that you know the visitor rate for this page, as opposed to the site as a whole.

WEB SITE CLASSIFIEDS

It's also possible to set up separate "classified" pages on your site. These pages will generally offer text ads (although you can, if you wish, include banners within the classified section). Classifieds should cost less than regular display ads. You may also find more creative types of advertising opportunities; Writing-World.com, for example, offers authors a chance to advertise their books on the "Author's Bookshelf" (which provides a separate page for each title).

---

[2]Note that graphics and advertisements are measured in terms of pixels, not inches or metrics. This allows them to adjust according to the browser parameters set by the user.

NEWSLETTER CLASSIFIEDS

These tend to look much like the classifieds in any print publication. Such ads are text-only, and usually cost less than online display ads. Fortunately, this type of ad involves only two serious design issues:

- **Where will you put them?** Some newsletters place ads at the top of the page; others place all classifieds at the very bottom. Others intersperse ads with content—e.g., an ad (or two) between every section or separate article. Advertisers, of course, prefer to be at the top of the page, but if you put too many ads at the top, readers won't be led directly into your content, and may not bother to read the newsletter.
- **How long should they be?** It's wise to set a line limit on newsletter classifieds— e.g., four sixty-five-character lines. If an advertiser wants a longer ad, you can charge a small fee for extra lines. Your line limit should include addresses, URLs, etc. (Make sure advertisers know that "sixty-five characters" *includes* spaces.)

FINDING ADVERTISERS

If you know your subject area, finding advertisers should not be too difficult. The first place to look is in other publications similar to yours. Check other e-mail newsletters or Web sites on your topic for advertisers; if someone is advertising with your competitor, they may be willing to advertise with you as well. Don't overlook print publications; I've found many advertisers for Writing-World.com by looking through the display and classified ads of print magazines for writers. Do a Web search on keywords related to your topic, and check the "sponsored" sites that come up, as well as any sites that appear to be commercial.

Once you've found a list of likely advertisers, develop a short, sincere e-mail describing the nature or purpose of your zine, its circulation (i.e., site hits or e-mail subscribers), and your rates. Again, be sure to offer discounts for multiple "insertions" (the ad-business term for placing an ad). I've included a sample solic-itation-letter e-mail at the end of this chapter.

AFFILIATE ADS

Another way to earn income through advertising is to sign up with various affiliate pro-grams that relate in some way to your publication's content. With an affiliate program, you will receive a fee or percentage for every sale that is made through your site. For example, many writers sign up with Amazon.com and advertise relevant books on their site, receiving a percentage of every sale made to a visitor who clicks through to Amazon from their site. However, you won't receive any money up front (as with reg-ular advertising); you'll only get paid *if* visitors actually choose to buy the product. You can find a list of companies that offer affiliate programs through COMMISSION JUNCTION.

ETHICAL CONSIDERATIONS

If you choose to place advertising on your site or in your newsletter, you have a responsibility to readers to make sure that your advertisers are honest. While it may not be possible to personally check out every company that places an ad, stay alert for "warning signs." Recently, I turned down an ad request from a company that "guaranteed" to get writers published (for a fee of nearly $300). Be prepared to take an ad down (and refund the balance of the advertiser's money) if you start to receive reader complaints about the advertiser, or if you discover that the company has a bad reputation.

Another ethical consideration is "special placement." Many advertisers will ask you to place their ad "at the top of the page"—above any other ads that are already running. Many will ask whether they can obtain such placement for an extra fee, or will make it a condition of signing up. While this is an individual decision, I recommend against offering special placement. Chances are, the ads at the "top" of your page are those that have been with you the longest—and it won't please your long-term advertisers to be "bumped" to a lower position just to please a new client.

SELLING SUBSCRIPTIONS

Another means of raising money from an online publication is to sell subscriptions. Unfortunately, this method hasn't worked well for many publications. With so much free information on the Web (and, quite likely, plenty of free information on your subject area), most readers don't feel inclined to pay for an e-zine or e-mail newsletter.

The exception is when the information you provide has a demonstrable "market" value. For example, while most "information" writing newsletters are free, those that focus primarily on market information (such as *Freelancing4Money* and *Write Markets Report*) charge for subscriptions, and have been very successful. The information those newsletters provide equates to potential income for the subscriber.

Trying to sell subscriptions to a Web-based publication can be even more tricky. Again, you'll need to have some type of content that readers consider "worth paying for." With so many free zines on every imaginable topic, that means that your content must have an obvious, preferably *financial* value to the reader. You'll also need to be able to set up a password-protected directory, so that the material will be available only to those who have actually paid for access.

Another problem with offering your zine on a paid-subscription basis is that this is likely to keep your circulation figures low. This, in turn, can affect the price you will be able to charge for paid advertising. It's a good idea to evaluate which is most likely to be profitable: paid subscriptions, or paid advertising.

Many editors have tried to convert a formerly free publication to a paid publication (often after discovering how much maintaining that publication "costs" in terms of both money and time). Sometimes this works, but not often; subscribers who are accustomed to receiving a publication for free are rarely pleased at the news that they must now pay for it.

SELLING A PRODUCT OR SERVICE

Many writers use their sites or newsletters as a means of promoting products—such as their own books. This approach makes particular sense if you are a self-published author, but it's also effective for writers who are commercially published. In this case, the primary ads in your zine or newsletter would be your own; your content would serve as a vehicle to carry your promotions.

Other writers choose to develop products specifically for sale through their site or newsletter. For example, many develop special reports or e-books that relate to the content of the publication. Since these can be "published" and transmitted to the reader at virtually no cost, they can be an ideal "fundraiser."

You may also use your site to promote a service—e.g., to market your writing, editing, or related skills. Many writers offer online classes through their sites, promoting them through their e-mail newsletters. Again, in this case, your publication would serve primarily as a promotional vehicle to market your service. Make sure that your publication has value to the reader, however, and doesn't come across as simply one big ad.

SEEKING CONTRIBUTIONS

We can thank Amazon.com for the proliferation of sites and newsletters that ask for reader contributions and support. Amazon.com developed the brilliant idea of allowing individuals to set up "honor pages," through which site visitors can make a contribution to a Web site, publication, cause, or whatever. One simply sets up an "honor system" account on Amazon.com, places a button or banner on one's Web site, and asks visitors to donate. Visitors make their payment through Amazon.com (which is especially easy if they already have an account). For this service, Amazon.com receives 15 percent of every transaction, plus 15¢.

I have tried this approach myself, with mixed results. I've found that, while my Web site receives around 80,000 visitors per month, most donations come only through the newsletter, and then only when actively solicited. (In addition, many people don't want to donate online, but request an address to which they can mail a check.) Unfortunately, constantly attempting to solicit donations can come across as "begging," which is likely to turn off some readers. While donations can supplement your zine income, you will probably need to consider other sources of support.[3]

THE BOTTOM LINE IS THAT running a Web zine can be hard on the bottom line, particularly if you choose to pay for content or for assistance. It's also important to consider how much *time* you must allocate to your e-zine, because this is time that you're *not* spending on other, possibly more lucrative projects. That doesn't mean that you *shouldn't* publish an e-zine; it simply means that before you embark upon such a project, you should weigh the costs as well as the benefits.

---

[3]It's also not entirely clear how to classify this sort of income with regard to taxes. I refer to this income as "voluntary subscriptions."

SAMPLE CONTRACTS AND AD SOLICITATION LETTER

WEB-ZINE/E-MAIL NEWSLETTER CONTRACT

The contract below is modified from the contract originally developed for the now-defunct Inkspot Web site by Debbie Ridpath Ohi. Paragraph 1 is used for contributions to the e-mail newsletter *Writing World*; paragraph 1b is used if the contribution is for use exclusively on the Writing-World.com Web site.

```
WRITING-WORLD.COM CONTRIBUTOR CONTRACT
Original Article: Newsletter

========================================

Moira Allen, Editor

[address]

[fax/e-mail]

DATE

ADDRESS

Dear NAME:
```

This letter confirms your agreement with Moira Allen, editor of Writing-World.com, concerning the publication of an article or articles tentatively titled "XXXX" ("the Work").

1) You hereby grant to Moira Allen: (a) first publication rights/first electronic rights to the Work, for publication in the "Writing World" newsletter; and (b) nonexclusive electronic rights to archive the Work on the Writing-World.com Web site for a period of twelve months after the article appears in the newsletter.

1b) You hereby grant to Moira Allen: (a) First electronic rights, including the exclusive right to publish the Work on the Writing-World.com Web site for a period of three months; (b) nonexclusive electronic rights for an additional period of nine months, for a total of one year; and (c) nonexclusive electronic rights thereafter, until such time as you request the article to be removed from the Writing-World.com site.

During the first three months, you are free to republish the Work in any nonelectronic medium; after three months, you are free to republish the work in any medium.

2) Once the Work has been published in the "Writing World" newsletter, you are free to republish the Work in any medium at any time.

3) You may request, in writing, the removal of the Work from the Writing-World.com Web site at any time after the first year.

4) Should Writing-World.com fail to publish the Work within six months of acceptance, the "three months exclusive electronic rights" clause will be waived, and you will be free to market the Work to other electronic publications. Should you sell the Work to another electronic publication that requires exclusivity, however, please notify Writing-World.com.

5) We agree to pay you a fee of $XXXX, for XXXX words at 5 cents (U.S.) per word, on acceptance.

6) We reserve the right to edit or otherwise change the Work, or to ask you to make reasonable changes to the Work, prior to publication. No changes will be made that affect the intent or meaning of the Work without consulting you.

7) You agree to allow the use of your photo (if provided), name (or pseudonym), and biographical data in connection with the publication, advertisement and promotion of the Work and of Writing-World.com.

8) You represent and warrant that: (a) you are the sole author of the Work (unless the Work is noted as a collaborative effort); (b) *to the best of your knowledge* the Work does not infringe upon any statutory or common law copyright, trademark right, proprietary right, or any other right of any other person; (c) you are the owner of the rights transferred via this contract, or have the authorization to transfer those rights; (d) the statements in the Work are true *to the best of your knowledge* (unless the Work is noted

as fiction), and the Work is not libelous and does not invade the privacy of any person; and (e) the Work has not previously appeared in any other publication, unless this has otherwise been noted. If any of the terms above are violated, the Work shall be removed from the Writing-World.com Web site, and you shall be liable for any payments provided and/or any costs incurred as a result of the violation of these terms.

Please indicate your agreement to these terms by signing in the space provided below and returning this form to me by mail or fax. I will return a signed copy with your payment. (If you would prefer payment by PayPal, please let me know. Or, if you are a non-U.S. contributor, you may opt to receive payment in the form of an Amazon.com or Amazon.co.uk gift certificate.)

Sincerely,

_____

Moira Allen, Editor, Writing-World.com

Agree to:

_____

Name/Date

SAMPLE ADVERTISING CONTRACT

When completing this contract, I check the type of advertising that has been selected, and then *remove* the paragraphs that do not apply to that type of advertising. For example, if an advertiser was advertising only on the Web site, I would remove the paragraphs discussing newsletter and Author's Bookshelf advertising. Note that if you have other payment options, such as the ability to accept credit cards directly, you should include those in the payment section.

WRITING-WORLD.COM ADVERTISING CONTRACT
======================================

Moira Allen, Editor

[Address]

[fax/e-mail]

DATE

NAME/ADDRESS

Dear ADVERTISER,

Thank you for your request to place an advertisement on Writing-World.com. You have chosen the following sponsorship option:

( ) Site-wide advertising (appearing on 700+ pages)

( ) Newsletter Classified

( ) Author's Bookshelf

Your DISPLAY advertisement is scheduled to run from the first day of MONTH through the last day of MONTH— for a total of *XX* months.

Your NEWSLETTER advertisement is scheduled to run for a total of XX issues, beginning with the issue dated XXXXX.

Your AUTHOR'S BOOKSHELF listing is scheduled to run from the first day of MONTH through the last day of MONTH—for a total of *XX* months.

All site ads will be posted within three working days of the first of the scheduled starting month.

Your total fee for the advertising specified above is: $XX.

Payment may be made by PayPal (to <e-mail>, last name "XXXX"), or by check to:

(Address)

Writing-World.com accepts advertising only for products and services that are useful and/or beneficial to writers (with the exception of Author's Bookshelf listings). We reserve the right to refuse (or remove) any ad that does not appear to be in the best interest of writers. You agree to indemnify Writing-World.com against any complaints or legal actions arising from the use or misuse of your service or product. If you accept these terms and conditions, please sign this agreement and fax or mail it to the address above.

Sincerely,
Moira Allen, Editor, Writing-World.com

Agree to:

_____

Name/Date

AD SOLICITATION E-MAIL

This simple e-mail explains the purpose of my site, and provides circulation figures. It also lists ad rates for single insertions, and directs the potential advertiser to a Web page with more information. (I would also recommend creating a form-letter e-mail with your ad rates and terms, which you can send to anyone who inquires.) The letter also includes a "testimonial" paragraph; it's a good idea to ask your long-term advertisers how their ads are "pulling" and include their comments (assuming they're positive!) in your quest for new advertisers. You may also wish to ask your regular advertisers whether they would be willing to act as references.

Dear

I recently came across your [Web site/advertisement in XXX/other], and wanted to let you know about a writers' site and newsletter that might interest you. Writing World is a biweekly e-mail newsletter from Writing-World.com; it currently has more than 13,000 subscribers (and is passed along to numerous newsgroups and discussion lists). The Writing-World.com Web site attracts more than 80,000 writers per month, and offers over 400 articles, a variety of columns, and a host of other resources.

We offer advertising opportunities on the Web site (120x120 pixel display ads) and in the newsletter. Newsletter advertising costs $XX for two issues, with discounts for longer terms. Web site advertising is $XX for a single month, with substantial discounts for longer terms. Our rates are listed in full at http://www.writing-world.com/admin1/adrates.shtml

Many of our advertisers have been with us for more than a year, and tell us their Writing-World.com ads have been more successful than those placed in Writer's Digest, The Writer, and Byline combined. Please drop by and take a look!

Sincerely,
Moira Allen

RESOURCES

TIPS ON PUBLISHING AN E-ZINE

Commission Junction
www.cj.com
Find affiliates and affiliate advertising for your e-zine or newsletter.

Ezine and Newsletter Publishing
www.worldwidelearn.com/ezine-publishing.htm
Articles, free courses, links, and loads of other information on e-zine publishing, promotion, and profit strategies.

EzineArticles.com
http://ezinearticles.com
Free content for newsletters and e-zines.

Ezine-Tips.com
http://Ezine-Tips.com/about
"Ezine-Tips strives to be the number-one source of free information for newsletter publishers. It covers content creation, format issues, list management, ezine promotion, advertising and other forms of revenue, and strategies to achieve success." This site is packed.

E-zinez.com
www.e-zinez.com/index.html
Subtitled "The Handbook of Ezine Publishing," this site offers tutorials and articles on building an e-zine or e-mail newsletter.

JimWorld
www.jimworld.com
Offers tools and techniques for Web site promotion.

New-List.com
http://New-List.com/instructions
Submit information about your e-zine to subscribers interested in your topic area.

So, You Want to Start an E-zine?
www.zinebook.com/roll.html
Loads of information and resources for e-zine producers.

E-ZINE DIRECTORIES AND RESOURCES

(See Resources, chapter 5, for a list of e-zine directories.)

SERVICES THAT HOST NEWSLETTERS AND MAILING LISTS

FREE SERVICES
Topica
www.topica.com

Yahoo! Groups
http://groups.yahoo.com

Zinester
www.zinester.com

FEE-CHARGING SERVICES
Ezine Manager
http://ezinemanager.com

Listbox
http://v2.listbox.com

<< CHAPTER 15 >>

ELECTRONIC PUBLISHING: IS IT FOR YOU?

WHEN I WROTE THE FIRST edition of this book, part of the task of this chapter was to answer the question, "What is an e-book?"[1] Today (thanks in part to Stephen King), there are probably very few people who haven't at least heard of e-books. However, the question facing *authors* today hasn't changed over the past four years: "Is e-publishing a viable alternative to print publishing?" Or, more specifically, "Should I publish my book electronically?" Four years ago, the answer was "it depends." Today, the answer is still "it depends."

BOOM AND BUST: FOUR YEARS OF E-PUBLISHING

IN 1999, THE E-PUBLISHING COMMUNITY (including e-publishers, e-published authors, and e-book fans) was filled with optimism. Authors were told that e-publishing was the wave of the future. Some predicted that by as early as 2003, e-books would outsell print books, and many boasted that e-books heralded the demise of print books altogether. Naysayers were resoundingly booed and generally considered "obstructionists" to the bright new electronic future that awaited authors.

By 2000 and early 2001, a writer could choose from more than a hundred electronic publishers. Larger companies like MightyWords, aka FatBrain, aka eMatter,

---

[1]It's probably still a good idea to offer a definition, as there are now several types of "electronic" books. In fact, a more appropriate title for this chapter might be "digital" publishing, as the general category of "e-publishing" is usually thought to include "print-on-demand" publishing, which produces print books from digital files (see chapter 16). It also includes "dBooks," or books sold on diskette or CD-ROM, and possibly "etexts," which are digital editions of older, classic works (including novels and nonfiction books that have gone into the public domain) and are generally offered for free. In time, this category may also include "eReplicas"—scanned images of ancient and classic books such as the original Gutenberg Bible.

offered thousands of electronic titles, ranging from ponderous treatises to slim pamphlets. In 2000, Stephen King added fuel to the fire by launching his own e-book, *Riding the Bullet*, which sold nearly half a million copies within the first week.[2] Perhaps inspired by King's success, a number of commercial print publishers, including Random House and Simon and Schuster, launched heavily funded e-publishing divisions. At the same time, companies like iUNIVERSE and XLIBRIS launched massive campaigns to woo authors to subsidy print-on-demand programs.

Unfortunately, this e-publishing boom (which corresponded to some degree with the dot.com boom) eventually busted. Stephen King's next e-project, a serialized novel titled *The Plant*, was shut down in mid-book due to lack of sales, much to the dismay of those who had wanted to find out how it ended. (King's idea of "poor sales" may not match that of most authors, since he was still selling something like 75,000 copies of each installment.) In 2001 and 2002, many of the major publishers shut down or dramatically scaled back their electronic divisions. In 2002, MightyWords closed, the Frankfurt Book Fair discontinued its e-book awards, and the International e-book Award Foundation folded (it was subsequently resurrected by Microsoft).

Smaller independent e-publishers began to collapse as well. In the fall of 2001, I put together a list of ninety e-publishers for an updated resource appendix to the first edition of *Writing.com*. When I checked that list in July 2002, thirty-five of the publishers had closed, and sixteen were not accepting submissions. While some were closed to submissions due to a backlog of manuscripts, others still had "temporarily closed" notices posted since 2001.

Does this mean that e-publishing is dead? Not at all. What it means is that the industry has gone through a necessary shakeup—and that it is still in the developmental stages. According to an article in the *Washington Post,* one problem contributing to the "bust" was that "e-book creators paid way more attention to publishers' requirements ... than to what readers really want from an e-book."[3] E-books (especially those from commercial publishers) were often seen by customers as overpriced—often costing nearly as much as a hardcover original. E-readers (such as the Gemstar e-book) were also slow to catch on, costing $300 to $600. Many booklovers undoubtedly wondered why they should pay that much money for a device on which to *read* books—when they could just as easily spend it on *books.*

As Deb Staples, publisher of SynergEbooks, points out, "Most of the larger companies that folded or scaled back had to do so because they put way too much money into starting the company up in the first place. Many of them started with offering too many digital choices, which means they would've had to purchase a lot of very expensive conversion software. Their marketing budgets were overpriced and caused them to lose most of their working capital very quickly."

---

[2]The word "sold" may be a misnomer, as many outlets offered the e-book for free for several days, so it's not clear how many copies were actually sold and how many were given away.
[3]Linton Weeks, "E-books Not Exactly Flying off the Shelves," *Washington Post*, 6 July 2002, sec. C, p. 1.

Arline Chase, publisher of EBOOKSONTHE.NET, agrees: "Conglomerates want big bucks and millions of customers. The market share isn't large enough for them to bother with right now." As for the demise of smaller companies, Sandy Cummins of WRITERS EXCHANGE E-PUBLISHING, a company based in Australia, notes that "most of the fly-by-night companies who hardly edited their books have shut their doors. Thus the overall quality of the e-books is improving—and our reputation is improving with it."

At the same time, the unbridled optimism of the early days of e-publishing seems to have vanished, or at least been toned down a bit. Chase says that "Most people have lost faith in [e-publishing]. They expected an overnight sweeping change from paper to e-books and that didn't happen any more than movies dying when TV was invented. We believe e-books are still in their infancy and they will become a part of the general publishing picture. We do not believe they will ever 'replace print books,' but they will become more popular and will become an entertainment and informational avenue many people will enjoy." She adds, "We do not expect to get rich on this venture, but we do expect to publish some good and important books and to have fun doing so."

BACK TO BOOM?

Despite all the bad news, e-book sales *have* continued to grow steadily over the past four years. Calvin Reid, who tracks sales for *Publishers Weekly*, reported in June 2002 that e-book sales were increasing by roughly 10 to 15 percent a year.[4] A *Wired* article by M. J. Rose in July 2002 quotes a number of positive sales statistics: FICTIONWISE, for example, was listed as selling more than ten thousand e-books a month, HARD SHELL WORD FACTORY as selling more than a thousand e-books a week, and PALM DIGITAL MEDIA as selling six hundred to a thousand units a day. BOOKLOCKER reported a 65 percent increase in revenues for that year.[5]

The real question, however, is what these numbers mean to authors. In the case of Fictionwise and Palm, the answer is "not much." Fictionwise does not publish original e-books (i.e., as an author, you can't submit an unpublished work to this company for publication). It publishes only "reprints of short stories and novels from professional fiction authors.... Fictionwise will now sell your work if you can offer a *minimum of 10 reprints* that are either novels published by established print publishers ... or short fiction works published in major professional genre magazines...." Nor does Palm Digital Media (aka PeanutPress) publish original titles; it offers electronic versions of works that are already available in print.

The other two figures are more promising. Hard Shell Word Factory has been one of the leading (if not *the* leading) publisher of e-books from the beginning. However, HSWF's front page offers the reader books on disk ("dBooks") and paperback titles; one must go to another section of the site to find e-books. In

[4]Ibid.
[5]M. J. Rose, "Promising Chapter in E-book Story," *WiredNews*, 9 July 2002, *www.wired.com/news/print/0,1294,53699,00.html*

addition, while HSWF offers approximately 196 fiction e-book titles, only *five* of those are actually published by HSWF itself (the other 191 come from other e-publishers), and of the rest, more than 50 are reprints of classic novels now in the public domain.[6] Much of HSWF's sales, therefore, seem to derive from its operations as a *distributor* rather than simply as a *publisher*. (This is not to assume that HSWF is doing badly in that regard either, as it is one of the most respected e-publishers in business; it's simply an example of how misleading oversimplified statistics can be.)

Booklocker.com also offers both electronic and print-on-demand formats. It is not strictly a "publisher," in that it does not offer basic commercial publishing services such as editing, proofreading, book design, etc. (see E-publishing Formats and Options, below). Instead, it functions more as a distributor—authors' books are posted "as is." However, Booklocker.com's success is based on its selectiveness; unlike many distributors, it won't accept "just any" title, but accepts primarily nonfiction titles that have a high sales potential.

Thus, glowing sales figures from those segments of the e-publishing industry that are offering reprints of previously published materials by top-name authors do not necessarily translate into glowing sales figures for authors of original e-books. Since the primary concern of many authors is to "get published," the question at hand is whether e-publishing is the best way to accomplish this.

E-PUBLISHING FORMATS AND OPTIONS

THE GENERIC TERM "E-PUBLISHING" COVERS a variety of publishing models and formats. E-books include downloadable books that can be transferred to your computer, a PDA (such as a Palm) or a handheld e-book reader; books on disk or CD-ROM; and books that are printed out in print-on-demand format. Some publishers offer e-books in a wide range of programs, including Adobe Acrobat and HTML, and formats tailored for handheld devices. (Some also offer books in Word or .exe files, but these formats are less popular.)

E-publishing models include commercial electronic publishers, subsidy publishers (which includes most print-on-demand publishers), "distributors," and self-publishers. (I will not be addressing electronic editions of books currently or previously offered in print, since authors in this case are not technically e-published, but print-published.)

COMMERCIAL E-PUBLISHING

Commercial e-publishers operate much like commercial print publishers, accepting books on the basis of quality and marketability. While authors do not receive an advance, they do receive royalties (often as high as 40 percent), and do not pay anything toward the cost of producing the book. Most commercial publishers provide the same process of review, editing, and proofreading before

---

[6]Though many e-publishers are issuing electronic "reprints" of classic novels that are now in the public domain, you can also obtain most of these for free at Project Gutenberg (*http://gutenberg.net*).

publication as a print publisher. Most also accept fewer than 10 percent of submissions. (A review of e-publisher acceptance rates by Karen Wiesner, published on Writing-World.com in 2001, shows that many accept as few as 1 to 3 percent of submissions.)[7]

Commercial e-publishers typically sell their books through their own Web site, as well as through AMAZON.COM, BARNES & NOBLE, and other electronic bookstores. Some also produce editions for handheld e-readers and other handheld formats (such as the Palm). Some offer both electronic downloads and disks or CD-ROMs, and some also offer print-on-demand services. Most provide such services as obtaining ISBN numbers, copyright registration, and (sometimes) a Library of Congress listing. While it is generally possible to order a commercially published e-book by ISBN through a bookstore, most bookstores do not actually carry them on the shelves.

SUBSIDY E-PUBLISHING AND PRINT-ON-DEMAND

Subsidy e-publishers will accept nearly any title, regardless of quality, and produce it for a fee, paying authors a royalty. Another form of "digital" subsidy electronic publishing is "print-on-demand," in which an actual printed book is created from a stored electronic file. Unlike traditional print publishing, however, in which hundreds or thousands of copies of a book are printed at once, a print-on-demand book is printed a copy at a time. Thus, books are printed only when ordered; the author isn't stuck with dozens of cartons of unsold books in the garage. These two options are discussed in more detail in chapter 16.

NO-FEE "DISTRIBUTORS"

A type of electronic publisher that is difficult to categorize is the "publisher" who accepts electronic manuscripts "as is," usually already formatted by the author, and provides a "bookstore" where those books can be purchased. Generally, such a distributor charges no fee to the author, but takes a percentage of royalties (usually around 25 to 30 percent). A distributor generally does not get involved in editing, designing, or producing the book, and the author can usually set the price (though the distributor may have a minimum price limit). Some distributors, like Booklocker.com, are highly selective about what books they will offer for sale; others will accept most manuscripts. This type of e-publisher/bookseller provides an excellent alternative for the author who is primarily self-published but doesn't wish to go to the hassle of setting up his or her own online "bookstore," accept credit cards, fulfill orders, etc. This also enables a self-published author to avoid registering as a retail business, as the author receives royalties from the distributor rather than direct sales from customers.

ELECTRONIC SELF-PUBLISHING

Many authors choose to electronically self-publish their books. This offers an excellent, inexpensive alternative to print self-publishing—for the obvious reason that one does not incur the cost (which usually runs to several thousand dollars) of getting one's book printed. Marketing costs are usually lower as well, as a

[7]Karen Wiesner, "E-publisher Acceptance Rates," *www.writing-world.com/publish/wiesner.shtml.*

self-published e-author generally does the majority of the marketing via the Web. Distribution costs are minimal (if the book is offered as a disk or CD-ROM) or nonexistent (if it is offered as a download). In addition, if one offers only downloads, rather than providing a "tangible" product such as a diskette or CD-ROM, one may be able to avoid the need to establish oneself as a "publisher" and a "retail business" (for which a business license is needed).

Most self-published e-authors publish in PDF or HTML format. Self-published e-authors are also eligible to participate in Amazon.com's Advantage program (see chapter 11); however, they must be able to provide a disk version of the book, with an ISBN.

It's important to be aware that many subsidy publishers attempt to promote their services as a form of "self-publishing." There is, however, a profound difference between subsidy publishing and self-publishing. The primary difference is in ownership. A self-publisher owns *all* rights to his or her book; no rights are licensed to another publisher. A subsidy publisher, however, receives a license of rights just like a commercial publisher. Another key difference is revenue—the self-publisher receives 100 percent of book sale revenues, while the subsidy-published author receives only a percentage of those revenues in the form of royalties. The self-publisher also retains complete control over the book—its cover, its design, its marketing process, its price and discounts—while the subsidy-published author may not have any say over these matters.

For more information on electronic self-publishing, see Creating Your Own E-book (chapter 17) and Promoting Your Book on the Web (chapter 11).

ADVANTAGES OF E-PUBLISHING

THE MOST OBVIOUS ADVANTAGE OF electronic publishing is the cost. Print publishing involves the cost of paper, expensive printing equipment, packaging, shipping, warehousing, and more. E-books, however, are created and stored electronically; even when such books are sold on diskettes or CD-ROMs, the cost of producing such a book is dramatically less than that of producing a comparable print book. Consequently, e-publishers can run a publishing business on a shoestring (at least compared to the cost of running a print publishing house), and can pass those savings on to readers in the form of lower prices, and to authors in the form of higher royalties. But e-publishers and authors cite a number of other advantages to this medium as well:

BETTER CHANCES OF ACCEPTANCE

"E-publishing is opening the doors for a lot of new authors," says Mary Wolf of Hard Shell Word Factory (HSWF). "It is also a home for those great stories that fall between the cracks with New York publishers for various reasons: don't fit the length requirements; wrong type of hero/heroine; wrong career, era, or setting; etc. We are free to push the envelope, resulting in fresh new voices. . . . At the same time, stories still need to be well-written!" Karen Wiesner, author of *Restless as*

Rain, Leather and Lace, and *Falling Star* (Hard Shell Word Factory) and *Electronic Publishing: The Definitive Guide {The Most Complete Reference to Non-Subsidy E-publishing}* (Avid Press) says, "I can sell things to e-publishers that I could never sell to mass market publishers. Since I'm gaining a strong fan following, this is definitely something I consider important." At the same time, she noted in her "E-publisher Acceptance Rates" survey that many e-publishers accept less than 10 percent of all submissions, which means that 90 percent or more of would-be e-authors are being rejected.

MORE OPPORTUNITIES FOR FIRST-TIMERS, UNKNOWN AUTHORS, OR AUTHORS OF "UNUSUAL" BOOKS

Arline Chase points out, "For writers whose stories don't fit the mold, e-publishing can be a way to find an audience and good reviews. As an instructor at Writer's Digest School for the past five years, I can tell you that there are many good writers with stories that don't fit the 'high concept' mold sought by print publishers today. There used to be about seventy-five to a hundred print publishing companies, owned by people whose tastes and criteria were varied. Most of those imprints are now owned by five major media corporations. It used to be that if an editor liked a book he or she could contract for it. Now titles are chosen by committees who consider content less important than demographics of the customer base. The major publishers want books that will *sell*. They are not interested in producing mid-list authors, or in keeping books in print, or in publishing a good book that won't find a wide audience, just because it *is* good."

Deb Staples believes that "e-books are a great way to put your foot in the door. Now you can say you are a published author, and begin the process of marketing and learning how the publishing business works . . . and you can start on your second book. I believe that e-books are a great way to get talented authors into a market that might otherwise never see them." Chase agrees: "Authors can then go back to traditional publishers with reviews and readers' comments, and may yet find a print publisher and a wider audience."

LESS EMPHASIS ON STANDARD NOVEL LENGTHS

E-publishing offers a market for books that are longer, or shorter, than traditional print novels. It is an excellent market for novelettes, which can be sold for a lower price than a paperback novel and are often more acceptable to the consumer because they are easier to read (or print out) than a full-length novel. This is the primary reason best-selling author Diana Gabaldon offered her story *Hellfire* (previously anthologized in Britain) to the now-defunct Dreams Unlimited: "Care to guess how many paying markets there are for 11,000-word historical mystery stories? Yes, exactly."

MORE CONTROL OVER THE PROCESS

"Writers have greater freedom with characters and plot, more 'say' in revisions, and more input in cover art and sales blurbs," says Wolf. While e-publishing editors may make suggestions for revisions in a manuscript, authors note that there is considerably more room for discussion and negotiation.

HIGHER ROYALTIES

Because the costs of e-publishing are significantly (if not monumentally) lower than those of print publishing, authors receive a far higher percentage of revenues. Royalties range from 20 to 40 percent (in some cases slightly higher); 40 percent is fast becoming the industry standard. Most e-publishers pay royalties every quarter rather than once or twice a year like print publishers. (However, Karen Wiesner, who has sold hundreds of copies of her romance titles and several thousand copies of her nonfiction e-book, notes that "I don't think the combined total of all my book royalties would equal what a standard mid-list author with a traditional publisher makes off a single advance.")

AUTHOR-FRIENDLY CONTRACTS

Most e-publishers ask only for electronic rights, leaving the author free to market print rights and subsidiary rights elsewhere. In addition, most e-publishing contracts are renewable rather than indefinite. Thus, instead of tying up an author's work until it "goes out of print" (a meaningless term in e-publishing!), either party usually has the option to renew or terminate the contract at the end of a specified time (usually a year). Most reputable e-publishers also post their complete contracts online, so that an author can review the terms before submitting.

SHORTER RESPONSE TIMES?

Most e-publishers attempt to respond to submissions within two to four months. Response times are lengthening, however, as the number of submissions increases. "We used to have a four-to-six-week turnaround time," says Marilyn Nesbitt of DiskUs Publishing, "but we get so many submissions now that this is changing. Still, we try to keep a manuscript no longer than four months."

FASTER PUBLICATION?

Some e-publishers will bring out a title within months of acceptance. However, this is becoming less and less common, particularly among the larger e-publishers, which are often backlogged with manuscripts. According to Wiesner, "None of my e-publishers has gotten a book finished and released in less than a year after it was accepted for quite some time." Even though a book could technically be "published" within weeks, many e-publishers prefer to space out their releases over time—some have already scheduled their titles through 2003, which means that manuscripts accepted now may not be published until 2004 or later.

MULTIMEDIA AND FORMAT OPTIONS

An electronic book—whether online or on CD-ROM—can include a variety of multimedia elements to "add to the experience," notes Siobhan McNally of DOMHAN BOOKS. Such elements might include music, graphics, animation, audio, or "interactive/clickable features." McNally also points out that downloadable formats for hand readers often include different fonts, a highlighter, Post-it notes, a clickable table of contents, and bookmarking capabilities. This allows the option of providing different formats for different customers. "DɪskUs publishing has reached out to the aged and those with visual difficulties, because the medium in which we publish allows readers to set the font size or type, which aids in their reading pleasure," says author Leta Nolan Childers.

INTERNATIONAL AVAILABILITY

"Readers in Australia can buy the book the same day it's released to a buyer in the United States," says Bonnee Pierson, former publisher of Dreams Unlimited. "They don't have to wait for export or foreign rights negotiations. This is a terrific advantage for families who are stationed overseas. . . . Vacationing in Europe and running out of reading material? Plug into the Net and buy a new book! It's immediately accessible to everyone, everywhere." Julie Ferguson, who published a book on naval history, says that her title is frequently downloaded by navy members serving at sea.

LONGER "SHELF LIFE"

Since it costs very little to keep an e-book "in stock," a book does not have to sell thousands of copies to remain "in print." As long as sales remain "good" (by e-book standards), most e-publishers are willing to keep a title in their inventory, rather than dropping it for a more profitable title.

DISADVANTAGES OF E-PUBLISHING

UNFORTUNATELY, AUTHORS (AND PUBLISHERS) ADMIT to a number of disadvantages to e-books as well, including:

LOWER SALES

"No, I'm not satisfied with sales—if I were to compare them to a traditional author's sales," admits Karen Wiesner. "I am satisfied by the fact that each royalty period, my earnings at least double. I'm gaining a following slowly, and with e-publishing being so new, I admit that I'm not expecting to become a best-seller for at least five years." As other authors point out, however, few print publishers would give a title five years to become a "success." According to Mary Wolf of HSWF, sales of five hundred are considered good. Two e-publishers surveyed listed average sales of thirty to fifty copies per title, and one described sales of her own e-book as "pitiful." Many authors have found that if a customer has a choice between a print edition (e.g., a POD version) and an electronic edition, the former will outsell the latter, indicating that customers would still prefer a print edition if they have the choice.[8] One question to ask yourself, therefore, is what "being

---

[8]When I offered an electronic version of the previous edition of *Writing.com*, the print edition still outsold the electronic edition ten to one in the first year, even though the electronic edition was less expensive and included an updated Web-resource appendix.

published" means to you. If it means reaching a wide audience with your work—e.g., hundreds or possibly thousands of readers—you may find that goal difficult to meet with an e-book.

LITTLE PUBLISHER PROMOTION

While most commercial publishers make some effort to market their books—often by sending out press releases and review copies to e-zines—all agree that the primary task of marketing falls upon the author. "Don't sit back like your job is over and expect the cash to roll in," warns Wiesner. "In a field this new, you have to do one hundred times more marketing than a traditional author. Don't allow opportunities to pass you by." Shery Ma Belle Arrieta says that marketing isn't a one-time thing, but a daily task. "Once you're done writing your e-book, you become a marketer/promoter." In interviews I conducted with e-book authors, nonfiction authors with experience in self-promotion (including active, popular Web sites) reported significantly higher sales figures than authors of fiction. (For more information on promoting your book online, including Arrieta's tips, see chapter 11.)

LACK OF AVAILABILITY IN BOOKSTORES

Though e-books are available through many online bookstores such as Amazon.com and Barnes & Noble, they are hard to find in traditional bookstores. Though all e-books can be ordered by their ISBN, this isn't the same as being "on the shelf." When traditional bookstores do accept e-books, it is usually due to the promotional efforts of a local author. Research on book sales by such firms as Forrester Research, however, indicate that up to 92 percent of all books are still sold through traditional bookstores—and e-book downloads still make up only a small fraction of the books sold online.

NO ADVANCE

Besides the obvious financial drawbacks of not receiving an advance, this can create other problems for authors. Many professional organizations, such as the ROMANCE WRITERS OF AMERICA, require a writer to have "commercially published" a certain number of books to be eligible for professional membership. However, these organizations also tend to define a "commercial publisher" as one that pays an advance (and that publishes a minimum number of copies). This automatically excludes e-publishers, which means that an e-published author is not considered "professionally" published by these organizations. E-books are excluded from many industry awards for the same reason.

FEWER REVIEWS

While some publications (especially online) review e-books, many traditional book review sources have been slow to accept them. "They're still under the impression that we're not selling 'real' books," says Pierson. Karen Wiesner agrees: "I doubt too many metropolitan newspapers would consider e-books at this time." Nor are e-books likely to be reviewed in major book and library trade publications, such as *Kirkus Reviews* or *Editor and Publisher*.

LACK OF SECURITY

Concerns about piracy deter many authors from considering e-publishing, and indeed, there is little to prevent someone from buying an e-book and making and distributing an unlimited number of copies. (Hackers cracked the security codes on Stephen King's *Riding the Bullet* within days, though this seemed a fairly pointless exercise, as the book was being distributed for free by many online bookstores anyway.) Some e-publishers (including King) attempt to increase security by adding more restrictions to downloads—such as making them nonprintable—which simply serves to annoy consumers. Most e-publishers don't consider this a serious issue, however. Sandy Cummins "recently had a run-in with a group of e-book pirates" and discovered that their main requirements were "cheaper books and the ability to get the well-known print authors' books."

CONSUMER RELUCTANCE TO READ "ONLINE"

Perhaps the biggest obstacle to e-book sales is the reluctance of many consumers to read a book on their computer screen—or pay the cost of paper and toner to print it out. "I love the quality of e-books, but I don't find e-books convenient," says Karen Wiesner. "I can't afford a dedicated reader or a PDA and have no real desire to purchase either of these types of electronic devices. I read on the computer all day, so I'd rather not read a book on a computer or a small PDA screen at night." Michele Johnson of the now-defunct Petals of Life notes that portability is another issue: It's difficult to read an e-book "in the car, in bed, or in the tub." Diana Saenger of SANDS PUBLISHING predicts that "if a reader does not emerge and become as popular as the Palm, e-books are dead. If one emerges, it could become the avalanche of a whole new technology."

Besides consumer reluctance to read a book on a computer screen, there is (as Wiesner notes) the understandable reluctance to pay $300 to $600 for a separate handheld reader. While many companies are working on the "ideal" e-reader, it still seems to be several years in the future.

WHAT TO LOOK FOR IN A COMMERCIAL E-PUBLISHER

THOUGH MANY E-PUBLISHERS HAVE GONE out of business in the past four years, more have arisen to take their place. There are still more than a hundred commercial, independent e-publishers to choose from—so how can you determine what to choose? Here are some pointers offered by publishers and authors:

- Does the publisher have a good Web site? Is it clearly laid out, so that you can tell what the publisher offers?
- When you visit the Web site, does it present an appealing "store front" that entices visitors to buy the books? (If a site doesn't make it easy or inviting to buy, chances are that visitors won't buy *your* book.)
- Did you learn about the publisher from outside publicity, or stumble across it by chance?
- Has the publisher been recommended to you by a reliable source?

- Have the publisher's books (or site) won any awards or achieved particularly favorable reviews or publicity?
- Does the publisher provide its contract either on the site or on request?
- Does the publisher ask for appropriate rights? (Most publishers ask for electronic publishing rights only.)
- Are the royalties "industry standard" (from 20 to 40 percent or higher)?
- Can you cancel the contract after a period of time (or at any time)?
- Does the publisher offer the type of books you write?
- Does the publisher offer the type of books you like to read?
- Are the covers on the site appealing?
- Review some of the excerpts or descriptions of other titles; do they appeal to you? Do they seem well written and edited?
- Are the books priced reasonably?
- Does the publisher offer a variety of formats (e.g., PDF, HTML, Palm, POD, etc.)?
- Has the publisher been in business for long?
- Will the publisher provide you with contact information for other authors, so that you can contact them for references?
- What is the experience of the publisher's editors?
- Are books edited and proofread before publication? (Will you have a chance to review corrections and "galleys" before publication?)
- If books are produced on disk or CD-ROM or in POD format, how many free copies will you receive? What is your author discount on subsequent copies?
- Does the publisher advertise, and if so, where?
- Does the publisher offer advance review copies to professional reviewers and review publications? Where are the publishers' books reviewed?
- What promotional assistance will the publisher offer you?
- Are the publisher's titles on Amazon.com and other online bookstores?
- Does the publisher provide an ISBN and copyright registration?
- Can you communicate with the publisher? Do they answer your questions? Do you feel that the publisher is being honest with you about your book's potential in this medium?
- Will you feel proud of the finished product?

It's also not a bad idea to purchase two or three sample books from the publisher (particularly in the genre in which you would be submitting) to read and review. Check the quality, both of the content and of the editing. Would you read another book by the same author? Or do the books contain grammatical and typographical errors? In short, would you consider your book to be "in good company?"

THINGS TO WATCH OUT FOR IN AN E-PUBLISHER

- A poor Web site that makes it difficult to shop for books or purchase books; a site that is slow to download; or a site that seems more interested in soliciting authors than buyers.

- Any request for money in advance, for *any* purpose.
- Inability to review a contract in advance.
- Inappropriate rights requests, such as requests for subsidiary rights (such as movie, audio, or translation rights) that the publisher is not likely to use. Watch out, as well, for a contract that asks the author to give the publisher a percentage of any subsidiary rights that the *author* sells.
- A contract that claims print rights, or prohibits you from selling print rights elsewhere.
- A contract that claims rights or revenues from the sale of your book *after* the contract itself has been terminated. (For example, one print-on-demand company claims the nonexclusive right to continue selling your book for a full year after you terminate the contract.)
- A contract that does not have a termination clause.
- A contract that claims the right to use your work in other publications offered by the publisher.
- A contract that requires the author to submit his or her *next* book to the same publisher for consideration ("right of first refusal").
- Poor customer service.
- Inability to communicate effectively with the publisher—e.g., e-mails not answered in a timely fashion, or questions not answered fully, honestly, or accurately.
- Anything that gives you an uneasy feeling!

While there are many excellent, professional e-publishers in the business, there are also plenty of individuals who have simply slapped together an "e-publishing business" in the hope that it will make money. Often, these companies are well-intentioned, but simply lack the skills to select high-quality titles, to edit those titles effectively, or to market them. When choosing an e-publisher, you want to find one that will be in business for a while, and that will "invest" in your book.

SHOULD YOU OR SHOULDN'T YOU?

Despite its "boom and bust" swing, electronic publishing is still an industry in its infancy—"in the toddler stage," says Bonnee Pierson—and also an industry that is undergoing rapid change. Technological advances are continually reshaping the industry. Consequently, it is extremely difficult to predict what will happen next or how the industry may change in the next few years.

Many commercial e-publishers are taking active steps to influence these changes and to improve the reputation and acceptance of e-books. E-publishers and authors consider "consumer education" (and industry education) to be a major part of their mission. Most are certain that consumer and industry acceptance of e-books will continue to grow, especially, as Mary Wolf says, "with the next generation, who are growing up with computers and taking reading on them for granted."

One thing is clear: It is a choice to be made carefully, after serious consideration of the potential advantages and disadvantages. It is not a venue to rush into out of desperation or excessive haste to be published. Decide, first and foremost, what you consider your measures of success as an author—and then decide what form of publishing is most likely to achieve those goals.

Electronic self-publishing can, indeed, be a path to success. It can also be a siren song that leads unwary authors onto some serious rocks. Opportunities for online publication should be assessed not on the basis of ego, desperation ("I'll never be published any other way"), or the ease with which such publication can be accomplished, but upon a serious evaluation of the pros and cons. How much effort will you have to expend, for what return? Will your rewards be tangible (more money) or intangible (an enhanced reputation that will lead to a wider audience and more or better assignments)? Knowing exactly what you must invest (time, money, energy, passion) and what you will receive for that investment is the key to making wise Web-publishing choices.

RESOURCES

E-PUBLISHERS REFERENCED IN THIS CHAPTER

Note: Several publishers referenced in this chapter have since closed.

Booklocker
www.booklocker.com

DiskUs Publishing
www.diskuspublishing.com

Domhan Books
www.domhanbooks.com

ebooksonthe.net
www.ebooksonthe.net

Fictionwise
www.fictionwise.com

Hard Shell Word Factory
www.hardshell.com

Palm Digital Media (Peanut Press)
www.peanutpress.com

Sands Publishing
www.sandspublishing.com

Writers Exchange
http://writers-exchange.com/epublishing
An Australian e-publisher offering a wide range of genres and subjects.

DIRECTORIES OF E-PUBLISHERS

ePublishers Yellow Pages
http://ebookdirectory.homestead.com/
Directorypageone.html
A directory of electronic publishers "approved" by EPPRO.

EPPRO: The Electronically Published Professionals
http://eppro.net
"A forum for electronic publishers, authors, editors, marketers, promoters or other professionals working within the e-publishing industry."

Epublishers
www.sff.net/people/Lida.Quillen/epub.html
This list offers links to submission guidelines and notices of publishers that are closed to submissions.

Mary Wolf's Guide to Electronic Publishers
http://my.coredcs.com/~mermaid/epub.html

GENERAL E-PUBLISHING INFORMATION

Binary Thing ePublishing Network
www.binarything.com
"A network of related Web sites dedicated to ePublishing, combining news, information, articles, discussion forums and an online store."

BitBooks.com
http://bitbooks.com
Search engine/directory for digital fiction.

Canadian eAuthors
www.ceauthors.com
Resources for Canadian authors who have been e-published.

Contract Issues: Books Published Online
www.nwu.org/docs/online-p.htm

Electronic Book Web
http://12.108.175.91/ebookweb
News, updates, and reviews of the e-book industry.

Electronic Text & Multimedia Collections
www.library.wisc.edu/etext
Academic electronic text collections, including historic and primary source documents, literature, etc.

Internet Publishing
www.hipiers.com/publishing.html

Piers Anthony's extensive list of electronic publishers, with a review of each (find out who doesn't pay, etc.).

KnowBetter.com

http://knowbetter.com
What began as a site for the Rocket eBook (and still host of the Officially Unofficial Rocket eBook FAQ) is now a source of information on e-book news (all formats and platforms), commentary, e-book reviews, information on freebies, and "E-book Informer," which scours the Web for new releases.

Planet eBook

www.planetebook.com
A site aimed at "Web publishing professionals" and self-publishers, with articles, Web-publishing tools, news updates, a forum and more.

Writer Beware/Epublishers

www.sfwa.org/Beware/epublishers.html
Warnings on the perils of subsidy e-publishing and unethical e-publishers.

CHAPTER 16

SUBSIDY ELECTRONIC PUBLISHING AND PRINT-ON-DEMAND

SUBSIDY E-PUBLISHERS, LIKE THEIR PRINT counterparts, produce and distribute books for a fee (generally ranging from $200 to $500 per book). Authors receive a royalty, which is usually comparable to that offered by commercial e-publishers (around 40 percent). Most subsidy publishers will accept any book, regardless of quality, except for pornography or hate material. Books are not edited or proofread, but published "as is." Many subsidy publishers have a range of extra charges—such as charges for formatting the book if the author has not done so, charges for illustrations, for cover designs, for editing, for an ISBN or copyright registration, etc. These charges can add up quickly. Subsidy publishers provide no promotion, and may offer a lower royalty rate for books that are not sold directly from the publisher's Web site (e.g., if they are sold through Amazon.com or another online bookstore). XLIBRIS, for example, offers 50 percent royalties for e-books sold from its Web site, but only 25 percent for e-books sold through other sites.

Another form of subsidy publishing that is becoming increasingly popular is "print-on-demand" (POD) publishing. This is considered a form of "electronic" (or "digital") publishing in that a book is submitted to the publisher electronically, and is stored as an electronic file, to be printed out in "book format" only when it is actually ordered by the customer. Many publishers offer both electronic and print-on-demand editions of the same book. While a handful of commercial publishers offer both print-on-demand and electronic editions, most POD publishers (including IUNIVERSE and Xlibris) are subsidy publishers.

While many authors and publishers advise against any form of subsidy publishing, many writers choose this route for a variety of reasons. Subsidy publishing can, for example, provide many of the advantages of self-publishing, including more control of the product, for less hassle and at a comparable cost. Subsidy e-publishers offer some of the same (or similar) advantages as commercial e-publishers, including:

- **High acceptance rates.** Many subsidy publishers will accept any manuscript, as long as it does not contain offensive material. In many cases, therefore, "acceptance" is virtually guaranteed.
- **Higher royalties.** A reputable subsidy publisher will offer similar royalties to a commercial publisher—usually 40 to 60 percent.
- **Fast turnaround.** A manuscript may be accepted within one to two weeks of submission and go online in as little as a month.
- **Author-friendly contracts.** Reputable subsidy publishers demand few, if any, rights to your work. Some may request a limited grant of electronic rights; others leave copyright entirely in the hands of the author. As with commercial publishers, subsidy publishing contracts can be renewed (or terminated) by either party after a specific time.
- **Availability.** Like any e-book, subsidy-published books are available worldwide, both from the publisher's Web site and through online bookstores. Nor are subsidized books dropped from inventory for lack of sales. It is usually the author's choice to keep a book "in stock" or to withdraw it.

These advantages, however, come with corresponding disadvantages, including:

- **Lack of quality control.** Since subsidy publishers accept nearly any manuscript, such sites offer little or no quality screening. Consequently, while your book may be of high quality, it may be sharing "Web space" with other books of much lower quality. Consumers who buy an inferior product are less likely to take a risk on another book from the same publisher. Thus, the presence of low-quality books on your publisher's site can actively detract from your own sales.
- **Lack of editing.** Subsidy-published e-books rarely receive any editing—a fact which many sites declare up-front. This means that not only will you not receive any editorial feedback on your material, but that your book will not be copyedited or proofread; it will be posted "as is." Be sure you know how to use a spellchecker! (Some subsidy publishers offer editorial services for an extra fee, or you can choose to hire your own freelance editor.)
- **Lack of promotion.** Most subsidy publishers offer no promotional services; they do not place ads for books in trade magazines or send out advance copies for reviews. The responsibility for promoting and marketing a book usually rests entirely with the author.
- **Lack of respect.** Subsidized e-books are held in extremely poor regard by the majority of the publishing industry (including genre organizations). Most organizations will not consider a subsidized book as a qualification for membership or for industry awards. Many consumers have also learned to avoid subsidized books, due to the lack of quality control.
- **Cost.** Subsidy publishing costs money—usually from $300 to $500 to have your book posted on the site, plus (in some cases) annual maintenance fees. If a site offers editorial services, these come at a cost as well—either an up-front fee or a portion of royalties. In addition, the author must still assume the full cost (in both time and money) of promoting and marketing the book.

PRINT-ON-DEMAND PUBLISHING

FOR MANY WRITERS, POD PUBLISHING offers the best of both worlds. As described earlier, this form of publishing is considered "electronic" (or at least "digital") in that the manuscript is stored as an electronic file until a customer places an order. The book is then printed and delivered. Since books are printed only when ordered, POD publishing avoids the massive up-front cost of printing several thousand copies. Customers, however, can still obtain a hard copy of a book, complete with a professional cover and a well-designed layout.

Many authors have found that if they offer customers the option of an electronic download or a POD edition, the majority will order the POD version. This suggests that most consumers still prefer a printed book to an electronic file if they are given the choice. Print-on-demand is also a good alternative for someone who basically wishes to self-publish, but wishes to avoid the costs associated with producing a printed book.

Many authors have also found that POD is an excellent way to revive out-of-print books. The AUTHORS GUILD offers its members a program through which out-of-print titles can be reissued in POD format, and such titles often sell extremely well. It's worth noting, however, that these titles (and authors) generally have a proven track record of sales, and (quite often) an existing readership.

Needless to say, print-on-demand publishing has a host of disadvantages. One of these is the cost: While POD rates started at around $200, many POD publishers are now asking for a base rate of $500 or more—and that's before the writer receives any "extra" services (such as ISBN, cover design, marketing assistance, proofreading, etc.). Other disadvantages include the following:

- **Your book will not appear in most bookstores.** Very few bookstores will carry print-on-demand titles, because they have a very low profit margin and can't be returned. They can't be purchased in quantity and "stocked" like ordinary titles, so while they can be *ordered* through a bookstore, they won't be found on the shelves. (Several subsidy POD publishers claim that their books are regularly stocked in stores like Barnes & Noble; be very wary of any such claims, and check for yourself.)
- **Your book will not be reviewed by most book reviewers.** Most newspaper book review sections will not consider print-on-demand books (or, indeed, any form of subsidy or self-published title). The *New York Times*, for example, has a policy of reviewing only titles that are "widely available in ... general-interest bookstores." A spokesman for *Publishers Weekly* noted in a *New York Times* article, "We started to review POD books, but we don't want to get inundated with them. There's still a standard of quality that must be met."[1] Other papers and major reviewers are equally reluctant to review POD titles.
- **Your book won't be sent for review.** Since print-on-demand books are expensive, your publisher generally won't be willing to print off more than a few copies

---

[1]Eric Taub, "Books for the Asking," *New York Times*, 17 October 2002; article available online at *http://donswa.home. pipeline.com/nytimes.epublishing.html*.

to send to reviewers. If you want to send more, you'll have to pay for them yourself, which will add up quickly, even at your author's discount.

- **You have little (or no) control over the price of your book.** The cost of a POD book is based on the number of pages (among other factors); the longer the book, the more expensive it is. Consequently, some books are nearly priced out of the market compared to similar books that have been commercially published. You also can't set quantity discounts (as you could with a self-published book), which limits your ability to make "bulk" sales to groups or organizations.
- **You have limited format options.** While some print-on-demand publishers are expanding their ability to handle more than black-and-white text, it can still be difficult (and expensive) to include illustrations, charts, or other nontext elements. At present it's almost impossible to include any sort of color artwork in a standard POD book, and the inclusion of any special elements often means hefty extra fees.
- **You'll receive one or two author copies at most.** Again, as POD books are expensive to produce, your publisher will rarely be generous with "author copies." While most commercial publishers offer at least ten free copies (and can generally be talked into providing more), a POD publisher will usually offer one or, at most, two. This limits the number of copies that you can give away for personal or promotional purposes; you'll have to buy any additional copies. (Your author discount may be anywhere from 40 to 50 percent, but if the price of your book is $18.95, that's still a substantial cost.)

Arline Chase (EBOOKSONTHE.NET) explains one of the primary disadvantages of print-on-demand publishing: the economic problems involved in getting POD titles into bookstores.

POD books never go out of print, but as of now the price is prohibitive and distribution is minimal at best, though that is changing. PODs are printed one at a time, as they are ordered. No book is printed until it *is* ordered and there is a "no returns" policy. Bookstores are reluctant about that.

Print publishers print thousands of copies and may pay as little as $1 each for a trade paperback. Most major distributors pay 30 percent of a sale price—about $4.50 for a trade paperback that sells at $15. They in turn give the bookstores a discount of 40 percent off list price. That $6 discount becomes the bookstore's profit when the book is sold to the customer at $15.

A POD book can cost $6 to print. Obviously, it can't be sold to a distributor for $4.50. The result is that in order to accommodate the distribution system, some POD paperbacks list prices as high as $25. Customers tend to frown on prices that high for a paperback. Bookstores are understandably reluctant to order directly from the POD publisher, because they have to pay full price and make nothing on the transaction.

Because of these bookstore discounts, many print-on-demand publishers offer lower royalties for books sold through bookstores (including Amazon.com) than for books sold directly from the publisher's Web site. Since print-on-demand royalties tend to be lower than e-book royalties (20 to 35 percent rather than 40 percent or more), this can cut significantly into an author's profits. On the other hand, the price of a POD book is generally higher than for an e-book, and many buyers will choose a print edition over an electronic edition even when the latter is less expensive.

Many would-be self-publishers choose the POD route because it involves so little upfront cost. It also enables an author to avoid setting up an entire retail "publishing" business (which involves getting a business license, establishing a "doing business as" name and more). The problem with using POD books in a "self-publishing" venture, however, is that the author cannot set deep enough discounts to sell multiple copies effectively. Similarly, the author must purchase any books used for promotional purposes (such as sending to reviewers). While some POD publishers (such as BOOKLOCKER) offer author discounts, others do not—which means that this could cost the author anywhere from $7 to $15 per review copy.

WARNING SIGNS OF SCAMS AND RIP-OFFS

While many subsidy publishers are reputable, this aspect of the business also lends itself to abuses. If you're considering this form of publishing, watch out for the following telltale signs of rip-off:

- **Excessive up-front cost.** The standard "registration" rates for subsidy e-publishers range between $300 and $500 per title for e-books, while the "base" rate for print-on-demand can be even higher. Be extremely cautious of higher fees, or of attempts to persuade you to buy extra options from a high-priced menu.
- **Excessive renewal fees.** Some subsidy publishers request annual renewal fees in addition to the initial "registration" fee (in addition to the profits that a publisher is earning, theoretically, from the ongoing sale of your book). These fees may range from $100 to $500 per year.
- **Additional "production" costs.** Your registration fee should cover the costs of production, including translating your book into the appropriate online format. (Most subsidy publishers insist that a manuscript be delivered in a specific electronic format, which means that transferring it into the final "published" form is a very simple matter.) It should also include the costs of obtaining an ISBN, copyright registration, and a Library of Congress number. Beware of any publisher who charges an additional "formatting" fee (usually per page) on top of the basic registration fee.
- **Low royalties.** The standard commercial e-publishing royalty rate is at least 40 percent, and some offer as much as 60 percent. Most reputable subsidy publishers pay similar rates. Beware of any publisher that offers a lower fee (10 to 20 percent). Some publishers claim that a 10 percent royalty is "standard"

for the industry, but this is not true. While 10 percent is standard for many parts of the print industry, it is not standard for the e-publishing industry and makes no sense whatsoever for an e-publisher who is receiving an up-front fee to produce your book in the first place.

- **An excessively binding (or demanding) contract.** Most commercial e-publishers use time-limited contracts that enable either party to terminate the agreement after a period of one or two years. Reputable subsidy publishers do the same. Some publishers, however, impose a considerably longer limit on the contract and may ask an additional fee or share of royalties if the author manages to sell the book to another publisher in the interim. Also, watch out for any contract that asks for a transfer of additional rights, such as print rights, translation rights, audio rights, movie rights, etc. By transferring these rights, you enable a publisher to claim a percentage of any of those rights that *you* happen to sell.
- **An incomplete contract.** Most reputable publishers post their contracts online. Some, however, post a "sample" contract that includes terms "to be negotiated." This prevents an author from determining in advance what those terms (often involving rights or royalties) might be.
- **Inflated hype.** Reputable publishers, both commercial and subsidy, are up-front about the difficulties in placing e-books in traditional bookstores. Beware, therefore, of any publisher who claims to offer "bookstore sales" or makes a big deal about getting your book into Amazon.com or Barnes & Noble. Inclusion in the Amazon.com catalog happens automatically as a result of obtaining an ISBN; it is not the result of any special effort on the part of a publisher. Also, be aware that inclusion in online bookstores does not constitute "bookstore distribution."

The bottom line is that if one wishes to embark on a subsidy publishing venture, regardless of the medium, one must be ready to take on far more than just the task of *writing* a book. The subsidy-published author is completely responsible for getting that book to market—and for generating customers. While a savvy author who is skilled in the art of promotion and marketing can often do very well, a great many authors who have gone the subsidy route "just to get in print" have been deeply disappointed by the results. Some authors are happy to simply hold a "published" book in their hands—but those who wish to get their books to readers must be willing to work very hard to accomplish that goal.

SUBSIDY AND PRINT-ON-DEMAND E-PUBLISHERS: SOURCES AND INFORMATION

1stBooks
www.1stbooks.com

Booklocker
www.booklocker.com
Offers electronic publishing and distributing and fee-based print-on-demand publishing.

Dehanna Bailee's Print-on-Demand Database
www.geocities.com/dehannabailee/pod.htm
Compares costs and services of several dozen subsidy POD publishers

iUniverse.com
www.iuniverse.com
Offers subsidy POD publishing.

Print-on-Demand Publisher Database
www.geocities.com/dehannabailee/pod.htm
Dehanna Bailee offers an excerpt from her book, *A Basic Guide to Fee Based*

Print on Demand Publishing Services, comparing production time, costs, submission requirements, etc., of a number of e-publishers and POD providers.

Xlibris
www.xlibris.com
Offers subsidy e-publishing and POD publishing.

Writer Beware/Epublishers
www.sfwa.org/Beware/epublishers.html
Warnings on the perils of subsidy e-publishing and unethical e-publishers.

Writer Beware/Print On Demand
www.sfwa.org/beware/printondemand.html
Cautions to keep in mind when seeking a POD publisher.

CHAPTER 17

CREATING YOUR OWN E-BOOK

THERE ARE A NUMBER OF situations in which you may find it necessary, or desirable, to be able to create your own e-book. If you wish to self-publish an e-book, you'll need to be able to format it attractively, and in an appropriate file format for the reader. Many subsidy e-publishers, e-book distributors, and print-on-demand publishers require the author to provide a ready-made e-book in a specified format, or will charge you for the costs of formatting. Or, you might wish to convert a book previously published in print to electronic format.

Fortunately, creating an e-book is not difficult. You may already have the software you need, and that software can also help you with a number of design issues. This chapter will focus on issues of design and production; actually *writing* your e-book is a completely different topic and won't be covered here.

E-BOOK SOFTWARE

WHILE E-BOOKS ARE AVAILABLE ACROSS a variety of platforms (including versions for handheld e-readers and other handheld devices such as the Palm), the majority of e-books sold online are still produced in Adobe Acrobat PDF format.[1] The reason for this is simple: PDF files can be read by the largest number of platforms (Mac, PC, and many handhelds), and the Acrobat Reader is free, which

---

[1]Some writers sell their e-books in Word format, which is also a good "cross-platform" program since most readers or buyers will already have Word. However, Word does not provide the same level of protection as PDF, which prevents a reader from modifying the text, so I would recommend using this format only for readers or buyers who simply can't handle PDF files. Some writers also make e-books available as .exe files; however, this format will make your e-book inaccessible to anyone using a Macintosh. Since it's simple to create a file that works across both platforms, there seems little point in excluding such a large category of potential readers.

means that your customer doesn't have to buy any special software or equipment to read your book. A PDF file also offers the closest approximation to the "printed page," which makes it easy to read, easy to print, and easy to use by folks who aren't big fans of "reading online."

It's not possible to actually *create* a book in PDF format, however. You must first create your e-book in another program, such as Microsoft Word, or a desktop publishing (DTP) program, such as PageMaker or Quark. I've tried both approaches, and each has advantages and disadvantages.

The advantage of Word is that it is a word-processing program, making it easy for you to actually write and format your e-book at the same time. You can create chapter headings and subheads and generate a table of contents and index within the same document. Word documents also offer more flexibility when converted to PDF: with a touch of a button, you can convert URLs to hotlinks (something that you can't do with a DTP program, which handles text differently).

If, however, your book involves complicated format issues, such as a special design, or lots of photos or illustrations, you may find a DTP program easier to work with. Word can be frustrating when working with illustrations, call-outs, or other special design concerns; a program such as PageMaker or Quark gives you a "what you see is what you get" image of your document, and allows you to drag and drop elements more easily. However, it is more difficult to generate a table of contents or index, or to work with your text once you have converted the document to Acrobat.

Once you're ready to convert your e-book to PDF format, you have two choices. One is to subscribe to ADOBE's online conversion service, which enables you to upload a document (such as a Word file) of no more than 100 MB to have it converted to PDF. You are allowed five free "tryouts" of the system; thereafter, the program costs $9.99 per month or $99.99 per year. The second alternative is to purchase the Adobe Acrobat program itself for $249. (Note that this is *not* the same program as the free Acrobat Reader, which is used to open and display PDF files.) The Adobe Acrobat Distiller, a less powerful version of Acrobat, is also bundled with several other Adobe programs, including PageMaker.

The advantage of the subscription program is, obviously, the price. However, once you've converted your file, you won't be able to make any modifications or enhancements to your e-book. To make any changes to your file, you'll need the actual Acrobat program, which allows you to do the following:

- Add or delete pages, and import pages created from another document or program. (For example, you can import a cover image created separately, in a program such as Photoshop.)
- Coordinate the pagination of your PDF file with the pagination of your actual document. For example, your actual e-book may not begin with "page 1"—it may have front matter that is not included in your pagination. If you simply convert the e-book to a PDF file, however, Acrobat will consider the first page of your document to be "page 1"—which means that your PDF pagination may be different from your text pagination (and thus confusing to the reader).

- Convert URLs to hotlinks. A URL must include the http://prefix to be automatically hot-linked. (This function doesn't work with documents converted from DTP programs.)
- Hot-link your table-of-contents entries to the appropriate pages within the text. You can also hot-link your index entries, and make internal links from one section of text to another (e.g., if you wanted to say, "See page XXX for more information").
- Hot-link any section of text to a Web site (or e-mail address).
- Establish different levels of security for your document. For example, you can disable the printing option (so that a reader can't print your document—an option which should be exercised with care, as it tends to irritate readers who prefer to read a hard copy). You can also password-protect the document to ensure that it isn't read by anyone who hasn't purchased the password.

As with any self-publishing expense, you'll need to weigh the cost of the full Acrobat program against your anticipated gains from the e-book itself. If you are creating only one e-book that you plan to give away, the expense may not seem worthwhile (although ultimately you'll be able to create a better product). Similarly, if the cost of Acrobat is approximately what you'd be charged by a subsidy or POD publisher for formatting your book, it may not be worthwhile. However, if you plan to produce or publish more than one e-book, the program is a sound investment.

DESIGNING YOUR E-BOOK

THE FIRST RULE OF E-BOOK production is: Write the book first, design it second. Get your book written; then, start to think about what you'd like it to look like. You also don't need to make a decision about software until your book is written. You can write your book in Word or some other word-processing program (e.g., WordPerfect) and then convert it to a DTP program. (If you do so, however, keep in mind that some of your formatting may be lost, such as headings and subheads, bold and italic fonts, etc.)

Once the words are on the page, however, you need to make some meaningful decisions about how that page is going to look. A badly formatted e-book will alienate readers more quickly than a badly designed print book. At best, a badly designed book will look amateurish; at worst, it may be difficult to read or "navigate," making your information inaccessible to the reader.

One reason PDF files are so popular is that they mimic the "look" of the printed page. (This in itself says much about readers: Even those who are willing to read electronic material still want it to look as much like "print" as possible.) To develop a pleasing design for your e-book, therefore, the best place to start is by looking at comparable printed books. You'll quickly be able to determine the elements you need to consider in your design, including:

PAGE SIZE

The first thing you'll notice is that printed books are rarely in the 8.5" x 11" format of the typical manuscript page (and, quite probably, the format of your current manuscript). Print books (especially nonfiction paperbacks) tend to have a page size ranging from 5" x 7" to 6" x 9". The reason for this is simple: Narrower pages are easier to read. (That's why magazines divide their pages into columns, so that the eye has less distance to travel.) Fortunately, it's easy to set different page-size parameters in Word or your DTP program; go to the "Page Setup" option and specify, for example, that you want your pages to be 6 inches wide and 9 inches deep.

One important thing to keep in mind when using Acrobat is that your pages don't have to be the same size. If, for example, you have a book flyer that is 8.5" x 11", there is no reason why you can't include that at the end of your book, even though the rest of the book is formatted at 6" x 9". Keep in mind as well that the reader has the option of adjusting the size of your page to fit the screen.

MARGINS

The most common mistake made in self-published print books is a lack of margins. For an attractive, professional layout, make sure that your margins are at least three quarters of an inch on all sides. For an e-book, you don't need to distinguish between "right" and "left" pages, so don't leave a larger "inside" margin as you would when designing a print book.

PAGE HEADERS

Your book should have a "running head" at the top of the page, perhaps a quarter of an inch below the page edge. That head can be located flush with the right margin, or the left, or centered. If your book is divided into chapters, create a new header for each chapter; otherwise, use the title of the book itself for the header. The header should look somewhat different from the main text of the book—for example, you might want to print it in a different-size font, or in italics, or both.

PAGE NUMBERS

You can include your page numbers in the page header, or in a separate footer at the bottom of the page. If you place them in the footer, it may be more appropriate to center them than align them with the left or right margin. (Aligning page numbers with a margin is usually done when you have "left" and "right" pages, a concept that has no meaning in an e-book.) If you choose to include the page number in the header, a good way to design this element is to align the text of the header (e.g., the chapter title) with the left margin of the page and the page number with the right. Be sure that your pagination makes allowances for any illustrations or pages that you will be importing from other types of files.

FONT

Choosing a font is one of the most important decisions you will make when designing your e-book. Take your time; go through the font menu of your word-processing or DTP program and try several typefaces, at different sizes.

Your font should be no smaller than 10 points; an 11- or 12-point font will be easier to read.

For the text of your book, choose a serif font (such as Times, Palatino, or Century Schoolbook), as these are easier to read. For heads and subheads, you can use either a serif or sans-serif font (such as Arial or Helvetica). Use a "proportional" font rather than "nonproportional" font (such as Courier); this is a book, not a manuscript, and readers prefer the font to resemble what they're accustomed to reading in print. Look for a font that is relatively clean and simple; the fancier (and more embellished) the font, the more likely it is to be difficult to read on the screen.

The challenge in choosing a font is that some fonts look good on the screen, while others look good on paper. You want to find a font that looks good on both—so that it will be easily read both by those who read your book online and by those who choose to print it out. Be sure to test your font both on the screen and on paper.

LINE SPACING

While most programs provide automatic line-spacing based on the size of your font, this isn't always the best spacing for an e-book. For ease of reading, it's often a good idea to "open up the page" by adding a little more space between lines than the automatic single-space setting provides—but not so much that the text appears double-spaced. Fortunately, both Word and DTP programs provide the option to set your own spacing. If you're using a 12-point font, experiment with setting your line-spacing at 15 to 17 points or higher. (In Word, you'll find this option under "Format » Paragraph".)

HEADS AND SUBHEADS

You'll undoubtedly be entering heads and subheads as you write your book. If you're using Word, it's a good idea to create "styles" for these headings. By defining "Heading 1" (which should be used for your chapter headings), "Heading 2," "Heading 3," etc., you'll be able to generate a table of contents based on those headings later—and you'll also be able to change the font, size, and spacing of those headings automatically throughout your document simply by redefining the specifications in your style menu. You can also establish styles for heads and subheads in a DTP program—but keep in mind that if you transfer a Word document into a DTP program, that style information will be lost.

ILLUSTRATIONS

One of the advantages of an e-book is that you don't have to pay extra print costs to include color photos, illustrations, drawings, diagrams, etc. However, there are trade-offs: While illustrations won't add significantly to your production costs, they *do* increase the file size of your finished book. If you are planning to e-mail your e-book to customers or readers, or expect to have those customers download it from a Web site, you will want to keep your file size as small as possible. Keep in mind that many readers may be using a slow modem—and won't be happy about the amount of time required to download a 10 MB e-book packed with photos.

If you have a scanner, you can scan your own photos and then convert them into GIF or JPEG files. A basic art or illustration program will enable you to crop those images, enlarge or reduce them, or make other modifications. It will also enable you to choose the "quality" at which you save those images; saving at a lower quality will reduce the file size of each image, and thus the overall file size of your finished book. Unless you need ultra-high quality reproductions, this is generally a good idea.

It's now easy to import scanned photos, illustrations, drawings, diagrams, etc., into either a Word or DTP document. It's not as easy to position those elements in Word as it is in a DTP document, however, so if you expect to have a lot of illustrations, you may find that a DTP program is easier to use. Generally, you will be able to resize your illustrations directly within the document.

When laying out photos or illustrations, be sure to leave an ample margin between the image and the surrounding text, and, where appropriate, include captions.

If an illustration or diagram will take up an entire page, you can format it separately, in an art program (or, in the case of a chart, Excel). Then, after you've converted your primary text to Acrobat, you can import those pages separately and insert them into the text. Be sure to leave a blank page as a "placeholder" where the imported page is supposed to go; this will ensure that your pagination remains correct. (Once you've imported the image file, be sure that you delete the blank page!)

FRONT MATTER

You'll notice quite a bit of "front matter" in a printed book, including a number of blank pages. An e-book doesn't need quite so much front matter, and there is no reason to leave blank pages (except as placeholders for files to be imported later). At a minimum, however, your front matter should include:

- A cover, even if it's simply black-and-white
- A title page (if your cover is black-and-white, a title page may not be needed)
- A copyright page
- Acknowledgments, if desired
- Table of contents

Most books don't physically begin with "page one." The front matter is generally numbered separately, often with small Roman numerals to distinguish it from the rest of the text. The actual page numbering usually begins with the first page of the first chapter (or introduction). However, as I mentioned earlier, this can be awkward when creating an e-book. An Acrobat PDF file will number pages from the first actual page of the book (which might be your cover)—so if your own pagination begins with chapter one, the page numbers in Acrobat won't correspond to the page numbers in your text. If you have the full Acrobat program, you can change this; if, however, you're simply using the conversion program through Word or PageMaker, you can't. In that case, it's better to number your pages from the very beginning of your book, so that the reader won't be confused.

BACK MATTER

If you wish to provide an index for your book, that is considered "back matter." You can automatically generate index entries in either Word or a DTP program, but these entries won't transfer from one program to another. Thus, if you want to export your Word document into a DTP program, you'll have to redo your table of contents and index entries.

The back of your book is a good place to include your bio and contact information. It's also a good place to include advertisements for any other books that you're selling, along with ordering information.

FORMATTING IN WORD

Most of the format elements listed above can be handled in Word. You can change the size of your page, select a font, set up your margins and headers and footers, and develop your table of contents and index, all within a single document. (If you own Adobe Acrobat, you can convert each chapter to PDF separately if you prefer, then import the chapters into your master document. Otherwise, you will have to format and convert the book as a single document; Word's "master document" function won't work here.) Even if you do have Acrobat, it's best to work with a single document rather than multiple separate chapters, as this ensures that your formatting (e.g., subheads, etc.) will be consistent.

To do this, you'll need to know how to use "sections" in Word. Word offers two different types of section breaks: "Next Page" and "Continuous." Use the "Next Page" section break between chapters. Then, you can go into the "Insert » Header/Footer" menu and create separate headers (and footers, if desired) for each chapter. To prevent your chapter headers and footers from appearing on the first page of each chapter, go into "Format » Document, select "layout," and click the "different first page" option under "headers and footers."

When formatting in Word, the key phrase is "check your document"—again and again and again. Whenever you make any change to your format—by changing line-spacing, by moving something to a new page, by inserting a graphic—it's a good idea to first repaginate your entire document, then go back and check it to make sure everything still looks okay. You'll be amazed at how often you end up with a line hanging over on a separate page, or something that has suddenly been bumped out of place. Word is effective in formatting text, but leaves much to be desired when the book includes many graphic elements.

FORMATTING IN ACROBAT

Technically, you will do very little actual formatting in the Adobe Acrobat program itself. Acrobat simply takes the file that you have formatted in Word, and displays it "as is." However, there are certain things you need to keep in mind when formatting *for* Acrobat.

First, if you wish to be able to automatically convert URLs to hotlinks, be sure to include the http:/ /prefix. Then, you can use a single command that will automatically hot-link every URL in your document. (Keep in mind that hotlinks increase the size of your finished file—so a document packed with URLs is going to be a larger file than a document of the same length that is only text.)

Unless you plan to offer your e-book in Word format as well, don't bother to hotlink your URLs in your Word document. These links won't transfer over to the PDF file, so you'll just be wasting your time.

Be sure to set the same page-size parameters in Acrobat as you've set in Word. Otherwise, you'll have a 6" x 9" page sitting in the middle of an 8.5" x 11" "paper." (However, you can include pages of different sizes within your PDF document.)

Acrobat also gives you the ability to hotlink within the text. Thus, you can link table-of-contents entries directly to the appropriate pages. You can also link index entries—but keep in mind that doing this will also dramatically increase the size of your finished file, because of the extra file space required for hotlinks.

DTP files treat text different from Word files. The one difference to keep in mind is that it is *not* possible to automatically hot-link URLs from a DTP file that has been converted to Acrobat. Otherwise, your format should transfer the same way; you'll simply have to hot-link URLs manually (by selecting them and then entering the link).

SHOULD YOU ZIP IT?

If you have a "long" e-book—i.e., a large computer file—you may wish to compress it before making it available to readers. Otherwise, your e-book may take too long to download (which can cause a reader's computer to "freeze" or even crash), or otherwise simply be too awkward to disseminate electronically. I'd recommend compressing any e-book file that is longer than 500 k (and there is no reason not to compress even shorter e-books). If your book is longer than 1 MB, you might even wish to split it into two or more sections and then compress those. Keep in mind that graphic files and hyperlinks take up a lot of file space.

Compressing your e-book is easy. All you need is a program such as DropStuff or DropZip; you can download free demo versions of these programs for Windows or Mac from ALADDIN SYSTEMS. DropStuff will create a .sit file; DropZip will create a .zip file. (I have found little difference between these two in terms of the amount of compression or the ease of reopening the compressed files.)

However, if you choose to compress your e-book file, your readers must be able to open those files again. Often, the necessary software to do this will be built into your reader's browser; however, it's a good idea to provide a link to a site where the user can download a free version of such programs as WINZIP or Aladdin Systems' StuffIt Expander (see Resources). It's also a good idea to give the reader or buyer the option to request or download either the compressed or the uncompressed file.

CONVERTING A PRINT BOOK TO E-FORMAT

MANY AUTHORS ARE FINDING A new electronic (or print-on-demand) market for books previously published in print. This can be a way to revive an out-of-print book, or to find a new market for a book that is still available in print. (Before attempting to offer an electronic edition of a published book, be sure that you own or have reacquired the necessary electronic rights to the work!)

It can be relatively simple to convert a print book to electronic format—or more complicated based on what you hope to achieve with the final document.

The easiest way to convert a print book to electronic format is simply to scan the entire book and save the scanned pages in PDF format. (Most writers find that it's best to actually take the book apart and scan the pages individually, rather than while the pages are still bound together.) This approach will give you an exact electronic facsimile of your original printed book.

This approach has its drawbacks, however. First, an exact facsimile may not be what you want. If you're self-publishing the electronic edition, or publishing it through another agency, you won't want to retain the copyright and publishing information of the original, so you'll need to create new "front matter." Another drawback is that no matter how good your scanner may be, scanned and converted pages are never as clear and easy to read as the original.

If you have an electronic version of your manuscript, another alternative is to format this electronically (as described above). If your book was published within the last ten years, you may also be able to obtain an electronic copy of the edited edition of your book (as opposed to your original manuscript) from the publisher. This approach will also work well if you want to make any changes to the new, electronic edition (something that you won't be able to do if you simply scan the pages).

Despite the claims of OCR (optical character reading) programs, scanning your book and then converting it to text doesn't work terribly well. OCR programs handle some fonts well, and other fonts not so well—and even at their best, they introduce a number of typos and glitches into a document. If you do decide to scan and convert to text, you'll need to proofread your document *extremely* carefully before turning it into an e-book.

If your book has an index that was not part of your original manuscript (i.e., it was added by the publisher), this can add another problem. However, it is actually relatively simple to format your e-book so that it matches the page layout of the original. First, measure the page dimensions of the original text, and use those as your own page layout. Next, count the number of lines of text per page. Create a set of test pages, and experiment with font style and size and line-spacing until you've achieved the same number of lines. Finally, adjust your font size until the content of your electronic pages matches that of the printed book (i.e., each page begins and ends with the same words as the printed pages).

DISTRIBUTING YOUR E-BOOK

IN MANY RESPECTS, AN E-BOOK is a self-publisher's dream come true. No longer does one have to invest thousands of dollars just to get one's book printed (and thousands more to advertise and distribute it). One can simply design it, save it as a file, slap up a Web site to advertise it, and presto! Pure profit!

Of course, it's never that simple. The Web is flooded with self-published and subsidy-published e-books; it can be tough to make a quality offering stand out from the crowd of mediocrity. Chapter 11 looks at ways to promote your book online; this section looks at some of the issues you'll need to resolve if you wish to distribute your own e-book—whether you're selling it or giving it away free.

SETTING UP SHOP

If you wish to sell your e-book, the first question you'll need to answer is "how will customers buy it?" When you offer a product for sale, you become a de facto "retailer"—and this has legal and tax implications. The good news is that there are different regulations governing the sale of purely electronic "information." Since you may not be dealing with a "tangible" product—an actual, physical book—you may be able to avoid having to obtain a retail business license, or registering a "doing business as" name, etc. And, indeed, many writers are doing just that, setting up e-shop on their Web sites and selling e-books without any thought given to business licenses.

Setting up shop can be a complex process in itself, however. If you plan to sell your self-published e-book, you need a mechanism by which customers can order and pay for it. And since you'll be selling primarily through the Web, most customers will expect to be able to pay for your book with a credit card. However, obtaining "merchant status" so that you can accept credit cards on your own can be nearly impossible for the self-publisher (as self-publishers of print books have discovered to their dismay for years). Credit-card acceptance and "shopping cart" services can also be expensive, taking a hefty chunk of your profits.

Two useful alternatives are PayPal and ClickBank. Needless to say, each has its advantages and disadvantages.

The advantage of PayPal (now owned by eBay) is its relative ease of use for the seller, and its low fees. For a premier or merchant account (required if you wish to receive credit card payments), the fee for receiving funds ranges from 2.2 percent (merchant) to 2.9 percent (premier) plus 30 cents per transaction. (International transactions are charged an additional 1 percent). There is no setup fee and no fee for sending money. You can also transfer funds from your PayPal account directly to your bank account.

The disadvantage is that many potential customers balk at the need to establish an account on PayPal before being able to send you money. Also, while PayPal does serve several countries besides the United States, the procedures for setting up a non-U.S. account can be complicated. (As of this writing, PayPal has indicated that, thanks to its purchase by eBay in July 2002, it will be able to streamline international transactions; but as yet, the process is still cumbersome, and PayPal is far from popular outside the United States.)

ClickBank offers a more streamlined approach to purchasing: Customers don't have to set up an account, but can use their credit card just as with any online store. This also makes ClickBank more accessible for international customers. Another advantage of ClickBank is the ability to set up affiliate accounts, which means that you can sign up other people to promote and sell your book through their own sites. The downside of ClickBank is its higher fee—$1 plus 7.5 percent per transaction, plus a $49.95 setup fee.[2]

ClickBank also restricts transactions to the sale of digital products only—i.e., your product must be "deliverable entirely over the internet via Web pages, downloadable files, or e-mail." You cannot use ClickBank to sell a physical product, such as a diskette or CD-ROM. PayPal makes no such distinction.

Both ClickBank and PayPal allow you to offer your customers secure transactions—as you aren't handling the transfer of funds through your site directly. All you need to do is provide an order page on your site with a link to the payment service of your choice.

Another option is to use the AMAZON.COM HONOR SYSTEM to handle your payments. The advantage of this system is that more people are familiar with, and comfortable with, Amazon.com, and may already have an Amazon.com account. The disadvantage is the fee: 15 percent plus 15¢ (which would cost $1.65 for a $10 book).

DELIVERING THE PRODUCT

Whether you're selling your book or giving it away for free, you need to determine how to actually deliver it to the reader or customer. The most common methods are via download or e-mail, or by mailing a diskette or CD-ROM.

To offer a downloadable version of your e-book, you'll need to set up a page on your Web site that explains how to download the book and offers a list of the format options available (e.g., different formats for different platforms, or a choice between a compressed file or a larger uncompressed file). Then, simply upload your e-book files to your Web site and provide a link to each file from the download page. For example, your download page might be "http://www.mydomain.com/ebooks/mybook.html," which would offer a link to "http://www.mydomain.com/ebooks/mybook.pdf" (for a copy of the book in PDF format) and "http:/ /www.mydomain.com/ebooks/mybook.zip" (for a zipped copy). Your download page should also provide links to any software that the buyer might need to read your book—including ADOBE Acrobat Reader, if the book is in PDF format, or any necessary unzipping/unstuffing programs such as WINZIP or ALADDIN SYSTEMS' StuffIt Expander to open a compressed file.

Provide clear instructions on *how* to download your file. If your book is in PDF format, remind buyers to "right-click" the file to download[3], so that it will be saved to their hard drive. Otherwise, the user's browser will attempt to treat the PDF file as an HTML page, and try to open and display it while it downloads. This can cause major delays in the downloading process, and in the case of a large PDF file, can cause the user's system to freeze or crash.

If you are selling the e-book, you can set up your ClickBank or PayPal payment page to redirect the customer back to your download page after they have paid.

---

[2]To compare costs, a $10 book sale would cost 59¢ through PayPal, and $1.75 through ClickBank.
[3]This instruction will have meaning only to Windows users. Mac users don't have a "right click" option—but neither do they have quite as many problems in downloading PDF files.

A more complicated approach is to set up a password-protected directory, so that no one can download the book until they have paid for it and received a password. However, not all ISPs allow this type of directory; you'll need to discuss this option with your ISP's technical support, or consider arranging such a page with another site that can provide an online "store" or "shopping cart."

No matter how clearly you spell out download instructions, however, you will find that a great many customers either can't download the book properly, or (amazingly) don't even seem to see the page. For these customers, you'll need to e-mail the book. Or, you may prefer to provide the book only via e-mail, either on request or after you've received confirmation that the customer has paid for a book. The downside of this approach is that you're responsible for getting the book to the customer in a timely fashion—usually within 24 hours of receiving the order. It means that you will have to respond to every order personally. This means that going on vacation can be a problem, as a customer won't want to wait a week or two to receive the book.

The other difficulty with e-mail is the problems and concerns many users now have with e-mail attachments. Many people have now set their systems to screen out *all* attachments, for fear of viruses. Others are unable to receive large attachments due to the size limits set by their ISPs.

The final option is to physically mail your e-book on a disk or CD-ROM. This option is technically precluded by ClickBank, but not by PayPal.[4] If, however, you wish to sell your book through Amazon.com, a physical disk (and ISBN) are required. (E-book self-publishers can sell such disks through the AMAZON.COM ADVANTAGE program—see chapter 11 for more information.)

Selling your own e-book has the advantage of putting you in complete control of your product, and ensuring that you receive 100 percent of sales revenues. However, it also puts you in the less pleasant position of being responsible for customer service: Making sure a customer has actually paid for a book, making sure the customer is able to receive the book, and dealing with customer complaints and questions. You may find that these aspects of self-publishing are more hassle than they're worth. If so, you may find the services of an e-book distributor (such as BOOKLOCKER.COM) worth the expense. Distributors generally claim 25 to 35 percent of revenues—but they also handle all the technical issues of accepting payments and delivering the product, as well as the majority of customer questions and complaints. And since such distributors may have additional marketing channels, you may even find that you sell more books through a distributor than on your own.

---

[4]You will undoubtedly encounter the occasional customer who can't successfully download the book *or* receive it as an e-mail attachment, in which case mailing a disk is the last resort—and should not violate ClickBank's rules against selling physical goods.

RESOURCES

BOOK PRODUCTION

Adobe
www.adobe.com
Produces Adobe Acrobat and the Acrobat Reader, as well as PageMaker and Photoshop.

Aladdin Systems
www.aladdinsys.com
Produces DropStuff, DropZip, StuffIt, and StuffItExpander.

How to Create PDF Files
www.etc.buffalo.edu/workshops/pdf/ How_to_create_PDF_files.html
This is a fairly complex explanation of a simple process, and applies only to Windows.

WinZip
www.winzip.com
A free, downloadable program enabling you to open zipped files.

BANKING AND CREDIT CARD SERVICES

#1 Credit Card Processing & Accept Credit Cards
www.1-credit-card-processing-accept-credit-cards.com/pricing.htm

Accept Credit Cards Today
www.accept-credit-cards-today.com

Amazon.com Honor System
http://s1.amazon.com/exec/varzea/subst/fx /home.html

CCNOW
www.ccnow.com

ClickBank
www.clickbank.com

PayPal
www.paypal.com

Total Merchant Services
https://application.acceptcreditcards.com

You Can Take Credit Cards Online
www.youcantakecreditcardsonline.com
E-book by Michael Knowles comparing and explaining various methods of accepting credit cards.

(See Resources, chapter 11, for book promotion resources, including Amazon.com's Advantage program.)

CHAPTER 18

WHERE NEXT?

I N THE FIRST EDITION OF this book, I noted that "Trying to make predictions about the future of the Internet is like trying to fish for eels with a wire hanger: The results aren't likely to be what you hoped for, and you're also likely to receive some serious shocks." Nevertheless, I'm going to take that hanger and go fishing—in hopes of providing a potential glimpse of what lies ahead for writers in cyberspace.

In the first edition, I asked several writers to share their predictions for the future. Some of those predictions were hits, some misses. For example, I predicted that the online marketplace would expand; instead, it seems to be shrinking. One author predicted that e-books would rapidly take a chunk out of the print publishing market; as yet, that hasn't happened. Another predicted that e-books might become the ghetto of midlist authors, which, fortunately, hasn't happened either. Predictions about a rising flood of "new styles" of creativity, blending multimedia with the written word, haven't come to pass *yet,* primarily because technology hasn't quite caught up with imagination. (When it becomes possible to *easily* manipulate and download multimedia elements, I suspect this prediction will come true.) Concerns about copyright protection being extended to cover *information* rather than just how that information is expressed (a move urged by several database companies) have also, fortunately, not come to pass.

The two predictions that proved most accurate were that electronic rights issues would become an increasing problem—and that the Internet would become increasingly important to writers. The latter was voiced by Debbie Ridpath Ohi, who declared that "Having online access will become a necessity for writers rather than a luxury." Ohi predicted that more and more editors would want to receive queries and submissions by e-mail, and that any writer who could not communicate by this means would be at a disadvantage. That prediction, indeed, could be considered the foundation of *this* edition—which is based on the belief that writers can no longer afford to stay offline.

With two hits and an abundance of misses, is it possible to attempt to guess what lies ahead in the *next* four years? I'll take a firmly ambivalent position here, and say "yes and no." Rather than trying to predict what will happen next in cyberspace, I'd like to take a moment to discuss some of the issues that will *affect* what happens in cyberspace—one way or another.

THEY CALL IT THE WORLD WIDE WEB ...

A GREAT MANY PREDICTIONS ABOUT the future of the Internet are made while looking primarily *just* at what is happening *on* the Internet. The Internet, however, does not exist in a vacuum. To look at the future of the Internet (and in particular, how that future will affect our future as writers), we have to look at the bigger picture as well—specifically, the global picture and the economic picture. (And those are so easy to predict—not!)

FOLLOW THE MONEY

The future of the Internet (and how that future affects writers) depends to a great extent on the economy outside the Internet. The dot.com boom and bust of 1999 to 2001 took down some of the Internet's major players, and left others scrambling in the wake of reduced revenues. This has had an impact on all of us.

Themestream, for example, thought it could sell ads for hundreds of thousands of dollars by attracting "eyeballs" to the site through "content." Thus, it allowed writers to post just about anything they wanted (unscreened and unedited) and paid them first 10 cents a hit and later 2 cents a hit. When the site died in 2001, it was the writers who were left with no means of collecting what they were owed. Pets.com thought it could make money by selling dog food online (though one wonders who *really* goes online to shop for a fifty-pound sack of kibble or rawhide chew toys). Again, it tried to attract customers by offering content—and for a time, Pets.com was a wonderful market for pet writers. Then it, too, crashed and burned.

The media conglomerate Primedia bought the "guide site" ABOUT.COM for $690 million in 2000; subsequently, Primedia stock dropped from $8.85 a share in 2001 to $1.35 in June 2002. Though About.com still pays its guides, it dropped hundreds of topics (and editors), and is currently facing a lawsuit from former guides. Primedia's hard times are affecting writers in other ways as well: The company has been dropping many of its titles, including *Cats* and *Teen Magazine*. Those magazines, which were profitable when managed by smaller, independent companies, just weren't bringing in the numbers for a huge corporation like Primedia—and when magazines die, writers lose.

The problem of finding effective revenue streams has affected most online publications. Some have tried to switch from free subscriptions to paid subscriptions—which often doesn't go over well with readers. Some ask for reader donations. Some respond by reducing the amount they pay writers, or by asking for more rights, or by ceasing to pay altogether. And some simply shut down.

Since I began tracking electronic markets for my biweekly newsletter, *Writing World*, I've seen this marketplace shrink rather than grow. E-zines disappear literally overnight, and as the older markets die, I'm not seeing new ones arising to take their place. In addition to economics, another (but not unrelated) issue is "burnout." Many editors began their publications as labors of love—but over time, found that the "labor" outweighed the "love." As the economy has gotten tighter, many of those editors have found that they needed to spend more and more time on paying projects—which meant less time for their e-zines. Thus many independent publications are changing hands, going under, or both (as in the case of Inkspot, which was bought by Xlibris and then shut down).

As I write this in July 2002, the stock market has just experienced one of its fastest and deepest plunges in history, and is being described as "the worst bear market in twenty-five years." Yet the last "worst plunge in history" occurred in 1997—just two years before the dot.com boom of 1999. By the time you actually read this, the economy could be worse—or it could be dramatically better. I wouldn't dare attempt to predict which. But even when the economy gets better, the situation for writers remains tenuous. In a "good" economy, multimedia conglomerates have more money with which to buy up smaller companies—thus, the "boom" times lead to media mergers and acquisitions that continue to shrink the market for writers. When the "bust" time comes, those companies hose off their less profitable publications and divisions, shrinking the market still further.

Whether we're in a boom or a bust, things seem to be steadily worsening for writers. Publications are turning increasingly to "all rights" or "work-for-hire" contracts, eliminating the writer's ability to resell material. At the same time, rates are not going up. A magazine I worked for from 1985 to 1987 paid an average of $200 for a feature article then—and pays the same today. Fiction magazines paid around 2 cents a word in the 1940s; today, the Science Fiction Writers of America considers 3 cents a word to be a "professional" rate. So whether you use the Internet to sell your work to online publications or to find more print markets, my prediction is "tighten your belt, it's just going to get worse."

CYBER SECURITY

Another global issue facing anyone who uses the Internet is the question of security. The events of September 11, 2001, reminded the world in general and America in particular that life isn't as secure as it seems—that we can be attacked when and where we least expect it. But the place that many experts *expect* to be attacked is not on the ground (or the air), but in cyberspace.

Cyberwars have already flamed up and sputtered out on a global scale. In 2001, Israeli hackers attacked Palestinian Web sites, and Palestinian hackers responded by declaring "cyber jihad" not only on Israeli sites, but on sites belonging to any country thought to be "friends" with Israel, including U.S. sites. This particular cyberwar involved not only Israelis and Palestinians, but hackers from many other countries who aligned themselves on one side or the other. While the effects on the United States were minimal, experts are well aware that the next "cyberwar" could be much more costly.

One area in which this may affect writers is that of privacy. Writers could be affected by government efforts to monitor chat rooms and e-mail, or by legislation that would make it more difficult to remain completely anonymous online. We could be affected if the government takes steps to find out who visits particular sites or gathers particular types of information (as is already happening in some bookstores and libraries).

Another area of concern is confidence in the safety and privacy of online transactions. Many people are still reluctant to use a credit card online, or to provide the amount of personal information required to set up an account in many online stores. As concerns about identity theft and selling of one's personal information increase, concerns about online transactions may increase as well. The online marketplace, however, thrives on the credit system. If the safety of that system is jeopardized, either by an outside attack, by hackers, by corporate greed, or by government surveillance, this could affect the ability of writers to sell their e-books or products, or to sell subscriptions or advertising for their e-zines, and so forth.

Again, it's impossible to predict how this is all going to turn out. What I *can* predict is that the debate over privacy vs. security is going to go on long after this book is published![1]

E-PUBLISHING: WILL IT BOOM OR BUST?

While it's not clear whether global security issues will greatly affect e-publishing, that industry is certainly affected by the economy. As I mentioned in chapter 15, several major print publishers attempted to launch e-publishing arms between 1999 and 2000, but shut them down or scaled them back by 2001 and 2002. But this isn't necessarily bad news for e-publishing; in fact, it could be very good news.

The whole purpose driving e-publishing was to provide authors with an alternative to the huge media conglomerates that had taken over the print publishing industry. In print publishing, even popular "midlist" authors find themselves squeezed out, as publishers search for the next mega-blockbuster-hit that will bring in millions. First-time authors find it harder and harder to get a break. So it would seem, really, that the last thing we want, as writers, is to have the major publishers take over the e-publishing industry and shape it according to their dollar-driven desires. If e-publishing becomes the domain of big publishers and big-name authors, then nothing will change for the rest of us.

The e-publishers that have risen to the top, however, are those who were able to operate on a smaller scale. There simply isn't a sufficient market for e-books to fuel the requirements of a huge corporation—but the market *can*

[1]For more information, see "Privacy vs. Security" in *E-Business Security Advisor,* *www.advisor.com/Articles.nsf/ aid/COBBM73,* and "Terrorist Threat Shifts Priorities in Online Rights Debate," *http://news.com.com/2009–1023– 272972.html* (and its sidebar on various Internet surveillance technologies).

sustain a publisher who literally works out of the garage, as Angela Adair Hoy did when she originally founded BOOKLOCKER.COM. It can't sustain a company that is accustomed to hiring full-time personnel in a single corporate office—but it can sustain a company that "outsources" editing and other tasks to a network of editors, proofreaders, and designers, who may live thousands of miles from the actual publisher.

The biggest problem facing the e-publishing market, in my opinion, is the fact that it has arisen primarily as a solution to problems facing *authors* (the difficulty in getting published)—but not problems facing *consumers*. Typically, a successful product moves into a niche that has not yet been filled—but it's hard to argue that the "book" niche is unfilled from the consumer's perspective. Rare is the reader who walks into Barnes & Noble and sighs that there is "nothing to read." Thus, many consumers don't buy e-books because they don't feel that they *need* e-books.

Another problem facing e-books is that, at present, they don't mesh well with the current "economic model" of how books are bought, sold, and handled by consumers. Consumers don't just view books as a collection of words (which could be read as easily on a screen as on a page), but as tangible products. A book is something one can buy, read, loan to one's sister, give to a friend, donate to the library, or sell to a used-book store. Avid readers use these same methods to *acquire* books (including books that can be obtained no other way, such as books that are out of print)—e-books may never be able to compete with the library book-sale, where you can buy a bag of paperbacks for $5. It's also hard to imagine, as yet, how one will be able to wrap up an e-book and give it to one's nephew for Christmas.

Economic factors may ultimately help in this regard as well. "Sticker shock" is becoming an increasing factor in the book market—it's hard to accept that a paperback novel now costs as much as $9. If e-books can offer a comparable value for a lower price, then they *will* begin to fill a customer need—the growing need for books that one can afford. However, even inexpensive e-books will still be in competition with the used-book stores (online and off) and the library book-sales.

Another niche that e-books have the potential to fill is in the nonfiction reference market. Having just transported forty boxes of books from one home to another, I can attest that if half of those books were electronic, it would have spared my back and my moving bill. It would also make looking up information far simpler—instead of having to thumb through three or four books on the shelf, one could do an electronic search of one's reference collection and find the answer to a question in minutes. It's no coincidence that Booklocker.com, which focuses almost entirely on nonfiction, is regarded as one of the most successful independent e-publishers and e-book distributors in the industry.

I believe the question facing the e-publishing industry, therefore, is whether it can become consumer-focused rather than author-focused. E-publishers need to stop asking, "How can we persuade consumers to buy the books that we publish?" and start asking, "How can we publish the kinds of books consumers will be willing to buy and read electronically?" E-publishing will become an author's dream when it becomes a consumer's dream.

E-RIGHTS: THE BATTLE CONTINUES

IF ANYTHING CAN BE PREDICTED "for certain," it is that writers haven't seen the end of the battle over electronic rights. If past skirmishes are any example, however, there seems a good chance that the battle isn't going to go our way. The problem is that even when we win, we lose.

The *Tasini* case (see chapter 8) is an example. It served more or less as the "test case" for electronic rights issues. Jonathan Tasini, head of the National Writers Union, et al., sued several major publishing companies over the unauthorized use of writers' materials in electronic databases. The first round went to the publishers; the second went to Tasini. But even though Tasini eventually *won,* it's hard to claim that his victory really helped writers.

Certainly, it established conditions under which one's work could and could not be reused without permission. But rather than acknowledge those conditions, the reaction of publishers has simply been to impose all-rights and even work-for-hire contracts upon freelancers and contributors. Some have even attempted (in some cases successfully) to impose *retroactive* all-rights contracts on their contributors. This is an insidious ploy that requires contributors to grant all rights to works that the publisher has *previously* purchased if they want the publisher to buy any *future* works.

In addition, rather than attempting to provide writers with any extra compensation for works that had been placed in electronic databases without permission, publishers responded to the *Tasini* decision by purging those databases of any material to which they did not already own the electronic rights. Publishers raised a great "woe is us" cry about how the *Tasini* decision thus damaged our collective information "heritage"—but few were impressed, including judges handling the *Tasini* case. The bottom line, though, was that for writers, there was no *improvement* to the bottom line.

The other landmark case referenced in chapter 8, *Random House v. RosettaBooks,* will also undoubtedly have negative repercussions for writers. The crux of this case was that RosettaBooks had published electronic editions of titles originally published in print by Random House before book contracts covered electronic rights. Random House argued that their contracts actually gave them the rights to *any* type of edition, including electronic editions, even though such rights were not specified. (It is worth noting, by the way, that Random House did *not* bother to sue its authors, who were the ones who granted RosettaBooks the electronic rights, even though, according to Random House, they should have had no right to do so.)

Random House was blocked from its efforts to prevent RosettaBooks from publishing the titles while the lawsuit proceeded, and the two publishers ultimately reached an agreement to work together. However, again, the result of this decision is likely to be to persuade book publishers that they must lock in every *imaginable* future book right, to preclude such problems in the future. And that, in fact, is precisely why some contracts include rights to media "as yet to be envisioned"—so that if, in the future, we really do start putting books on data crystals, that will be covered in our old contracts.

Thus, while writers are winning in court, they're losing in the marketplace. The reason for this, again, goes back to global economic factors. Publishing houses—whether book or periodical—are no longer small, author-friendly family affairs. Giant media conglomerates such as Primedia and Bertelsmann are gobbling up the independents at a terrifying rate—and imposing their own, company-wide contracts on everyone concerned. Thus, when an author tries to negotiate a contract, he or she can no longer simply talk it over with an editor and come to an agreement—because that contract was most likely issued by the media conglomerate's legal department, leaving the editor no "say" over its terms and conditions.

Having watched this trend for more than four years now, I can only believe that things are going to get worse for writers before they get better. The reason is simple: Writers lack clout. Even the major writing advocacy groups have little real power against the multimedia conglomerates dominating the industry. While groups like Author's Guild and ASJA have had some effect on industry contracts, the overall trend is toward larger rights demands—with little or no increase in compensation.

Ironically, the answer to this problem could lie in a worsening economy. Media mergers have been the result of "boom" times—times when larger companies have the funds to gobble up their smaller competitors, and when the desire to own everything in sight seems to make economic sense. However, as the economy grows tighter, this approach tends to backfire—as we've seen in the highly publicized World.com failure, and as we're seeing in the publishing world with Primedia, which has hosed off several publications that it previously "gobbled," for not being sufficiently profitable.

When a major corporation gobbles up publications and then shuts them down, that reopens the market niche for those publications. It opens the door for smaller independent companies to launch new publications, because they are no longer facing impossible competition from the "big guys." While a sluggish economy is not the best time for a small company to launch a publication, as that economy swings back, there is a chance once again for more author-friendly independents to make a comeback.

In the meantime, all we can do as writers is be alert to excessive demands upon our rights, and resist them whenever we can. However, authors must also weigh "high principles" against the very simple need to earn a living. And no matter how often we say "no" to unreasonable contracts, editors know that there is always a writer somewhere who will say "yes." And so, as I said before, it seems to me that this situation is going to get worse before it gets better.

IF THERE IS ONE PREDICTION I can make with confidence, it is the same one that Debbie Ridpath Ohi made four years ago: The Internet is here to stay. Writers can no more ignore it than they could ignore the arrival of personal computers. Being able to function effectively in cyberspace is no longer a luxury; it's a necessity. Fortunately, it can also be intensely rewarding, extremely helpful—and at times, just plain loads of fun. Happy surfing!

<< Appendix A >>

ALPHABETICAL LIST OF ONLINE RESOURCES

#1 Credit Card Processing & Accept Credit Cards—
www.1-credit-card-processing-accept-credit-cards.com/pricing.htm

@Submit!—*http://uswebsites.com/submit*

1.2.3.Count.com Traffic Analysis—*www.123count.com*

13 Warning Signs of a Bad Poetry Contest—
www.winningwriters.com/warningsigns.htm

About.com—*http://beaguide.about.com/index.htm*

ABYZ News Links—*www.abyznewslinks.com*

Accept Credit Cards Today—*www.accept-credit-cards-today.com*

AcqWeb—*www.library.vanderbilt.edu/law/acqs/email-ad.html*

Acrobat Reader—*www.adobe.com/products/acrobat/readstep2.html*

AddAll Book Searching and Price Comparison—*www.addall.com*

Adobe—*www.adobe.com*

Adobe/Tryouts—*www.adobe.com/products/tryadobe/main.jhtml*

Aladdin Systems—*www.aladdinsys.com*

Alta Vista—*www.altavista.com*

Amazon.com—*www.amazon.com*

Amazon.com Advantage program—
www.amazon.com/exec/obidos/subst/partners/direct/direct-application.html

Amazon.com Associates program—
www.amazon.com/exec/obidos/subst/partners/associates/associates.html

Amazon.com Catalog Guide—
www.amazon.com/exec/obidos/subst/partners/publishers/catalog-guide.html

Amazon.com Honor System—
http://s1.amazon.com/exec/varzea/subst/fx/home.html

Amazon.com Look Inside the Book program—
www.amazon.com/exec/obidos/subst/partners/publishers/look-inside.html

American Bar Association/Lawyer Referral Services—
www.abanet.org/legalservices/lris/directory.html

AnalogX Whois Ultra—*www.analogx.com/contents/download/network.htm*

Antivirus Software—*http://antivirus.about.com*

AOL Instant Messenger—*www.aim.com/index.adp*

ASJA Contract Watch—*www.asja.org/cw/cw.php*

Assignment Editor—*www.assignmenteditor.com*

Association of American University Presses—*http://aaupnet.org*

Association of Research Libraries/Copyright and Intellectual Property—
www.arl.org/info/frn/copy/copytoc.html

AT&T—*www.linksys.com/attbroadband*

Audio Publishers Association—*http://audiopub.org*

Australian Writers' Guild—*www.awg.com.au*

Authorlink—*www.authorlink.com*

Author-Network.com/Agents—*www.author-network.com/agents.html*

Author-Network.com/What an Agent Can Do for You—
www.author-network.com/litagent.html

Authors—*http://contemporarylit.about.com*

Authors Guild—*www.authorsguild.org*

Authors on the Highway—
http://publishersweekly.reviewsnews.com/index.asp?layout=authorsMain

Auto Submit—*www.autosubmit.com/promote.html*

Avoiding Writing Scams: Advice from Those Who Know, by J.A. Hitchcock—
www.writing-world.com/rights/scams.html

Awesome Writers—*www.topica.com/lists/AwesomeWriters*

Bare Bones Guide to HTML, The—*http://werbach.com/barebones*

Barnes & Noble—*www.barnesandnoble.com*

Barron, Stephanie (Francine Matthews)—*www.francinemathews.com*

bCentral Free Web Tools—*www.bcentral.com/products/free.asp*

Before You Write that Check—*www.writer.org/scamkit.htm*

Beginner's Guide to Effective E-mail/Acronyms and Jargon—
www.webfoot.com/advice/email.jargon.html?Email

Beginner's Guide to Effective E-mail/Domain Names—
www.webfoot.com/advice/email.domain.html?Email

Beginner's Guide to Effective Email/Greetings and Signatures—
www.webfoot.com/advice/email.sig.html?Email

Beginner's Guide to HTML—
http://archive.ncsa.uiuc.edu/General/Internet/WWW/HTMLPrimer.html

Berry, Jeanine—*http://clik.to/Jeanineberry*

Binary Thing ePublishing Network—*www.binarything.com*

BitBooks.com—*http://bitbooks.com*

Blogger—*www.blogger.com*

Blogphiles Webring—*www.blogphiles.com/webring.shtml*

Blogspot—*www.blogspot.com*

Blogstyles—*http://blogstyles.com*

Bobby—*http://bobby.watchfire.com/bobby/html/en/index.jsp*

Book Marketing Update—*www.bookmarket.com/index.html*

Book Promotion Resources—*www.writing-world.com/promotion/index.html*

BookFinder.com—*www.bookfinder.com*

Booklocker—*www.booklocker.com*

BookWire/Book Publisher Index—
www.bookwire.com/bookwire/publishers/publishers.html

Building a Writer's Website—
www.sff.net/people/victoriastrauss/victoria%20strauss%20whywebsite.html

Bullhorn Exchange—*http://talent.bullhorn.com/BullhornExchange*

Calculators On-Line Center—*www-sci.lib.uci.edu/HSG/RefCalculators.html*

Canadian Authors' Association/Canadian Writer's Guide—
www.canauthors.org/pubs.html

Canadian eAuthors—*www.ceauthors.com*

CataList, the Official Catalog of LISTSERV Lists—*www.lsoft.com/lists/listref.html*

CCNOW—*www.ccnow.com*

Celebhoo.com/Your Gateway to Celebrities—*www.Celebhoo.com*

Charles Petit's copyright information site—*www.authorslawyer.com*

Children's Book Council Authors and Illustrators Page—
www.cbcbooks.org/html/links.html

Children's Book Insider—*www.write4kids.com/aboutcbi.html*

Children's Publishers—*http://susettewilliams.com*

Children's Writers Marketplace—*http://write4kids.com/wmarket/index.html*

ClickBank—*www.clickbank.com*

Coffeehouse for Writers/Our Critique Community—
www.coffeehouseforwriters.com/groups.html

Coffeehouse for Writers/Workshops—
www.coffeehouseforwriters.com/courses.html

Color Specifier—
http://users.rcn.com/giant.interport/COLOR/1ColorSpecifier.html

Colossal Directory of Children's Publishers Online— *http://childrenspublishers.signaleader.com*

Commission Junction—*www.cj.com*

Computer User ISP/Web Hosting Directory—*www.computeruser.com/resources/isp*

Concise, Scannable, and Objective: How to Write for the Web— *www.useit.com/papers/webwriting/writing.html*

Contest Report Card—*www.moviebytes.com/ReportCard.cfm*

Contract Issues: Books Published Online—*www.nwu.org/docs/online-p.htm*

Coolsig—E-mail Signature Files—*www.coolsig.com*

Copyright and Fair Use—*http://fairuse.stanford.edu*

Copyright Basics—*www.copyright.gov/circs/circ1.html*

Copyright Clearance and Fair Use—*www.lib.rochester.edu/copyright/default.htm*

Copyright Code, The—*www.loc.gov/copyright/title17*

Copyright Infringement— *www.computerbits.com/archive/1999/0400/copyright.html*

Copyright Terms and Expirations—*www.authorslawyer.com/c-term.shtml*

Correspondent.com—*www.correspondent.com*

Council of Literary Magazines and Presses—*www.clmp.org*

Cox Communication Services—*www.cox.net*

Creative Screenwriting—*www.creativescreenwriting.com*

"C" Rights in "E" Mail—*www.ivanhoffman.com/rights.html*

Critiquing Others' Work— *www.geocities.com/Area51/Labyrinth/6977/writing11.html*

Critters Workshop—*http://brain-of-pooh.tech-soft.com/users/critters*

Dave Barry on the International Library of Poetry— *http://windpub.org/literary.scams/D-Barry.htm*

Dehanna Bailee's Print-on-Demand Database— *www.geocities.com/dehannabailee/pod.htm*

Del Rey—*www.delrey.com*

Dembling, Sophia—*www.YankeeChick.com*

Derivative Rights and Web Sites—*www.ivanhoffman.com/derivative.html*

Digital Millennium Copyright Act (overview)—*www.gseis.ucla.edu/iclp/dmca1.htm*

Digital Millennium Copyright Act (summary)—*www.arl.org/info/frn/copy/band.html*

Directories—*www.nwu.org/links/lnkdirs.htm*

direct search—*www.freepint.com/gary/direct.htm*

DiscussionLists.com—*http://discussionlists.com*

DiskUs Publishing—*www.diskuspublishing.com*

Do We Need to Copyright Our Works?—*www.spawn.org/marketing/copyright.htm*

Dogpile—*www.dogpile.com*

Domain Registries—*www.domain.registries.net*

Domhan Books—*www.domhanbooks.com*

Done Deal—*http://Scriptsales.com*

DSL Service Providers and Availability Search—*www.dsl-service-providers.net*

Easysearcher—*www.easysearcher.com*

ebooksonthe.net—*www.ebooksonthe.net*

Eclectic Writer, The—*www.eclectics.com/writing/writing.html*

eLance—*www.elance.com*

Electronic Book Web—*http://12.108.175.91/ebookweb*

Electronic Journal Miner—*http://ejournal.coalliance.org*

Electronic Publishing and the Potential Loss of First Serial Rights—*www.ivanhoffman.com/first.html*

Electronic Text & Multimedia Collections—*www.library.wisc.edu/etext*

E-Mail Attachments: Your Questions Answered—*http://everythingemail.net/attach_help.html*

E-mail File Attachments—*http://telacommunications.com/nutshell/email.htm*

E-mail Newsletters: A Growing Market for Freelancers—*www.contentious.com/articles/1-10/editorial1-10.html*

E-mail Signatures—*www.apromotionguide.com/sig.html*

EPPRO: The Electronically Published Professionals—*http://eppro.net*

ePublishers Yellow Pages—*http://ebookdirectory.homestead.com/Directorypageone.html*

Epublishers—*www.sff.net/people/Lida.Quillen/epub.html*

Evaluating Internet Research Sources—*www.virtualsalt.com/evalu8it.htm*

Evaluating Web Pages—*www.lib.duke.edu/libguide/evaluating_web.htm*

Evaluating Web Sites—*http://servercc.oakton.edu/~wittman/find/eval.htm*

EventCaster—*www.netread.com/calendar*

Everything E-mail—*http://everythingemail.net/index.html*

Everything E-mail/E-mail Discussion Groups and Newsletters—*http://everythingemail.net/email_discussion.html*

Ezine and Newsletter Publishing—*www.worldwidelearn.com/ezine-publishing.htm*

Ezine Manager—*http://ezinemanager.com*

EzineArticles.com—*http://ezinearticles.com*

E-zinez.com—*www.e-zinez.com/index.html*

eZINESearch—*www.refer-me.com/members/e-zine-master*

Ezine-Tips.com—*http://Ezine-Tips.com/about*

Ezine-Universe.com—*http://Ezine-Universe.com*

Fear of Writing Online Courses—*www.fearofwriting.com/course/index1.htm*

Featurewell.com—*www.featurewell.com*

Ferguson, Julie H.—*www.beaconlit.com*

Fiction Critiquing 101—*www.cyberus.ca/~alette/Critique.htm*

Fiction Factor: The Online Magazine for Writers—*www.fictionfactor.com*

FictionAddiction.net—*http://FictionAddiction.net*

Fictionwise—*www.fictionwise.com*

Film Industry Central—*www.IndustryCentral.net*

Film Stew—*www.filmstew.com*

Film Tracker—*www.filmtracker.com*

Find an ISP—*www.findanisp.com*

FindLaw's Find a Lawyer—*http://lawyers.findlaw.com*

Fleet Street Online—*www.fleet-street.com/top.htm*

Flying Inkpot's Zine Scene—*www.inkpot.com/zines*

Foreign Language Internet Search Engines—*www.bizforms.com/search.htm*

ForTheLoveOfWriting.com—*www.fortheloveofwriting.com*

Forwriters.com—*www.forwriters.com*

Freelance Success Institute—*www.freelancesuccess.com*

FreelanceWriting.com/Magazine Guidelines Database—
www.freelancewriting.com/guidelines/pages

Freelancing4Money—*www.freelancing4money.com*

From FADE IN through FADE OUT—
http://members.aol.com/anniraff/contents.htm

Gabaldon, Diana—*www.dianagabaldon.com*

Gaylinkcontent.com—*www.gaylinkcontent.com*

Getting Permission to Publish: Ten Tips for Webmasters—
www.nolo.com/encyclopedia/articles/ilaw/pub_permission.html

Giving Credit and Requesting Permission: Guidelines for Using Material Other than Your Own—*www.oreilly.com/oreilly/author/permission*

Go Net-Wide—*www.gonetwide.com/gopublic.html*

Google—*www.google.com*

Google Groups—*http://groups.google.com*

Gotta Write Network—*http://hometown.aol.com/gwnlitmag/index.html*

GovSpot—*www.govspot.com*

Guru—*www.guru.com*

HandHeld Crime—*www.handheldcrime.com*

Hard Shell Word Factory—*www.hardshell.com*

Hardcore Critique Advice—*www.crayne.com/download/casiltip.txt*

Hazen, Burr—*www.windsurfingbible.com*

Historic Events and Birth-Dates—*www.scopesys.com/today*

History/Social Studies For K–12 Teachers—*http://my.execpc.com/~dboals*

Hoaxbusters—*http://hoaxbusters.ciac.org*

Hollydex Directory—*www.hollywoodnet.com/search*

Hollywood Creative Directory—*www.hcdonline.com*

Hollywood Script Readers Digest—*www.screenscripts.com*

HollywoodLitSales.com—*http://Hollywoodlitsales.com*

Homestead—*www.homestead.com*

Horror Writers Association—*www.horror.org*

Hotmail—*www.hotmail.com*

How to Create PDF Files—
www.etc.buffalo.edu/workshops/pdf/How_to_create_PDF_files.html

How to Critique Fiction—*www.crayne.com/howcrit.html*

How to Protect Yourself from Questionable Agents, by Marg Gilks—
www.writing-world.com/publish/agent/agents.shtml

How to Write a Screenplay—*www.visualwriter.com/descript.htm*

HTML Goodies—*www.htmlgoodies.com*

HTML Goodies/Ad Banners—*www.htmlgoodies.com/primers/bannerprimers.html*

ibiblio: the public's library—*www.ibiblio.org/collection*

ICQ—*www.icq.com*

Infomine: Scholarly Internet Resource Collections—*http://infomine.ucr.edu*

Inside Film Magazine Online/Screenwriting—
www.insidefilm.com/screenwriting.html

International News Links—*www.inkpot.com/news*

Internet Hollywood Network—*www.hollywoodnet.com/indexmain.html*

Internet Movie Database—*http://imdb.com*

Internet Publishing—*www.hipiers.com/publishing.html*

Internet Smileys—*http://members.aol.com/bearpage/smileys.htm*

Internet Tools for the Advanced Searcher—*www.philb.com/adint.htm*

Internet Writing Workshop—*www.manistee.com/~lkraus/workshop*

Is Your Work on the Web?—*www.sarahwernick.com/web.htm#article*

iUniverse.com—*www.iuniverse.com*

iVillage Readers and Writers Channel—*www.ivillage.com*

Jacqui Bennett Writers Bureau/UK Markets—*www.jbwb.co.uk/markets.html*

Jakob Nielsen's Alertbox—*www.useit.com/alertbox*

JimWorld—*www.jimworld.com*

JournalismNet—*www.journalismnet.com/papers/index.htm*

Journalist Electronic Rights Negotiation Strategies—*www.nwu.org/journ/jstrat.htm*

KnowBetter.com—*http://knowbetter.com*

Labyrinth, The—*http://labyrinth.georgetown.edu*

Lavene, Joyce and Jim—*www.joyceandjimlavene.com*

Librarians' Index to the Internet—*http://lii.org*

Library of Congress—*www.loc.gov*

Library of Congress/American Memory: Historical Collections for the National Digital Library—*http://memory.loc.gov/ammem/ammemhome.html*

LibrarySpot—*www.libraryspot.com*

List, The—*http://thelist.internet.com*

Listbox—*http://v2.listbox.com*

Literary Times—*www.tlt.com/news/itiner.htm*

Looksmart ISP Finder—*www.looksmart.com/ispfinder*

Magazines of Europe—*www.travelconnections.com/Magazines/Europeindex.htm*

MagazineWriting.com—*www.MagazineWriting.com*

MagoMania: Canada's Magazine Search Engine—*www.magomania.com/english*

Major Search Engines—*http://searchenginewatch.internet.com/facts/major.html*

Mandy's—*http://mandy.com*

Market List, The—*www.marketlist.com*

Markets for Writers—*www.chebucto.ns.ca/Culture/WFNS/periodicals.html*

Martindale-Hubbell—*http://lawyers.martindale.com/xp/Martindale/home.xml*

Mary Wolf's Guide to Electronic Publishers—*http://my.coredcs.com/~mermaid/epub.html*

Matt's Script Archive—*www.scriptarchive.com*

McAfee—*www.mcafee.com*

McArthur, Nancy—*http://junior.apk.net/~mcarthur*

Media UK—*www.mediauk.com*

Mercator—*www.aber.ac.uk/~merwww/allang.htm*

Meta Medic—*www.northernwebs.com/set/setsimjr.html*

MetaCrawler—*www.metacrawler.com*

Midwest Book Review—*www.midwestbookreview.com*

Midwest Book Review/Publisher Resources—*www.midwestbookreview.com/bookbiz/pub_res.htm*

Midwest Book Review/Publishers—*www.midwestbookreview.com/links/publish.htm*

Misc. Writing—*www.scalar.com/mw/index.html*

Misc. Writing Mailing Lists—*www.scalar.com/mw/pages/mwmlist.shtml*

Moore, Carole—*www.thehumorwriter.com*

MovieBytes—*http://moviebytes.com*

MoviePartners.com—*http://filmpartners.com*

Multnomah Cty. Library Electronic Resources—*www.multcolib.org/ref/quick.html*

My Virtual Reference Desk—*www.refdesk.com*

My Writer Buddy—*www.writerbuddy.com*

Mysterious Home Page/Publishers—*www.cluelass.com/MystHome/Publishers.html*

Mystery Writers of America—*www.mysterywriters.org*

NASA—*www.nasa.gov*

National Association of Women Writers—*www.naww.org*

National Writers Union—*www.nwu.org*

NetLab—*ftp://ftp.ccit.edu.tw/Windows/Windows95/WinSite/netutil/netlab95.zip*

Network Solutions—*www.networksolutions.com*

Never Heard of Them—*www.neverheardofthem.co.uk*

NewJour/New Journals and Newsletters on the Internet—
http://gort.ucsd.edu/newjour/NewJourWel.html

New-List.com—*http://New-List.com/instructions*

NewsDirectory.com—*www.newsdirectory.com*

Newsletter Access Directory—*www.newsletteraccess.com*

Newsletter Directory—*www.newsletter-directory.com*

NewspaperLinks.com—*www.newspaperlinks.com/home.cfm*

Newspapers.com—*www.newspapers.com*

Nolo Law—*www.nolo.com*

Noveldoc.com—*www.noveldoc.com*

Novice Writer's Guide to Rights—*www.writerswrite.com/journal/dec97/cew3.htm*

One Woman's Writing Retreat—*www.prairieden.com*

Online Books Page, The—*http://digital.library.upenn.edu/books*

Online Communicator—*www.online-communicator.com/writvid.html*

Online Writing Workshop for Romance—*http://romance.onlinewritingworkshop.com*

Online Writing Workshop for Science Fiction, Fantasy and Horror—
http://sff.onlinewritingworkshop.com

Overbooked Book Links: Mystery, Suspense, Thrillers, Crime Fiction Publishers—
http://freenet.vcu.edu/education/literature/mystpub.html

OzLit—*http://home.vicnet.net.au/~ozlit/agents.html*

Palm Digital Media (Peanut Press)—*www.peanutpress.com*

Paperboy, The—*www.thepaperboy.com/welcome.cfm*

PayPal—*www.paypal.com*

Periodical Writers Association of Canada—*www.pwac.org*

Phone Book, The—*www.the-phone-book.com*

PicoSearch—*www.picosearch.com*

Pitsco's Ask an Expert—*www.askanexpert.com*

Planet eBook—*www.planetebook.com*

Poetry Awards/Frequently Asked Questions—*www.poets.org/awards/faq.cfm*

Poetry Contest Scams—*http://windpub.org/literary.scams/ilp.htm*

PPPP.Net/Ultimate Collection of News Links—*http://pppp.net/links/news*

Preditors and Editors—*http://anotherealm.com/prededitors*

Preditors and Editors/Agent Listings—
http://anotherealm.com/prededitors/pubagent.htm

Preditors and Editors/Writing Workshops—
http://anotherealm.com/prededitors/pubwork.htm

Preparing E-mail Queries, by Moira Allen—
www.writing-world.com/basics/email.shtml

Press Kit—*www.writing-world.com/press/index.html*

Professional Directory—*http://filmindustry.com*

ProfNet—*www2.profnet.com*

Project Gutenberg—*http://gutenberg.net*

Promotion World—*www.promotionworld.com*

Proper Use of a Domain Name for Trademark Protection—
www.arvic.com/library/domanuse.asp

Publicly Accessible Mailing Lists—*http://paml.alastra.com*

Publishers' Catalogues Home Page—*www.lights.com/publisher*

Publishers on the Internet—*www.faxon.com/title/pl_am.htm*

Publishers Online—*www.peak.org/~bonwritr/pub.htm*

Publishing Law and Other Articles of Interest—*http://publaw.com/copy.html*

Quixotics—*www.quixotics.com*

Random House v RosettaBooks—*www.rosettabooks.com/pages/legal.html*

Readmywriting.com—*www.writersworld.tv/authors/ukireliteraryagents.htm*

RedInkWorks—*www.redinkworks.com/writing_tips.htm*

Regards.com—*www.regards.com*

RegSelect—*www.regselect.com*

Research and Facts—*www.nwu.org/links/lnkfacts.htm*

ResearchBuzz—*www.researchbuzz.com*

Rights and Why They're Important, by Marg Gilks—
www.writing-world.com/rights/rights.shtml

Rights Marketplace—*www.authorlink.com*

Romance Publishers—*www.rwanational.com/pub_links.stm*

Romance Writers of America—*www.rwanational.com*

Romance Writers of America/Author Webites—
www.rwanational.org/author_websites.stm

RX4Scripts—*www.Rx4scripts.com*

Sands Publishing—*www.sandspublishing.com*

School for Champions—*www.school-for-champions.com/writing.htm*

Science Fiction Writers of America—*www.sfwa.org*

SciFi_Discussion—*www.topica.com/lists/SciFi_Discussion*

Screenplayers—*www.screenplayers.net*

Screenwriters Market—*www.screenwritersmarket.com*

Screenwriter's Master Chart—*http://members.aol.com/maryjs/scrnrite.htm*

Screenwriters Utopia—*www.screenwritersutopia.com*

Screenwriters Web—*http://breakingin.net*

Screenwriting—*http://screenwriting.miningco.com*

Screenwriting Contests Directory—*www.moviebytes.com/directory.cfm*

Scriptapalooza—*www.scriptapalooza.com*

Scriptiverse Spec Script Marketplace—*www.scriptiverse.com*

SCRNWRiT—*www.panam.edu/scrnwrit*

Search.com—*www.search.com*

Search Engine Colossus—*www.searchenginecolossus.com*

Search Engine Tutorial—*http://northernwebs.com/set*

Search Engine Watch/Search Engine Submission Tips—
http://searchenginewatch.internet.com/webmasters

Selling International Rights, by Moira Allen—
www.writing-world.com/international/intrights.shtml

SFF Net—*www.sff.net*

SFF Net/People Pages—*www.sff.net/people.asp*

SF Novelist—*www.sfnovelist.com/index.htm*

SFWA Statement on Electronic Rights—*www.sfwa.org/contracts/ELEC.htm*

SFWA/Workshops—*www.sfwa.org/links/workshops.htm*

Siglets—*www.siglets.com*

Site Owner Link Tester—*www.siteowner.com/badlinks.cfm?LID=229*

Smarterwork—*www.smarterwork.com*

So, You Want to Start an E-zine?—*www.zinebook.com/roll.html*

Sources and Experts—*http://metalab.unc.edu/slanews/internet/experts.html*

Spicy Green Iguana—*www.spicygreeniguana.com*

StuffIt Expander—*www.stuffit.com/expander*

SubmitAway!—*www.submit-away.com/auto-submit.htm*

Suite101—*www.suite101.com/editorapp/member.cfm*

Supreme Court Opinions on *New York Times Co., Inc., et al. v. Tasini et al.*—
http://laws.findlaw.com/us/000/00-201.html

Symantec—*www.symantec.com*

TalkCity—*www.talkcity.com*

"The *Tasini* Decision: Implications for the Future—An Interview with Charles E. Petit"—*www.writing-world.com/rights/tasini.shtml*

Tile.Net—*http://tile.net*

Top 10 Ways to Irritate Your Visitors—*www.virtualpromote.com/top10.html*

Top 101 Experts—*www.bookmarket.com/101exp.html*

Topic Specific Directories—*http://jlunz.databack.com/netresources/topic_specific_directories.htm*

Topica—*www.topica.com*

Total Merchant Services—*https://application.acceptcreditcards.com*

trAce Online Writing School—*http://trace.ntu.ac.uk/school/index.htm*

TulipStats Web Stats—*www.tulipstats.com*

UCLA Extension—*www.onlinelearning.net/CommunitiesofStudy*

United States Copyright Office—*www.loc.gov/copyright*

United States Postal Service—*www.stampsonline.com, http://shop.usps.com*

Unmovies—*www.unmovies.com*

Urban Legends Reference Pages—*www.snopes.com*

Usable Web—*http://usableweb.com/index.html*

Useful Links for Romance Writers and Readers/Authors—*www.jaclynreding.com/links*

US Newspaper Links.com—*www.usnpl.com*

Vallar, Cindy—*www.cindyvallar.com*

Vanity Poetry Contests—*www.poets.ca/pshstore/sidebar/vanity.htm*

Viruses online and offline—*www.lctn.com/util/virusfaq.html*

Vmyths: Truths about Computer Security Hysteria—*www.vmyths.com*

Volunteer Lawyers for the Arts—*http://arts.endow.gov/artforms/Manage/VLA2.html*

Web Resources that Help You Identify Scams—*www.winningwriters.com/scambustingsites.htm*

Web Style Guide—*http://info.med.yale.edu/caim/manual/contents.html*

Web Wonk: Tips for Writers and Designers—*www.dsiegel.com/tips/index.html*

Webmonkey Reference: Domain Registry—*http://hotwired.lycos.com/webmonkey/reference/domain_registries*

WebScout Lists—*www.webscoutlists.com*

Webtracker—*www.fxweb.com/tracker*

WebTrends—*www.netiq.com/webtrends/default.asp*

WebWombat/Magazines—*www.webwombat.com.au/magazines*

Who Owns the Copyright in Your Web Site?—*www.ivanhoffman.com/website.html*

whoRepresents?com—*www.WhoRepresents.com*

Who's Buying What—*www.moviebytes.com/wbw/wbwfaq.cfm?*

Whose Property Is It Anyway?—*www.online-magazine.com/copyright.htm*

WickedMoon.com—*www.wickedmoon.com*

WinZip—*www.winzip.com*

Wooden Horse Publishing—*www.woodenhorsepub.com*

WordsWorth—*www.wordsworth.com/www/present/interviews*

WordWeaving Archive—*www.wordweaving.com/archives_index.html*

Working List of Speculative Fiction Markets—
http://home.att.net/~p.fleming/Sfmarket.html

Workshell Whois—*www.workshell.co.uk*

Worldcrafter's Guild (formerly Romance Writers Homepage)—
www.simegen.com/school/index.html

World Publishing Industry—*http://publishing-industry.net/Publishers*

Worldwide Freelance Writer—*www.worldwidefreelance.com*

Write Biz, The—*www.thewritebiz.com*

WriteLink—*www.writelink.dabsol.co.uk*

WriteLinks—*www.writelinks.com/Creative/Links/crea06.htm*

WriteLinks/Commercial Book Publishers—
www.writelinks.com/Creative/Links/BookPublishers/crea06_02.htm

Write Markets Report, The—*www.writersweekly.com/shop/forwriters.html#4*

Writer, The—*www.writermag.com*

Writer Alerts!—*www.nwu.org/alerts/alrthome.htm*

Writer Beware—*www.sfwa.org/beware*

Writer Beware/Epublishers—*www.sfwa.org/Beware/epublishers.html*

Writer Beware/Print On Demand—*www.sfwa.org/beware/printondemand.html*

Writer Space—*www.writerspace.com*

Writer's BBS—*www.writers-bbs.com/chat.html*

WritersCollege.com—*www.WritersCollege.com*

Writers.com—*www.writers.com/writing-classes.htm*

Writer's Digest—*www.writersdigest.com*

Writers Exchange—*www.writers-exchange.com/epublishing*

Writers' Groups—*www.writers.com/groups.htm*

Writers Guild of America—*www.wga.org*

Writers Guild of America/Guild Signatory Agents and Agencies—
www.wga.org/agency.html

Writers Guild of Canada—*www.writersguildofcanada.com*

Writers' Guild of Great Britain—*www.writersguild.org.uk*

Writers' Information Network/[Christian] Publishers—*www.bluejaypub.com/win/publishers.htm*

Writer's List—*http://web.mit.edu/mbarker/www/writers.html*

Writer's Market—*www.writersmarket.com*

WritersMind, The—*www.thewritersmind.com*

WritersNet—*www.writers.net*

Writer's Resource Center—*www.poewar.com*

Writers Script Network—*www.writerscriptnetwork.com*

Writer's Village University—*http://4-writers.com*

Writers Weekly—*www.writersweekly.com*

WritersWeekly/Markets & Jobs—*www.writersweekly.com/markets/markets.html*

WritersWeekly/Warnings—*www.writersweekly.com/warnings/warnings.html*

Writers Workshops—*www.nwu.org/links/lnkwks.htm*

Writers Write—*www.writerswrite.com*

WritersWrite/Greeting Cards—*www.writerswrite.com/greetingcards/ecards.htm*

Writers Write/Writers' Groups Online—*www.writerswrite.com/groups.htm*

Writers Write/Writer's Guidelines Directory—*www.writerswrite.com/guidelines*

WritingClasses.com—*www.writingclasses.com*

Writing for DOLLARS!—*www.writingfordollars.com*

Writing for DOLLARS!/Guidelines Database—*www.writingfordollars.com/Guidelines.cfm*

WritingSchool.com—*www.WritingSchool.com*

Writing World—*www.writing-world.com/newsletter/index.shtml*

Writing-World.com—*www.writing-world.com*

Writing-World.com/Class Links—*www.writing-world.com/links/classes.shtml*

Writing-World.com/Classes—*www.writing-world.com/classes/index.shtml*

Writing-World.com/Critique Groups—*www.writing-world.com/links/critique.shtml*

Xlibris—*www.xlibris.com*

Yahoo!—*www.yahoo.com*

Yahoo! Australia & NZ Directory—*http://au.dir.yahoo.com/news_and_media/magazines*

Yahoo! Directory/Genres—*http://d1.dir.dcx.yahoo.com/arts/humanities/literature/genres*

Yahoo! Directory/News and Media—*http://d1.dir.dcx.yahoo.com/news_and_media/by_region*

Yahoo! Directory/Virtual Cards—
http://d1.dir.dcx.yahoo.com/entertainment/virtual_cards

Yahoo! Groups—*http://groups.yahoo.com*

You Can Take Your Credit Cards Online—*www.youcantakecreditcardsonline.com*

You Too Can Sniff Out Scams!—*www.yudkin.com/scams.htm*

Young Writers' Clubhouse—*www.realkids.com/critique.htm*

Your Free Book Promotion Countdown Checklist—
www.geocities.com/~lorna_tedder/virgins.html

Zinester—*www.zinester.com*

TWO THOUSAND ONLINE RESOURCES FOR WRITERS: THE ELECTRONIC DIRECTORY

This book is accompanied by an electronic guide to online resources for writers. It presently offers nearly two thousand listings and is available as a PDF file that can be downloaded directly from the Allworth Press Web site. Simply go to *www.allworth.com/Catalog/WP280A.htm.* Follow the instructions for downloading the book. You'll be asked for a username and a password: Simply enter "reader" as the username and "resource" as the password. The directory will be updated at regular intervals; you can check the site for the latest version or add your name to a mailing list to be informed of future updates.

CONTENTS OF THE DIRECTORY

PART I: GENERAL WRITING, REFERENCE AND "GETTING STARTED" SITES

General Writing Sites · Articles · Business/Finance · Dictionaries · Exercises · Grammar · Writing Publications · Query Letters

PART II: GENRES AND CATEGORIES

Business/Tech Writing · Children's Writing · Christian Writing · Editors · Essays/Journaling · Flash Fiction · Historical Fiction · Horror · Journalism · Mystery · Poetry · Romance · SF/Fantasy · Screen/Script Writing · Songwriting · Speechwriting · Travel Writing

PART III: MARKET INFORMATION

Agents · Author Showcase Sites · Book Publishers · Book Publishing Tips · Columns/Syndication · Contests · Electronic Publishers & Publishing · Ezines

· Freelance Marketplace · Games · Greeting Cards · Guideline Databases · Handheld Content · Jobs · Magazines · Newspapers · Market Publications · Web Guides

PART IV: RIGHTS, COPYRIGHT, AND SCAMS
Contracts · Copyright · Electronic Rights · International Copyright · Libel & Defamation · Scams

PART V: RESEARCH
Citing Electronic Sources · Directories & Databases · Evaluating Web Sites · Experts · History & Lore · Literature & E-texts · Libraries · Search Engines · International Search Engines · Search Engine Tips

PART VI: NETWORKING
Associations · Author Sites · Chats · Chat Software · Classes · Conferences & Colonies · Critiquing · Discussion Groups · E-mail Tips · Mailing List Hosts

PART VII: PROMOTION, SELF-PUBLISHING, AND WEBSITE DEVELOPMENT
Book Promotion · Book Clubs · Book Reviews · Booksignings · Bookstores · Interviews and Public Speaking · Press Releases · Self-Publishing · Website Development/Promotion

PART VIII: INTERNATIONAL RESOURCES
International Writing Sites · Int. Bookstores · Business/Finance · Int. Journalism · Language/Translation · News Sources · Regional/Travel Information · World Literature

PART IX: MISCELLANEOUS
Awards · Character Development · Crossword Puzzles · E-zine Publishing · Ghostwriting · Grants & Funding · Names · Photography · Quotations · Sample Magazines · Viruses & Hoaxes · Young Writers

PART X: ONLINE MARKETS
Paying Electronic Markets · Literary Magazines & E-zines

Note: This list may change as the directory is updated and new categories added.

CONTRIBUTING AUTHOR BIOS

Shery Ma Belle Arrieta has been writing since she was ten. The founder of The e-Writers Place (*http://ewritersplace.com*)—recognized by *Writer's Digest* as one of the best sites for writers in 2001—Arrieta is also the author of several e-books, and offers e-mail workshops for writers. Arrieta is based in the Philippines and, when not writing, designs Web sites and offers Web development consulting. Her work has appeared in a variety of local and international print and online publications.

MaryJanice Davidson (*www.usinternet.com/users/alongi*) has sold eleven manuscripts to five different publishers in three years. Her nonfiction book for writers, *Escape the Slush Pile*, is available from The Fiction Works (*www.fictionworks.com/escapetheslush.htm*), and her novella, *Love's Prisoner (Secrets 6)*, was the 2000 winner of the Sapphire Award for excellence in Science Fiction Romance.

Debbie Ridpath Ohi (*www.electricpenguin.com/ohi*) is a freelance writer and editor, author of *The Writers' Online Marketplace* (Writer's Digest Books) and creator of the writers' Web site Inkspot. Her columns include "Press Kit" (for Writing-world.com), "Market Watch" (for WritersMarket.com) and "Songwriting Music Theory 101" (for MusesMuse.com).

Charles Petit (*cepetit@authorslawyer.com*) practices intellectual-property and publishing law, complex litigation, and civil white-collar-crime and antifraud litigation, almost exclusively on the plaintiff's side. He graduated magna cum laude from the University of Illinois College of Law, and is admitted in Illinois and ten federal courts scattered across the country. Prior to law school, he served as a commissioned officer in the USAF. Find out more about copyright issues from his Web site, *www.authorslawyer.com*.

Loralei Walker (*www.just-write4you.com*) is a full-time freelance writer from Vancouver, British Columbia. Her work has appeared in a number of online magazines, such as *Freelance Jobs News* and *Absolute Write*, as well as numerous corporate Web sites.

Lenore Wright has fifteen years' experience writing and selling screenplays in Los Angeles and New York. She offers more screenwriting advice on her Web site, The Screenwriters Web, at *http://breakingin.net*. To subscribe to her newsletter, *Script Market News*, send a blank e-mail to *newsletter@breakingin.net*.

INDEX

BOOKS FROM ALLWORTH PRESS

The Author's Toolkit: A Step-by-Step Guide to Writing and Publishing Your Book, Revised Edition
by Mary Embree (paperback, 5 ½ × 8 ½, 192 pages, $16.95)

The Writer's Guide to Queries, Pitches, and Proposals
by Moira Allen (paperback, 6 × 9, 288 pages, $16.95)

Making Crime Pay: The Writer's Guide to Criminal Law, Evidence, and Procedure
by Andrea Campbell (paperback, 6 × 9, 304 pages, $19.95)

The Journalist's Craft: A Guide to Writing Better Stories
edited by Dennis Jackson and John Sweeney (paperback, 6 × 9, 256 pages, $19.95)

The Writer's Legal Guide: An Authors Guild Desk Reference, Third Edition
by Tad Crawford and Kay Murray (paperback, 6 × 9, 320 pages, $19.95)

Business and Legal Forms for Authors and Self-Publishers, Revised Edition
by Tad Crawford (paperback, 8½ x 11, 192 pages, includes CD-ROM, $22.95)

The Copyright Guide: A Friendly Guide for Protecting and Profiting from Trademarks
by Lee Wilson (paperback, 6 x 9, 208 pages, $19.95)

Marketing Strategies for Writers
by Michael Sedge (paperback, 6 × 9, 224 pages, $16.95)

Writing for Interactive Media: The Complete Guide
by Jon Samsel and Darryl Wimberly (paperback, 6 × 9, 320 pages, $19.95)

The Writer's Guide to Corporate Communications
by Mary Moreno (paperback, 6 × 9, 192 pages, $19.95)

Writing Scripts Hollywood Will Love, Revised Edition
by Katherine Atwell Herbert (paperback, 6 × 9, 160 pages, $14.95)

So You Want to Be a Screenwriter: How to Face the Fears and Take the Risks
by Sara Caldwell and Marie-Eve Kielson (paperback, 6 × 9, 224 pages, $14.95)

The Screenwriter's Guide to Agents and Managers
by John Scott Lewinski (paperback, 6 × 9, 256 pages, $18.95)

The Screenwriter's Legal Guide, Second Edition
by Stephen F. Breimer (paperback, 6 × 9, 320 pages, $19.95)

Please write to request our free catalog. To order by credit card, call 1-800-491-2808 or send a check or money order to Allworth Press, 10 East 23rd Street, Suite 510, New York, NY 10010. Include $5 for shipping and handling for the first book ordered and $1 for each additional book. Ten dollars plus $1 for each additional book if ordering from Canada. New York State residents must add sales tax.

To see our complete catalog on the World Wide Web, or to order online, you can find us at *www.allworth.com*.